Praise

The Facts of Life in

"I'm nuts about Portland. This book right."

- *Neil Goldschmidt, Former Governor of Oregon*

"This fabulous compendium amply demonstrates Portland's special place in the universe."

- *Richard H. Meeker, Publisher, Willamette Week*

"...an entertaining, in depth look at our great city, from top to bottom. If you think you know Portland, you'll be surprised!"

- *Will Vinton, Creator of Claymation®*

"Even more interesting than the 'Facts of Life' book your parents gave you when you turned 13....I always knew I loved Portland. After reading this book, I finally understand why."

- *Margie Boulé, The Oregonian*

"A cornucopia of fascinating facts about the people, places and politics of Portland. This is a must for people who want to learn what makes Portland such an open and friendly community."

- *Carl Abbott, Portland State University Professor of*
  Urban Studies and Planning, and Portland Historian

"A serious, saucy, encyclopedic celebration of Portland!"

- *Joe Uris, Talk Show Host, Writer*
  and Curmudgeon Extraordinaire

"No one has been here long enough to claim that there's nothing left to learn about Portland. This book will tell you things you never knew!"

- *Ethan Seltzer, Director, Institute of Portland*
  Metropolitan Studies, Portland State University

"Reading this book is almost as much fun as living here."

- *Jonathan Nicholas, The Oregonian*

"...this book is must reading for Portlanders because it presents the city with all its facets...."

- *Nohad Toulan, Dean, School of Urban Studies,*
  Portland State University

"If at the end of the 21st century an enquirer should ask a librarian for the most comprehensive book on Portland at the end of the 20th century, the librarian could do no better than recommend Elaine Friedman's The Facts of Life in Portland."

- *Terence O'Donnell, Writer and Oregon Historian*

THE FACTS OF LIFE
IN
PORTLAND
OREGON

ELAINE S. FRIEDMAN

Portland Possibilities, Inc.
Portland, Oregon

First edition. Copyright © 1993 by Elaine S. Friedman.

Printed in the United States of America

Published by Portland Possibilities Inc.

Send inquiries to:
Portland Possibilities Inc.
Editorial Department
6949 SW 11th Drive
Portland, Oregon 97219
(503) 697 3391

Cover photo by Tobin Floom, IMAGES By Floom, Portland, OR
Cover design by L. Grafix, Portland, OR
Printed by Artline Printing, Beaverton, OR

Aerial photo on pages xii-xiii © Copyright Bergman Photographic Services, Inc., 1992. Used by permission of Bergman Photographic Services, Inc.

Map on pages 46-47 © Copyright Erwin Raisz, 1941. Used by permission of Raisz Landform Maps.

Map on pages 68-69 © Copyright Nancy Smith Goldman & Nancy Weigel, 1980. Used by permission of Nancy Smith Goldman.

Map on pages 70-71 © Copyright Nancy Smith Goldman, 1992. Used by permission of Nancy Smith Goldman.

Publisher's Cataloging in Publication Data
Friedman, Elaine S., 1951-
The Facts of life in Portland, Oregon / by Elaine S. Friedman. – 1st ed.
p. cm.
Bibliography: p.
Includes index.
ISBN 1-881512-14-2 (pbk) : $14.95
1. Portland (Or.)--Description and travel. 2. Portland (Or.)--Politics and government. 3. Portland (Or.)--Civilization. I. Title
F884.P83   917.9549

Dedication

To my husband, who got me started and kept me going; and who gave me sound advice, countless clippings and promising ideas from start to finish;

To my daughter, who urged me on with wise, encouraging words well beyond her mere twelve years;

To my son, who shared his mom with what seemed like a never-ending project; and offered to lend his name to an endorsement if we needed one from a five year old;

And to my parents, who, as always, were there whenever I needed them.

Pondering Portland

I have seen a lot of scenery in my life, but I have seen nothing so tempting as a home for man in this Oregon country....You have here the basis for civilization on its highest scale, and I am going to ask you a question which you may not like. Are you good enough to have this country in your possession? Have you got enough intelligence, imagination and cooperation among you to make the best use of these opportunities? Rebuilding our cities will be one of the major tasks of the next generation....In providing for new developments you have an opportunity here to do a job of city planning like nowhere else in the world.

> Lewis Mumford, addressing the City Club of Portland in July, 1938.

It was a going town, but it probably would be wrong to say that it was a "bustling" one. Portland has never bustled. It doesn't today. It ambles...with some loitering on the way. Throughout the city's history visitors have remarked on the slowness of the pace. Perhaps it is the valley's great fertility, requiring by comparison to other locations less effort, the clement seasons, a lushness, the sometimes tropical summer, the soft rains and muffling fogs, something soothing, soporific which slows men down, tempting them to be rather than to act. There were, and indeed are now, men of "push" – as the old boosters used to say – who have tried to hurry the place, to hustle it on to some large and brilliant destiny. The weight of the town's content usually defeats them.

> Terence O'Donnell and Thomas Vaughan, *Portland, an Informal History & Guide*, 1984.

Without sounding too corny or sentimental about it – and well aware of pressing social and environmental problems – my hunch is that if Plato were around today, writing *The City* instead of *The Republic*, he'd come up with a plan along the lines of Portland, an urban environment where a person can still move with relative ease through the private and public realms of life.

> Doug Marx, *Willamette Week*, November 2-8, 1989.

How Portland achieved this state of urban grace is a tale made up in equal parts of design and accident. One accident was the site picked for the city by the New Englanders who settled it. Tucked between rolling, forested hills and a bend in the Willamette River, the city was forced into a compact shape that followed the contours of the land. Another fluke was the small, 200-foot blocks selected for the nascent town. Intended to create more high-priced corner building sites, they also ensured that some 40% of the city centre was given over to streets and public rights of way. Portland is devoid of the concrete canyons that characterize San Francisco and New York.

The Economist, September 1, 1990.

Conservative, respectable, independent, the character of Portland combines pioneer grit and Yankee propriety. The former is a part of the legacy of the midwestern pioneers who survived the westward trek over the Oregon Trail, the latter a trait of the New England merchants and sea captains who traveled to the Pacific Northwest in ships around Cape Horn.

Those early settlers came west to farm and trade, not to seek a fortune in gold. If Seattle and San Francisco benefit from the more flamboyant legacy of the gold rush entrepreneurs by displaying glitzy, cosmopolitan facades, Portland reflects the sober values and work ethic of its founding fathers by restricting building heights, recycling trash, and preserving neighborhoods, stately old trees, and an aging bronze elk that stands in the middle of a busy downtown street, forcing traffic around it like a stone in midstream.

Julie C. Sterling, *T.W.A. Ambassador*, September 1989.

...Portland resembles a little Lego Land that begs for fondling. Once downtown, however, everything takes on a substantiality – stone and metal, wood and more metal. All is considered, and there is no excess. Mildew? No. And Portlanders would never consider building anything their grandchildren might not deem worthy of preserving.

Doug Coupland, *Western Living*, November 1988.

Portland is so maddeningly confident about what's best for Portland, voters continue to inconvenience themselves for the public good, spurring their politicians and planners to tear out their old "wrongs" to build new "rights." Pioneer Courthouse Square was just one of the better ideas: The city flattened a serviceable, two-story parking garage to liberate the open space. At even greater sacrifice, they ripped out four lanes of good, solid highway...to free up the river banks for Riverplace and an adjoining park. And not only did they divert millions of dollars in freeway allocations (potential concrete) to build mass transit, but they dared to restrict new downtown parking. In the meantime, dozens of leaders in San Francisco, Los Angeles and New York have won and lost elections on some, or all, of these issues for decades – with none of these triumphs.

Barbara Flanagan, *Metropolitan Home,* January 1988.

From one corner of Pioneer Courthouse Square, the spiritual if not exact geographical center of Portland, Oregon, rises a whimsical, 25-foot kinetic sculpture called *Weather Machine.* Each day at noon, clots of the curious gather here to wait for the forecast. As the hour begins to turn and nearby church bells herald its coming, there's a puff of mist from the column, and then one of three symbols appears at its top: a sun for fair skies, a dragon denoting rain, and – if barometric readings are uncertain – a blue heron.

Could it be a coincidence that the blue heron, Portland's official bird, stands for the unpredictable? This has got to be the artist's joke on a place renowned for its shifts of direction, its constant squirming between big-city aspirations and small-town conservatism.

J. Kingston Pierce, *Travel & Leisure,* April 1991.

In his *Inside USA* series of the 1950s, John Gunther wrote that Portland is to Seattle as tea is to gin. Close that book and open another; since that writing, the tea has been spiked. Portland can no longer be dismissed as a boring place in Seattle's shadow.

Yvonne Michie Horn, *T.W.A. Ambassador,* April 1991.

I take comfort in the purely speculative notion that, per capita, Portland has more social, cultural and political grassroots activists than other cities of comparable (or larger) size.

Doug Marx, *Willamette Week*, November 2-8, 1989.

...with the implementation of the light rail system, Portland has taken on the character of an urban theme park par excellence. It is this feeling of freewheeling exploration within a controlled, rational environment dotted with contiguous urban synapses that gives Portland its architectural charm and makes it, one could argue, the quintessential humanistic 20th-century American city. Like a well-run theme park, Portland is a clean and rational city. Its downtown is stitched together by a transportation system that efficiently circulates people through a wide range of archetypal urban episodes. There is a functioning specimen, usually no more than one, for every facet of metropolitan life: a public plaza, a performing arts center, a grand 10-theater movie house, a scientific research institute, a university, a historic-cum-public market, and many other attractions. For the most part, each specimen in this architectural microcosm is well crafted and engages in a dialogue with its surrounding neighbors.

Gideon Bosker and Lena Lencek, *Architecture*, November 1987.

The truth is, we match the portrait of middle America almost feature for feature. It has been said that the Portland metropolitan area could be picked up and dropped in the Midwest and nobody in the neighborhood would notice....

In another way the Portland area is not exactly typical. As a group, we're almost entirely white, of Anglo-Saxon descent. Historically, Portland has had a notable lack of ethnic diversity, be that black, Greek or Lithuanian. We're more like the majority of Americans than the majority of Americans.

Bill Redden, *Willamette Week*, November 3-9, 1990.

Few if any cities in the world with a metro population of a million have a downtown from which you can look out through the streets into wooded hills – in downtown Portland to the north, the south, the west and to the east, of course, the river and the mountain. And beyond. For what lies beyond is there, too, in the mind's eye, while we walk the city streets: to the east the desert and rim-rock, the rushing streams and sage-scented air; to the west that little valley as fertile as anywhere, while beyond the boom and roar of the Pacific surf. And these visions, this knowledge of what exists around us, is essential to our sense of where we are, reminding us that this huddle of humans called a city is not unto itself but is part of the land in which it lies and to which it owes its life. It is a realization perhaps well to keep in mind, and which Portland helps to keep there for the simple reason that, from this city, we can still look out.

Terence O'Donnell, *Northwest Magazine*, August 12, 1990.

...Portlanders still insist that a city is not for networking or catching planes to other places, but for living in. What they prize about the place is not its per capita income but its rivers, its neighborhoods, its live jazz, its microbreweries, and its pro basketball Trail Blazers. The last may be an acquired taste, but all the rest comes *naturally* – one of Portland's favorite words.

David Sarasohn, *Portland Best Places*, 1990.

Ultimately, Portland is a city of remembrance and of sorting out, where only the finest is kept and remembered, and where the substandard is simply not allowed. It comes as no surprise, then, that Portland is one of few North American cities with a Vietnam war memorial....The genius of the monument, and the reason it says so much about Portland's soul, is that when walking through the monument, visitors share a temporary agreement that reminds them of the necessity to protect and cherish what one has....On the stone is written, "As long as they are not forgotten, they are still alive." Portland has chosen to remember the 20th century.

Doug Coupland, *Western Living*, November 1988.

Aerial photo on the previous page was taken on May 14, 1992 by Bergman Photographic Services, Inc., Portland, Oregon.

Table of Contents

List of Maps

Acknowledgements

A book like this can only happen if people are willing to help. And help they did. From the enthusiastic encouragement of friends and family to the reams of information mailed to me by incredibly helpful strangers, this book owes its completion as much to the helpers as to the author.

At the beginning, I vowed to thank everyone individually. I was truly impressed with the accessibility of just about everyone I contacted, and the wealth of information they made available to me. I made lists and verified the spelling of names. I kept notes and updated the online acknowledgements file religiously. But it soon became apparent that there were just too many people to try to thank everyone by name.

But as readers, you should know that literally hundreds of Portlanders answered questions, mailed information, explained policies, returned phone calls, and generally went beyond the call of duty to get me what I needed to research and write this book. Many of the people I spoke with helped me as part of their jobs; others because of an avocation. But just about everyone was willing to take time out of an already busy day to help. While very occasionally I had to make a second request, I can recall no brusque or curt conversations. Even Marjabelle Young Stewart, whose rankings list Portland as the most polite city, would have been impressed.

The accessibility of Portlanders – in both the public sphere and private industry, from the receptionist to the president – was truly remarkable. After more than two years of research, I have come to believe that this accessibility is a fact of life in Portland, Oregon that is as important as the temperate climate and the growing population. As a native New Yorker, I can't help but think that a project of this magnitude could not have been completed as easily in my hometown. And I trust that it would be a hard task in many other places too.

So I send a heartfelt thank you to all the people who were kind enough to help me. I hope you'll understand that there were just too many of you to thank you all individually.

While I can't thank everyone by name, some people do stand out in my mind, because their contribution was particularly important. They include friends and family as well as people I met only because I called them up for help. Starting at the beginning of the alphabet, I send my sincerest thanks to: Hesha Abrams, Jeff Abrams, Mary Brelsford, Sandy Carlson, David Chaklai, Nancy Chapman, Sandy Christopherson, Terry Drake, Lorraine Duncan, Rich Eichen, Robin Esterkin, Abe Friedman, Sylvia Friedman, Suretta Geller, Nancy Goldman, David Goodman, Florence Goodman, and Don Gould.

Also to Judy Horowitz, Lanita Hyatt, Ron Kibert, Sandy Koo, Michael Liebman, Robert Liebman, Sarah Liebman, Sylvia Liebman, Andrew McKnight, Michael D. Ogan, Anthony Orum, Joseph Poracsky, Ravid Raphael, Dan Riordan, Deborah Robboy, Charles Rynerson, Lin Sanders, Elayne Shapiro, Leonard Shapiro, Bob Smith, Paul Taylor, Rick Van Sant, Ethel Watters, Judy Weinsoft, Meryl Weiss-Pearlman, and Howard Wineberg.

I'd also like to add a few collective thank yous. The first goes to the librarians and staff members at the Multnomah Public Library, the Portland State University Library, the Lake Oswego Public Library, and the Oregon Historical Society Library. Special thanks go out to the folks at the Hillsdale and Capital Hill branches of the Multnomah Public Library. I began my professional life as a librarian. With that background, I know that this book could not have been completed without their expertise and the resources available in their collections.

The second group thank you goes to the Northwest Association of Book Publishers and the Portland PC Users Group. NWABP provided a forum in which to learn and people who were willing to share their expertise. They were the enablers that allowed us to turn *The Facts of Life in Portland, Oregon* from an idea into a real book between covers. And folks from the PPCUG were extremely helpful as I learned my way around WordPerfect for Windows.

The third collective thank you goes to Portland State University. There has been much talk, of late, of PSU's urban mission. PSU wants to be an integral part of the city, accessible to all and bringing the university's vast resources to bear to solve problems and enhance livability. While the terminology of an urban mission may be new, my experience shows that the people at PSU do this already. And they do it very well.

Throughout this project, I was directed to people at PSU. When I was evaluating software, I asked a vendor to recommend a local user who could really tell me about the product. The vendor referred me to a person from Computer and Information Services at PSU. He graciously directed me to a few people on the staff, who were happy to share their evaluations of the software. Members of the Sociology Department spoke with me about cities in general, and Portland in particular. When I needed maps and a quick geography lesson, PSU people from Continuing Education and the Geography Department were glad to help. Their colleagues at the International Trade Institute provided statistics and reports.

A number of people at the PSU School of Urban Studies heard about my project and offered their assistance. Others from the School willingly answered my many questions when I showed up at their doors. Based on my experience, the folks at PSU are succeeding – with little fanfare but lots of smarts and sincerity – at their urban mission.

One more collective thank you. Much of the early work on this book was done – appropriately, as we'll see, for coffee-loving Portland – at espresso bars and cafes. Some of my most productive hours were spent reviewing huge piles of information at tiny cafe tables, a tall latte near at hand. So my final thanks are to the kind waitpersons and proprietors who never seemed to mind the portable office I brought with me, and who always remembered to go easy on the foam.

When one collects this much data, and contacts literally hundreds of people in the process, mistakes are inevitable. I checked and double-checked; read and reread. But I'm sure I made a few mistakes along the way. They are my mistakes, and my apologies for them. If you are willing to set me straight, I'll be sure to correct them the next time around. And if you happen to be one of the people who helped, I thank you.

Introduction

"It's too bad," mused my husband, "that no one has written a book that pulls together all the facts and figures on Portland. You're a librarian. Why don't you do it?" And so this book was born. It was originally christened *Portland By The Numbers*. But to understand Portland, we need much more than numbers. We need facts and we need context. We need history and we need stories. We need excerpts from what others have said and we need pointers to the future. Put it all together and you have *The Facts of Life in Portland, Oregon*.

I readily admit that as a relative newcomer to Portland who has been here just six years, I am not an expert. Rather, I aim to be a compiler of a grand bouquet of information that describes the Rose City – a city I came to by chance, and have come to love.

And while I'll also admit to anyone who will listen that I am an unabashed fan of Portland and the Northwest – and I'll offer them endless reasons why – Portland is by no means the perfect city, and the metropolitan area has its share of problems. We usually score very well on the city lists that have become so popular of late, that rate cities on everything from raising kids to rising real estate values. But we cannot deny that we miss the mark in some critical areas, which are as varied as the lack of a first-class university and the fact of gang violence.

Assembling information on Portland, I hope to give you a feel for this city. Just why is Portland winning so many livability awards? What makes Portland unique? Why do people come for a visit and decide to stay? Will we be able to maintain the high quality of life here? Are there serious threats on our horizon? Just what is life like in Portland, anyway? *The Facts of Life in Portland, Oregon* answers these questions. It describes the city, from the ways we shine to the areas where there's room for improvement, and everything in between.

I have tried to include a reference to just about everything that you might want to know about Portland. A truly enormous task. Like all surveys, I couldn't cover everything as thoroughly as I would have liked. But I always list sources, so you'll be able to find more information on particular topics if you are so inclined. I also made a decision early on that this book would focus on facts rather than addresses and phone numbers. You might want to keep a phone book near at hand if you are prone to follow up calls.

On a recent visit to Portland, sociologist Anthony Orum spoke to me about what he calls "indoor and outdoor" cities. Indoor cities are cities where winter is present much of the time. Residents stay indoors more, and there is often little to do besides work. Outdoor cities are more open. They are relaxed and expansive, and retain a sense of how people and nature interact to form an overall environment. People are not crowded together, and the pace of life is a bit slower. There is often a sense of youthful vitality among the residents. Of course there are exceptions; Minneapolis comes quickly to mind. But Orum's characterization of Portland as an outdoor city rings true. As you read, consider, if you will, how fortunate we are that Portland is an outdoor city.

April 16, 1993
Portland, Oregon

Winning

on the

Willamette

In the Beginning

Just about everyone in Portland knows the story of the 1845 coin toss. Two years earlier, Asa Lawrence Lovejoy and William Overton had filed a land claim for an area known as The Clearing. Overton soon sold his share to Francis W. Pettygrove. When Lovejoy and Pettygrove couldn't agree on a name, they flipped a coin – now known as the "Portland penny" – to decide. Lovejoy, who was from Massachusetts, would have picked Boston. But Pettygrove won, and he chose Portland, after the city of that name in his native state of Maine.

The other popular story describes a fork in the road on the Oregon Trail. A few gold pieces indicated the way west to California, while the words *To Oregon* led north. The implication, of course, is that those immigrants who could read were the ones who went on to Oregon.

In *The Facts of Life*, we focus on Portland today. But as these stories suggest, the city's short history is colorful and revealing. Those who have studied Portland's history write of contradictions and paradox, of opposites together. There are several wonderful histories you may want to read, which we list at the end of the chapter.

In the meantime, here are a few excerpts. They are included not to recount the history of Portland, for we cannot do it justice in just a few pages. Rather, they are here to entice you into finding a history of Portland soon, and as a bit of a backdrop or counterpoint for Portland in the 1990s.

A Glimpse at the Past

We begin before Portland came to be, with the opening of the northwest frontier:

> The Lewis and Clark expedition had opened the Pacific Northwest for the future westering of America....The sea otter, and later the beaver, were viewed much in the same way the mother lode in the Sierra Nevada in California would be during the gold rush. Fortunes were to be made. A country was waiting to be won.

> Gordon DeMarco, *A Short History of Portland*, 1990.

Fewer than thirty years after the Lewis and Clark expedition brought back reports of the Chinooks and Kalapooias and less than a decade after the building of Fort Vancouver, disease virtually exterminated the population of northwestern Oregon. The spread of the Anglo-American trading system opened the possibility of both immediate economic gains and ultimate catastrophe for the Indians.

> Carl Abbott, *Portland: Gateway to the Northwest*, 1985.

Portland had originated as a rest stop for traders and Indians at a clearing on the west bank of the Willamette between Oregon City and the Hudson Bay Company's Fort Vancouver on the Columbia. Asa Lovejoy, a 35-year-old Massachusetts lawyer, recognized the townsite worth of The Clearing after a lanky Tennessee drifter, William Overton, pointed it out in mid-November of 1843. Returning to Oregon City from Fort Vancouver, Lovejoy had offered the sick Overton a ride in his big canoe. Approaching The Clearing, Overton grew sicker and suggested they go ashore. Lovejoy could then examine "the best claim...around here." As Lovejoy later recalled, "It took my eye. I had no idea of laying out a town there, but when I saw this I said: 'Very well, sir, I will take it.'"

> E. Kimbark MacColl, *Merchants, Money and Power: The Portland Establishment 1843-1913*, 1988.

There was one problem, however, and it suggests that the description of Overton as a "desperate, rollicking fellow" was not too wide of the mark. He lacked the 25-cent filing fee. Lovejoy did not. Over Portland's first business luncheon an arrangement was worked out whereby Lovejoy would pay the fee and in return receive half the claim, 320 acres of what was to become downtown Portland.

> Terence O'Donnell and Thomas Vaughan, *Portland: an Informal History & Guide*, 1984.

If the *Oregonian* gave Portland equal standing with Oregon City as an information center for the territory, then a few miles of unfinished plank road were enough for Portland to gain victory over the town's nearest rivals. At the start of the 1850s, Americans throughout the Midwest and South were seized by a mania for plank roads – highways with a surface of sawed planks spiked to wooden stringers....The first planks, from Portland's own steam sawmill, went down with great fanfare and suitable oratory on September 27, 1851. The company ran out of money after planking only a few miles of this first version of Canyon Road, but even the rutted track that continued into the rich agricultural lands of the Tualatin Valley made Portland the most accessible port for Washington County farmers, who shipped their abundant wheat to San Francisco.

Carl Abbott, *Portland: Gateway to the Northwest*, 1985.

...the staid residents who made the city were men and women of a morality, religious conviction and sturdy force of character not exceeded by any class of people in America. But it must be noted...that Portland has been a most cosmopolitan spot. From the first it was the landing place for ships, and they came from all ports....Sailors...felt the usual jubilation of the jolly tar off duty, and sought whom and what he might devour....infamous means of satisfying the long denied passions of the seafarer, were sought and supplied....

In the face of all that has been said above, [including three colorful pages on "grossness and coarseness of speech" and "indulgences" carried to "violent and wild excess"] the general quiet and tranquility, and good order of the place is quite marked. Affairs of blood are not common; house breaking, violent robbery, or affrays are but few. Popular tumults are unknown. The order in processions, or excursions, or in public assemblies is good. A general spirit of urbanity and civility prevails, and the virtue of hospitality is nowhere more marked.

H. W. Scott, *History of Portland Oregon*, 1890.

Portland was, in fact, an immigrant city by the end of the century. The 1880s ushered in a thirty-year surge of European immigration to the United States, with a new influx of immigrants from Italy, Greece, Hungary, Poland, and Russia joining the established streams from Germany, Ireland, and Scandinavia. Portland never welcomed the volume of newcomers who landed in New York or clambered off the trains in Chicago, but nevertheless, by 1900, 58 percent of its residents – 52,000 out of 90,000 – had either been born outside the United States or were the children of immigrants.

Carl Abbott, *Portland: Gateway to the Northwest,* 1985.

It all seemed a contradiction, this mixture of conservatism and progressiveness; and yet it was typical of the city's ethic and for that matter of the state's. A town that went to bed very early in the several senses of that phrase, it nonetheless founded the most academically radical college in the United States. A state of farmers with a fondness for old ways, Oregon put into law in this period the "Oregon System" – the initiative, the referendum, the direct primary, the recall – legislative reform placing Oregon in the vanguard of the nation.

Were these contradictions? Perhaps only if one thought in stereotypes which Oregon and Portland, still isolated and independent, often did not. To outsiders, conservatism and liberalism might seem strange bedfellows. In Oregon it was thought – and still is to a considerable degree – that there was no reason why these two should not be occasional companions.

Terence O'Donnell and Thomas Vaughan, *Portland: an Informal History & Guide,* 1984.

As a sedate, maidenly and respectable city whose first families like to trace their roots back to the Puritan villages of New England, Portland had long boasted of having the world's longest bar, Erickson's, just two blocks from the waterfront. The liquor trade was so profitable that before state prohibition took effect in

January 1916, about 25 percent of the city's general operating funds were derived from liquor license fees. And yet when the teetotalling lumber baron, Simon Benson, donated 20 beautifully crafted bronze drinking fountains to the city so that his loggers and other citizens would not have to resort to bars in order to quench their thirsts, he was proclaimed a local hero.

> E. Kimbark MacColl, *The Growth of a City: Power and Politics in Portland, Oregon 1915 to 1950*, 1979.

...In November, 1922, the voters, with a large plurality in Multnomah County, succumbed to the enticements of the Ku Klux Klan and approved an anti-Catholic, anti-private school initiative measure that was to be declared unconstitutional by the U.S. Supreme Court in 1925. The Klan, with strong lower middle class and blue collar appeal, pledged itself to do battle against "Koons, Kikes and Katholics."

* * * * *

Less than a decade later, an Independent Republican Jew, department store executive Julius Meier, was overwhelmingly elected governor on a public power platform in a state dominated by the private utilities that subsequently emasculated almost every effort to organize people's utility districts.

> E. Kimbark MacColl, *The Growth of a City: Power and Politics in Portland, Oregon 1915 to 1950*, 1979.

At the peak of wartime production in 1943 and 1944, metropolitan Portland counted 140,000 defense workers....The Kaiser [shipbuilding] yards placed help-wanted ads in eleven states. The response almost emptied the rest of Oregon, and drew the unemployed from small towns in Idaho and Montana. Workers were brought in by chartered trains from the East Coast. Portland's population grew from 501,000 to 661,000 between 1940 and 1944. One could safely assume, in the war years, that every third person standing in line for the bus or a double feature was a newcomer to the city.

> Carl Abbott, *Portland: Gateway to the Northwest*, 1985.

On the site of the Pioneer Courthouse Square the town erected its first real schoolhouse, a big, white New England building with cupola and bell. Thirty years later the block became the site of the town's beloved Portland Hotel, a seven-story, steep-roofed Queen Anne chateau with an iron-railinged courtyard, complete with a *porte-cochere* – fit for an alighting monarch. Nothing in town, with the exception of the extinct farmers' market, is more missed by Portlanders who remember the 1951 demise.

For the next thirty-odd years this, the central block of the city served as a parking lot. Finally, the city, awakening to the fact that its heart should be something more than an expanse of oil-stained asphalt, purchased the block to convert it to a square....

> Terence O'Donnell and Thomas Vaughan, *Portland: an Informal History & Guide*, 1984.

Neil Goldschmidt took office as mayor four days after the city council approved the *Downtown Plan*. The timing presented him with a politician's dream – a detailed agenda of projects for which there was wide approval and deep support and to which most opposition had been neutralized. Goldschmidt had not originated any of the components of the plan, but he had monitored its progress during his two years as city commissioner and had developed a proprietary interest by helping to shape the detailed guidelines. The *Downtown Plan* meshed with his goals for neighborhood revitalization and regional planning as part of an overall growth strategy. It appealed to his established supporters among neighborhood associations and civic activists and allowed him to develop new ties with Portland businessmen. In return, Goldschmidt contributed his extraordinary political sense for picking the best sequence of projects and finding the means for implementation.

> Carl Abbott, *Portland: Planning, Politics, and Growth in a Twentieth-Century City*, 1983.

Goldschmidt was the right man at the right time to push Portland forward. The combative conservative downtown business and real estate interests no longer had the cohesion to get down and fight like they had in the past. When [Mayor Terry] Schrunk stepped down in 1972, Goldschmidt stepped into a vacuum of power. The old aristocracy was dying off and the business interests were vulnerable to the right challenger. With the Goldschmidt election victory a new era in Portland city history had begun.

Gordon DeMarco, *A Short History of Portland*, 1990.

More than 140 years have passed since Lovejoy and Pettygrove tossed their penny into the air to give a name to the new settlement on the Willamette. Over those decades, Portlanders have made their share of mistakes, but they have also managed to build one of the country's most attractive and livable cities. The challenge for the future is to do as well.

Portlanders care about their city. They worry about their neighborhoods, about access to the Willamette, about the preservation of parks and views, and about the impact of new development. They may disagree about specific political issues, but they participate actively in political campaigns and elections. Citizens who invest their time and energy can make their voices heard, whether they've lived in Portland for just a few years or a lifetime. The inscription on the Skidmore Fountain at First and Ankeny tells us that "good citizens are the riches of a city." Portland's greatest strength is that its residents take the message seriously.

Carl Abbott, *Portland: Gateway to the Northwest*, 1985.

If you'd like to delve into Portland's history, you might enjoy one of the books described on the next page. Or stop by the Oregon Historical Society, where you'll find exhibits, a research library, and a wealth of other resources on the history of the city of Portland, the state of Oregon, the Oregon Trail, and the Pacific Northwest.

For History Buffs

E. Kimbark MacColl's books are the best choice for those who want a detailed, in-depth study of business, politics and power in Portland from 1843 to 1950. *The Shaping of a City: Business and Politics in Portland, Oregon 1885-1915* was published in 1976. *The Growth of a City: Power and Politics in Portland, Oregon 1915 to 1950* came out in 1979. *Merchants, Money and Power: The Portland Establishment 1843-1913* was published in 1988, in collaboration with Harry H. Stein.

Those who prefer a briefer look will enjoy Gordon DeMarco's *A Short History of Portland*, which tells Portland's story in a delightful but no-holds-barred, nothing-is-sacred way.

Carl Abbott's *Portland: Gateway to the Northwest* is another great choice. The very readable text is supplemented by wonderful old photos and profiles of selected Portland businesses.

Portland: an Informal History & Guide, by Terence O'Donnell and Thomas Vaughan, is the choice for those who want a short, beauifully written portrait that combines a sense of history with a sense of place. It's a little dated, but it's still the one to carry around with you as you explore the Rose City. Unfortunately, it is out-of-print, but used copies occasionally turn up at Powell's Books, and the public library has quite a few in its collection.

Finally, a book from the urban studies perspective may also be of interest. *Portland: Planning, Politics, and Growth in a Twentieth-Century City* is another excellent book by Carl Abbott. His focus here is on planning efforts from 1900 on; the discussion includes geography, land use issues, city planning projects, and politics.

A Rose By Any Other Name . . .

Nicknames are usually revealing. Portland has many, and each one is indeed descriptive of the city, its history or its character. Some, like Stumptown and the Rose City, have been in use for decades. Others, like Beirut, U.S.A. and the Carousel Capital of the World, are newer monikers. As a group, Portland's nicknames are a good place to begin our look at Portland today.

First, the real name. The history books credit a man by the name of Francis W. Pettygrove. Along with Asa Lawrence Lovejoy, he owned the land that would eventually become Portland's central business district. Lovejoy was one of the two men who originally staked out the claim. Pettygrove entered the picture when Lovejoy's first partner, William Overton, decided to head for California. Overton gave Pettygrove his share of the land claim in exchange for the provisions he'd need to make the trip south.

Lovejoy and Pettygrove couldn't agree on a name. We've already told the story of their famous coin toss in the history section. Since Pettygrove won, he picked Portland, after the city of that name in his native Maine. But it wasn't long before Portland had its first nickname – an unflattering one at that.

Stumptown

Within a few years, Portland was nicknamed Stumptown. The name referred to the many fir tree stumps that remained, sometimes for years, in the middle of the newly laid out streets. Promoters of other townsites in the area are credited with originating the unflattering nickname, in hopes of discouraging potential settlers from choosing Portland over their own struggling townsites. Little Stump Town was a variant. Portland persevered, and Stumptown remains one of our more popular nicknames.

Puddletown

Puddletown, another Portland moniker, may have similarly early roots. As Terence O'Donnell and Thomas Vaughan note in their *Portland: an Informal History & Guide,* an 1852 *Oregonian* editorial argued that it was not appropriate for ladies to raise their skirts to avoid puddles. Instead, the editorial urged Portland women to stay at home when it rained. Given the climate, this was a problematic solution at best.

The Rose City

The most popular nickname for Portland is the Rose City, or its variant, the City of Roses. When Portland hosted the Lewis and Clark Centennial Exposition in 1905, some prominent, rose-loving Portlanders – including Frank E. Beach, president of the North Western Insurance Company; Frederick V. Holman, attorney, historian and above all rose enthusiast; and the city's Mayor, Harry Lane – launched an informal campaign to nickname Portland "the Rose City." With roses blooming throughout the city, a successful annual rose show, and an active Portland Rose Society, the name took hold, and it has been in regular use ever since. And every June, Portland celebrates its world famous roses with the annual Rose Festival.

The Mythical Realm of Rosaria

Each year during that festival, Portland becomes, for just a few days, the Mythical Realm of Rosaria. Royalty – including kings, queens and princesses, in varying combinations – have reigned over the festival since its inception in 1907. *The Oregonian* boldly announced in 1909 that "Portland will cease to be a municipality" and will become instead "an absolute monarchy." But the term Rosaria was not used in contemporaneous accounts of the festival until 1913, when the *Night in Rosaria* parade was sponsored by the United Artisans and a few other organizations.

1913 was also the first year that the newly formed Royal Rosarians were involved in the festival. Although they greeted Rex Oregonus, the festival king, with great pomp and pageantry, descriptions of his triumphant arrival and festival reign do not identify him as the King of Rosaria. But the *Night in Rosaria* parade was a huge success, and Rosaria crept into the language, both in connection with the festival and the Rosarians. In 1925, the festival featured *Rosaria*, a monumental pageant mixing history and mythology, depicting "the influence of the rose upon the progress of civilization." And so each year, we too bow to the traditions, and for a few June days Portland becomes the Mythical Realm of Rosaria.

Rip City

The words Rip City were made popular by Bill Schonely, who was the Portland Trail Blazers radio announcer for 22 years. The "Schonz" – who now calls the games on TV – uses Rip City to indicate a successful shot, when the ball touches nothing but net. But Rip City has also come to mean Portland, especially during basketball season. If the team is doing well, Blazermania reaches its high during the NBA playoffs and finals. Huge Rip City signs and banners span office buildings downtown, Rip City placards appear in car windshields, and the words Rip City adorn everything from hats to underwear.

There was a bit of a flap during the 1991 playoffs, when the Trail Blazers management tried to crack down on unlicensed use of the phrase. Although they had only just applied for a trademark, Blazer management claimed common law ownership of Rip City. Dozens of articles appeared in the local press, bad-mouthing the attempted crackdown. Indignant fans and business owners reported hearing Rip City long before the Blazers were shooting hoops, in places as far away as Chicago.

In fact, it seemed that the fans were talking more about the Rip City issue than the winning team. In the end, after four or five days of what some were calling Rip-off City, the Blazers backed down, and the fans went back to the serious business of cheering the team on. The less colorful Blazertown also owes its origins to the Portland Trail Blazers, Portland's only professional, major league team.

River City

At a May, 1991 lecture, Terence O'Donnell recalled that in the early days one could actually see a working port when looking down toward the waterfront. Nowadays, we seem less aware that Portland is a true river city. Portland is located at the confluence of the Columbia and Willamette Rivers. The depth of the Willamette factored into Lovejoy and Pettygrove's decision to file their claim where they did. Since then, the river has been vital to Portland's economy, and it remains so today.

As Carl Abbott explains in *Portland: Planning, Politics, and Growth in a Twentieth-Century City*, "River cities are usually working cities, and Portland is a city built around a working river." According to the Port of Portland, 10,000,000 tons of ocean cargo pass through Port facilities each year. Dividing the city into two very different east and west halves, the Willamette – which means River of Life – not only shapes the economy. It also serves as a basic frame of reference for all Portlanders.

City of Bridges

The river may give life to a city, but bridging the river is critical too. While we don't hear the City of Bridges nickname as often as we hear some of the others, it is most suitable. One of the goals of the 1988 *Central City Plan* is to create a downtown that truly spans the river. And, for better or worse, Portlanders will be inconvenienced during the 1990s by a variety of major bridge maintenance projects.

The number of bridges we have depends on how you choose to count them. Within the city limits, there are ten that span the Willamette. But, as Sharon Wood points out in *The Portland Bridge Book*, we should also count the two bridges that cross the Willamette just south of the city, as well as the two that cross the Columbia to connect Portland with Vancouver. That brings the bridge total to fourteen. Three railroad bridges complete the picture. They all have their own stories; we'll mention a few when we consider Portland's physical landmarks.

Frascaland

According to *The First Portland Catalogue*, "so much of the southern end of downtown Portland is Zimmer Gunsul Frasca's work that it is sometimes known as 'Frascaland.'" While the Frascaland nickname may be most popular in architectural circles, ZGF's contribution to Portland is well known both locally and nationally.

In 1991, the firm was honored by the American Institute of Architects with its most prestigious Architecture Firm Award, for its "high standard of work and its impact on the Northwest region." The AIA announcement quoted *San Francisco Chronicle* architecture critic Allan Temko, whose words explain not only why ZGF was deserving, but why Frascaland is so appropriate: "If Portland is a superior place to live and work, and it is surely one of the finest urban environments in the United States, much of the credit for its civility and handsomeness belongs to Zimmer Gunsul Frasca."

Carousel Capital of the World

Portland has been called the Carousel Capital of the World by Charles Kuralt, and for good reason. The International Museum of Carousel Art is located in the Carousel Courtyard on Portland's east side, and local carousel lovers have been heard to boast that there are more restored, operating wooden carousels in Portland than in any other city. Currently there are four permanent carousel locations, but during some summers there have been as many as seven operating carousels in the city. As Portland historians often point out, and as other nicknames reflect, early Portlanders loved parades, pageants and amusements. Apparently present day Portlanders do too.

PDX and Ptld

PDX is what you'll see on airport baggage tags when your destination is Portland. But it also shows up fairly often as a shorthand version of the city's name. And the unimaginative "Ptld" is frequently found scrawled in return addresses, on signature-gathering petitions, and on sign-up sheets. Ann Arbor's A^2 serves the same purpose, but it's much more fun.

America's Best City

Do we need to christen Portland with a new nickname? *Northwest Magazine* tried to do just that. The January 6, 1991 issue of that section of *The Oregonian* announced the "A Rose City by Any Other Name" contest, and the February 24th issue listed the winners. Interest in the contest was reflected by "nearly hundreds of entries" and the judges had little difficulty agreeing on the winners. Here are the five winning entries that were reported by compiler Peter Carlin, with the grand winner topping the list, and the submitter's name in parenthesis:

- ▸ America's Best City (fourth grader Katoune Bounma)
- ▸ City of Disillusioned Californians (Susan Courtney)
- ▸ City With Hope (Lucio Lent)
- ▸ Fully Incorporated Urbanized Zone of Biochemically Manufactured/Organically Composible/Ecologically Sound (Yet Still Cost Effective and Job Producing) Rose-Like Plant Synthetics (Joe VanderZanden)
- ▸ Whoopee World (Beverly Harris)

We assume that Whoopee World owes its derivation to "Whoop, whoop," which was Mayor Bud Clark's favorite expression. Katoune Bounma may be on to something with America's Best City, but from the looks of the other winners, the more established nicknames are probably safe for a while. (You may have noticed the rose that's painted on the side of all our buses, taxis and police cars. We just can't imagine replacing them with pictures of disillusioned Californians.)

Beirut, U.S.A.

Northwest Magazine may not have coined a new nickname, but the January 16, 1992 *Oregonian* reported that, according to Craig Berkman, Portland does indeed have another new moniker: Beirut, U.S.A. Berkman, who chairs the Oregon Republican Party, claims that that's how they refer to Portland in the White House. Little Beirut is a variant. During 1990 and 1991, both Bush and Quayle were met by noisy, sometimes vulgar protestors. Eggs, rocks, burning flags, arrests and efforts to vomit in red, white and blue were part of the scene when demonstrators protested their visits. All things being equal, disillusioned Californians on police cars don't seem so bad after all.

There are a few more Portland nicknames worth mentioning, including Rainville, Swooshville, and Slugville. Anyone even remotely familiar with Portland will understand the allusion to rain. Swooshville is a play on the basketball term, and Slugville honors the many slugs that infest Portland gardens. The last three are not used very widely. They appear most often in *Oregonian* columns by Jonathan Nicholas, who clearly likes nicknames enormously.

Looking at Livability

...he described it as a "solid and reliable town." It would never be the center of fashion, he explained, but the blue river and the sublime Monarch of the Mountains, (Mt. Hood), glistening above the dark green forests forty miles to the east, were more than adequate compensation. Portland's good citizens, Deady told his readers, would "sleep sounder and live longer than in San Francisco."

> Carl Abbott, *Portland: Gateway to the Northwest*, 1985, quoting Judge Matthew Deady's article "Portland-on-Wallamet," *Overland Monthly*, 1868.

The Lure of Livability

Livability has become a hot topic. There are articles on the best cities for everything from business to jogging. And there are "top ten" city lists for categories as varied as civility, taxes, child rearing and good complexions. The *Places Rated Almanac* has become almost required reading for mobile Americans who are considering a cross country move. Amidst all this, the concept of livability may seem an idea born in the 1980s, that will help guide our choices in the 90s. But as the above quote shows, ours is not the first generation to compare life in different cities.

As Nancy J. Chapman and Joan Starker explain, the whole question of livability has been addressed before. Their article "Portland: The Most Livable City?" appeared in a 1987 book called *Portland's Changing Landscape*. They point to E.L. Thorndike's 1939 study *Your City* as one of the earliest efforts. Thorndike used indices to determine the "general goodness of life for good people." As it does so frequently today, Portland fared well back in 1939. Chapman and Starker report that "Portland ranked 42nd, tied for 15th place, out of the 310 cities."

They also note Portland's top ranking in Ben-Chieh Liu's *Quality of Life Indicators in U.S. Metropolitan Areas, 1970.* Liu's study, which was done for the Environmental Protection Agency, used over 100 categories to evaluate 65 U.S. cities.

Evaluating Livability

Critical to any analysis are the criteria on which cities are judged. Chapman and Starker explain that results can vary for several reasons, including the following:

- Some studies use data for cities only; others use information for metropolitan areas.
- Criteria vary, as does the weight given to each factor that is evaluated.
- Values vary. In the words of Chapman and Starker, "Is it more important to have an excellent opera or a professional football team? Lakes for boating or mountains for climbing? We would not all agree."

Portland's Livability

But it is also true that there is a consensus about Portland. After evaluating the physical and social environment in Portland, Chapman and Starker report "that national experts as well as Portlanders rate Portland as among the top 25 percent in livability, although they may disagree somewhat on where it ranks within that top quartile."

Portland's rank in the 1989 *Placed Rated Almanac* – 24th out of 333 metropolitan areas – is consistent with the 1987 findings of Chapman and Starker. Scoring in the *Almanac* is often based on supply or quantity, rather than quality. For example, the education score is derived from a count of metro area college students rather than a critique of school districts or higher education options. The health care score uses a formula to count hospitals and the number of physicians per patient. And the arts score awards points based on the number of radio stations, museums, new library books and the like. Although it lacks a qualitative component to balance the numerical results, Portland's score in the *Places Rated Almanac* fits with Chapman and Starker's evaluation.

Portland continues to earn kudos in the 1990s. We've won many awards, and the Rose City appears at or near the top of a large variety of city ranking lists. The following pages report these accolades, for your information and amusement.

We're Number One!

The Mayors' Favorite

Portland appears to be a favorite of the U.S. Conference of Mayors. In 1988, their **City Livability Award** was presented to Mayor Bud Clark, for "outstanding mayoral leadership in the arts." Mayor Clark also received their 1991 **City Livability Outstanding Achievement Award**, in recognition of Portland Future Focus, which is a community-based, strategic planning process. And in 1992, Portland won the U.S. Conference of Mayors **Award for Excellence in Financial Reporting**.

Praises for Planning

Portland has a national reputation – which is well-deserved – as a well-planned city. The 1972 *Downtown Plan* won the 1989 **Rudy Bruner Award for Urban Excellence**. According to the Bruner Foundation, awards are given to urban projects that create "socially supportive, physically pleasing, and economically viable urban places." Because the award is given to completed projects, city planners did not apply until 1988. This award is one of the few that brings more than recognition – it comes with a $25,000 prize!

Portland's *Central City Plan*, which was adopted in 1988, won the American Planning Association's 1990 **Planning Implementation Award**. About 20% of the plan's almost 300 projects were in process or completed at the time the award was made in November, 1990.

Polite 'n Pretty

Portland also has a national reputation as **a particularly polite city**. Although we don't win every time Marjabelle Young Stewart compiles her list of polite cities, we won the top spot in both the spring, 1989 and fall, 1990 listings. The list is compiled from rankings by business executives who attend Stewart's corporate etiquette seminars. Pittsburgh, Cheyenne, and Charleston are among some of the other top ranked cities.

According to the Collagen Commission for the Study of Beauty, of Palo Alto, California, Portland topped the 1989 list of cities that are **easiest on the complexion**. Seattle, Pittsburgh, Cleveland and Cincinnati followed Portland. Miami was the worst, with Dallas, Los Angeles, Salt Lake City and Sacramento also at the bottom of the list.

A Good Investment, Too

Indeed, we're not just another pretty face. According the 1991/92 *Portland Metropolitan Chamber of Commerce Membership Directory*, 1990 rankings by the Federal Deposit Insurance Corporation rate Portland as top on the west coast, and number five in the nation, for **"the lowest commercial real estate risk."**

People Movers

Tri-Met, the Portland metropolitan area transit system, was named **America's Best Large Transit Agency** by the American Public Transit Association. The September, 1989 award – the transit industry's highest honor – recognized Tri-Met's ridership increases, successful light-rail line, and good management. The award also cited the success of the downtown transit mall, and of Fareless Square, the free-ride zone downtown.

And Mail Movers

Even the U.S. Post Office gets into the act! The Portland Division received top honors in a national rating of **overnight postal delivery performance**. With a 94.19% rating, Portland was number one for the first quarter of fiscal year 1991, topping the performance of 73 other divisions. The Portland Division, which encompasses most of Oregon and southwest Washington, serves more than three million customers in an area of 91,000 square miles.

Portland is also "number one" in a vast variety of different categories, for which awards are not usually given. The box on the following page includes some of the famous particulars.

Marks of Distinction

Portland has **more small breweries and brewpubs** than any other U.S. city.

The Saturday Market is **the biggest open air crafts market** in continuous operation in the U.S.

There are **more restored, operating, wooden carousels** – seven during the summer of 1990 – than in any other city.

Encompassing 4,683 acres, Forest Park is **the largest park within a city** in the United States.

With a diameter of only 24 inches, Mill Ends Park, at the intersection of SW Front and SW Taylor streets, has the opposite distinction: it is **the world's smallest park,** and probably the only one that was originally a utility pole hole.

Thanks to Mt. Tabor in southeast, Portland is **the only city in the United States to have an extinct volcano** within its city limits.

With one-third of all U.S. wheat exported through the Port of Portland, Portland is **the largest grain port** in the United States.

The Port also **imports cars to more states** than any other port in the U.S.

Portland is bisected by the Willamette River – **the longest north-flowing river** in the continental U.S.

Portland's most famous bookstore – Powell's City of Books – is also **the largest independent bookstore** in the U.S.

The Junior Parade at Portland's annual Rose Festival is **the biggest children's parade** in the world.

Finally, on January 12, 1991, anti-war protesters rallied in cities all over America to protest the impending war in the Persian Gulf. Although we are the 30th largest city in the U.S., Portland's Pioneer Courthouse Square was the site of the largest anti-war demonstration in the country. It was a typical rainy winter day, but 12,000 to 15,000 people gathered.

Even those holding the opposite political position were impressed with the turnout, and the fact that no arrests or injuries were reported. Apparently Portlanders can be polite even during political rallies. (Unfortunately, as the nickname Little Beirut implies, Portlanders are not always so well-behaved during demonstrations.) But in this instance, both the turnout and the crowd's behavior rated number one.

The Most Climbed Mountain

Although it's not in Portland, many Portlanders feel that Mt. Hood is truly "their" mountain. So we mention it here, both because it is **the highest mountain in the state**, and it is **the most climbed peak in North America**. In fact, among mountain climbers, it is **the second most popular mountain worldwide**: the only other mountain that is more popular with climbers is Mt. Fujiyama, in Japan.

With an elevation of 11,245 feet, Mt. Hood has been called the "crown jewel" of the Cascade Mountains. On clear days, this majestic mountain is visible from many places in the city. It's one of the most popular year-round destinations for natives and visitors alike.

Top Ranks

If you can't be "number one," showing up among the top ten is the next best thing. Some people east of Idaho still wonder whether Portland is in Maine or the state of Washington. But that's changing, as Portland gets the nod from many prominent national publications. Whether for business, pleasure, or just plain daily living, Portland appears with great frequency on the "best city" lists that have become so popular lately. We've added the bold-faced emphasis:

▸ The February 6, 1989 issue of *Newsweek* listed Portland among "America's hot cities." Other cities that were among "the best places to live and work" were Sacramento, Columbus, St. Paul, Providence, Albuquerque, Fort Worth, Birmingham, Orlando, and Charlotte.

▸ ***Kiplinger's Personal Finance Magazine*** echoed the praise. The November, 1991 cover story on "super cities" predicted that "the top places – for job-hunting, launching or relocating a business, starting a second career or investing in local companies – will be smaller, second-tier cities and regional capitals." Portland is among the 15 cities profiled. *Kiplinger's* liked the relatively low cost of "office space, utilities, housing, and taxes" and the fact that Portland is "still uncrowded and generating the jobs."

▸ For three years in a row, Portland came in third, with a grade of A-, on *Financial World* magazine's city "report cards." The February 19, 1991 issue graded cities on budgeting, infrastructure, accounting and performance evaluation. Although Portland's grade point average was identical to those of Phoenix and Seattle, those cities were ranked first and second because they are larger and thus more difficult to run. Detroit, with a D, was at the bottom of the 1991 class.

▸ Dallas and Phoenix topped both the 1992 and 1993 *Financial World* rankings, but praise for Portland was sprinkled throughout the articles. The Rose City was praised for smooth handling of the budgetary upheaval caused by Measure 5. And the editors liked the fact that Mayor Clark responded personally to a small company's inquiry regarding relocation. Philadelphia took last place in 1992; Detroit had the honor in 1993.

▸ *Business Week's* October 25, 1991 issue, which was devoted to quality, liked Portland for similar reasons. It profiled Portland as a city "on the cutting edge of quality in municipal government." *Business Week* liked the "private-sector techniques" used by the city, like customer surveys, performance audits that evaluate city services, department reorganizations that encourage cooperative work, and the new community policing policies.

▸ *City & State* echoed the refrain. Looking at "financial health" and "how well each city runs its financial operations," the November 18, 1991 issue found Portland and Dallas in a tie for sixth place, among the 50 wealthiest U.S. cities. Portland was number three for 1988-90 job growth. *City & State* liked Portland's "Aaa credit rating, minimal long-term debt burden per capita, and revenues that are rising faster than expenditures."

▸ The October 1, 1990 issue of *Newsweek* called Portland a "boom town." An article on hot housing markets included Portland as one of the "five hottest metropolitan areas in the last year." Using figures provided by the National Association of Realtors, *Newsweek* reported that Portland's housing values increased 15.8%, number five after Seattle/Tacoma (up 35.3%), Honolulu (33.2%), Sacramento (30.8%), and Indianapolis (16.1%).

▸ *U.S. News & World Report* liked Portland's housing market too. With the assistance of the WEFA Group, an economics consulting firm, the April 1, 1991 issue of *U.S. News* ranked 95 metropolitan areas on projected appreciation in home prices from 1990 to 1991. With a projected increase of 6.6% for 1991, Portland ranked fifth, behind Philadelphia, Honolulu, Fort Myers (Florida) and Chicago.

▸ Portland also made a strong showing in "Gloom and Boom Towns," a *U.S. News & World Report* analysis of cities most and least likely to withstand a recession in the 90s. The October 29, 1990 article listed Houston, Minneapolis, and Indianapolis along with Portland on the "boom" list; Philadelphia, New York, Detroit and Boston were the "gloom" towns.

‣ People who can withstand the recession can keep paying the mortgage. The April 12, 1991 issue of *American Banker* reported on a study of mortgage delinquency rates, which found Portland to be the third safest market in the U.S. Mortgage Information Corp., the firm that did the study, ranked Honolulu and Richmond ahead of Portland; Boston, New York and Atlanta were among the riskiest.

‣ *Flower & Garden* profiled Portland, and a number of Portland's gardens, in its September-October 1990 article on "Great Garden Cities." While the article noted that the featured cities "are by no means the only great garden cities in this vast country," the editors did suggest that "it would be worth going out of the way to visit a garden or two." Their picks in Portland included the Portland International Rose Test Garden, the Japanese Garden, Hoyt Arboretum, the Shakespearean Garden, Crystal Springs Rhododendron Garden, the Berry Botanic Garden, Leach Botanical Garden, and Elk Rock.

‣ Portland was included on *Parenting* magazine's list of the "ten best family cities." Using "good schools, affordable housing, a healthy economy, a low crime rate, and a clean environment" as criteria, the March, 1990 issue evaluated small cities, and determined that the best metropolitan areas for families have populations under about 500,000. The other top cities for raising a family were: Syracuse, Tallahassee, Boise, Roanoke, Cedar Rapids, Austin, Omaha, Colorado Springs, and Stamford.

‣ Portland also showed up on Peter Dragadze's list of underrated cities. Portland was in good, cosmopolitan company: his article in the April, 1987 issue of *Harper's Bazaar* also mentioned Genoa, Athens, Berne, Oslo, East Berlin, and Avignon. According to Dragadze, these "cities that travelers too often neglect" are "well worth visiting and even making a detour to see."

‣ The editors at *Travel & Leisure* apparently agree with Peter Dragadze's appraisal. The January, 1991 issue included

You Win Some, You Lose Some

In 1989, *Fortune* magazine ranked Portland as the ninth best American city for business. While we haven't made the *Fortune* top ten since then, the news is not all bad. In 1990, Portland was considered "near the top" among the remaining cities. The 1991 survey found Portland "third for quality public education," and "local executives [ranked] it fourth for overall satisfaction." The negatives? High taxes, and a pro-business rank of only 36 out of a possible 50.

Fortune reported that "cost has become far more important than it was in the Eighties." While quality of life remained important to the 600 executives queried for the 1991 survey, it was last on the list of considerations, which included the work force, nearby markets, business attitudes, good public schools, airline connections, costs (of living and doing business), and highways.

Atlanta topped the list in 1991, with Dallas/Fort Worth a close second. Recognizing that such new cities have their critics, who see them as "formless blobs of synthetic culture," *Fortune* came down squarely on the business side. "What they lack in refinement, they overcompensate for with energy, mostly directed toward turning a buck." And later, "Atlanta ... has 29 fiber-optic telephone paths, vs. only eight in New York. No problem if they need more; Atlanta is always eager to dig up its street for progress." It's beginning to sound like this was a contest that Portland did not need to win.

Although it was too small to qualify for the main rankings, *Fortune* liked neighboring Beaverton, which is home to Nike and many high tech firms. Portlanders rarely rave about sprawling Beaverton. But *Fortune* suggests that "lifestyle is Beaverton's main attraction, with coast and mountains both about an hour away. Nike chief Phil Knight believes that is part of the area's business magic. 'I think it's a creative place to do business.'" Beaverton must be doing something right.

More on Business Cities

Portland did better with the 400 CEOs queried for Cushman & Wakefield's annual survey on the best business cities. According to the 1991 Executive Summary, the CEOs were asked, among other things, "which cities are best for locating a business."

In the 1990 survey, Portland was ranked third out of 31 cities – a significant jump from 27th in the 1989 rankings. The 1991 rankings put Portland at number five. But the execs agreed with *Fortune* on Atlanta; the Georgia city was ranked number one in 1991, as it was in 1987, 1988 and 1989.

Portland in its "Where to Go Next" feature. Noting that "clean, safe and civilized Portland is the new jewel of the West," *Travel & Leisure* was impressed with the cultural scene. Urging readers to "get there now," the magazine suggested that they will appreciate Portland's architecture, galleries, Performing Arts Center, and "warehouse-size bookstore." (Powell's, for the uninitiated, is the biggest new and used bookstore in the U.S., complete with a cafe where you can drink a cafe latte or nibble a brownie while you browse through the as yet unpurchased books that caught your eye.) Praise for Portland's neighborhoods, ethnic restaurants and boutiques rounded out the magazine's recommendation.

▸ Boutiques interest *Playboy* too. The August, 1991 issue told its readers that Portland's Old Town is the place for hot shopping. *Playboy* suggested that readers check out Old Town stores as well as the Saturday Market, for northwest products and buys "that you won't find anywhere else."

▸ Portland is also a top city for walking. The August, 1991 issue of *The Walking Magazine* profiled the ten best walking cities in America. Their picks were: San Francisco, Savannah, Washington, D.C., Portland, Boulder, New York, Boston, Chicago, Philadelphia, and New Orleans. *The Walking Magazine* liked Portland's 200 foot blocks; the many fountains; China-town, Old Town and the Yamhill Historic District; the parks system; the transit mall; and the 40-Mile Loop. Powell's and a view of Mt. Hood were also among the highlights of a down-town walking tour. *The Walking Magazine* mentioned one other fact that merits repeating here: Portland's Chinatown is "the second largest in the U.S. after San Francisco."

▸ Those who prefer a drive should be sure to get direc-tions to the Gorge. Along with seven other roads, the Columbia Gorge Highway was listed in the 1991 *Rand McNally Road Atlas* as one of the country's most scenic routes. Other western winners included the Pacific Coast Highway in California and the Going to the Sun Road in Glacier National Park, Montana. But you might want to avoid the Columbia Gorge Highway during bad weather. According to geographer Daniel M. Johnson's article in *Portland's Changing Landscape*, climate and topography can make it "the most treacherous stretch of highway in the country."

▸ *World Trade* magazine did not include Portland among "North America's 10 Best Cities for International Companies." But the Rose City did rate a mention in the August, 1990 feature. *World Trade* was impressed by plans to improve the Port of Portland's marine and air facilities and to deepen the Columbia River channel. The winners? Atlanta, Baltimore, Charlotte, Columbus, Huntsville, San Jose, Seattle, Toronto, Tucson, and the twin cities of Minneapolis/St. Paul. The other places to watch besides Portland? Irvine and Memphis.

▸ Maybe it became a self-fulfilling prophecy. When *World Trade* looked again at international cities in December, 1991, Portland was on the list. (Irvine didn't make it, but Memphis did.) We made the list because, as the article noted, "Portland backs up beauty with brawn." Among other factors, *World Trade* liked Portland's good rail, air, water, and road connections; the "Pacific Rim influence"; and the "municipal commitment to global thinking." The other winning cities in 1991 were Little Rock, Louisville, Norfolk, Orlando, Raleigh, Sacramento, Salt Lake City, and San Antonio. "In the interest of diversity" the 1990 winners were excluded from the running, but all seven judges would have included both Atlanta and Seattle again if given the choice.

▸ Portland also got high marks in the July, 1992 issue of *Outside* magazine. In "You Could Be Living Here," Portland was ranked number four among ten U.S. cities "where you don't have to give up a good living to live a good life." Boise, Flagstaff and Asheville topped the list. Juneau, Ventura, Hilo, Beaufort, Traverse City, and Cornwall were the other winning cities. According to the article, all have "good schools, respectable employment opportunities, a little culture, and proximity to wild places." But Portland beat the bunch in one other area: with the exception of Cornwall – which is in New York State – Portland was the only city on the list where you can get *The New York Times* delivered to your home every day of the week!

▸ Finally, Portland popped up on May 14, 1992 in *Rolling Stone's* annual "Hot Issue." Citing Puddletown for its "Hot Music Scene," *Rolling Stone* mentioned some of the bands and clubs that are part of the alternative music scene here.

More Nods

National publications are not the only ones to give nods to Portland. Here are a few more winning mentions:

▸ According to an article in the June 9, 1992 *Oregonian*, sailors consider Portland to be "one of the top U.S. ports to visit." Many Navy, Marine and Coast Guard personnel get the chance to see Portland during Rose Festival, when their ships dock here to participate in the festivities. A total of twenty-three ships were in Portland for the 1992 festival. Unfortunately, festival planners expect fewer ships in 1993, due to military budget cuts.

▸ Portland has been recognized by the National Arbor Day Foundation as a tree city. Tree city awards are given to cities that encourage tree care and planting programs. Two other metro area cities – Lake Oswego and Tualatin – have also won tree city designations. In case you're curious, Portland has approximately 150,000 street trees.

▸ Speaking of neighboring cities, Milwaukie was profiled in *50 Fabulous Places to Raise Your Family*, a 1993 book by Saralee and Lee Rosenberg. The authors evaluated 300 small cities and towns. Among other things, they liked Milwaukie's schools, housing, and easy commute to jobs in Portland.

To sum up, there is indeed a consensus that you can start a business, buy a house, get a mortgage, withstand the recession, enjoy quality government, raise a child, take a walk, shop the boutiques, stroll the galleries, browse the bookstores, plant a tree, visit a garden, think globally, read *The New York Times* and hear hot music – all in the award-winning City of Roses.

A is for Architecture . . . and Advertising

Creativity in advertising isn't dead; it's just head-
quartered in a *Bell Epoque* building in Portland, Oregon,...

Bernice Kanner, *New York*, March 16, 1992.

...the quintessential humanistic 20th-century American
city.

Gideon Bosker and Lena Lencek, *Architecture*, November 1987.

Many Portland firms, companies, agencies and individuals
win top honors. We can't possibly list them all here. But in two
fields – architecture and advertising – Portland has attained
a reputation unusual for a medium-sized city. Portland architects have designed many of the award-winning buildings that
grace our city. And Portland ad agencies have become famous
for a host of winning national ad campaigns, which are often
advertising Portland products.

Business Week's January 14, 1991 issue illustrates the point.
Among the "Best of 1990" was a Nike ad from the shop of
Wieden & Kennedy. The new Convention Center's Twin
Towers, designed by the Zimmer Gunsul Frasca Partnership,
also made the list. Both firms, as well as the objects of their
attention, hail from Portland.

Winning Advertising

Wieden & Kennedy isn't the only Portland ad agency with
a national reputation, but it is certainly the most famous of the
Portland agencies, and the one that put the Rose City on the
advertising map. Both *Ad Week* and *Advertising Age* named
Wieden & Kennedy Agency of the Year for 1991.

The W&K awards list could go on and on. But, as Jack D.
Welch explained in the March 13, 1991 *This Week Magazine*,
"Wieden hasn't the slightest clue how many awards W&K has
won for creative excellence. 'Hundreds. Thousands,' Christine
Barrett, creative manager suggests. 'Maybe more. Tons. They
probably stopped counting.'" After assembling a long list of
advertising awards for other Portland shops, we've decided to

stop counting too. Instead, we'll mention just two of the more unusual ones.

First, Will Vinton's Claymation® characters are known throughout the world. According to Will Vinton Studios, the California Raisins™ were "some of the most successful commercial characters of all time, ranking among the top three most popular commercials three years in a row." In November, 1991, they danced into the Smithsonian, "in honor of the significant role the California Raisins™ have played in American pop culture." While Bart Simpson, brainchild of Portland's Matt Groening, may be giving the Raisins a run for their money, the Raisins clearly have their place in history.

There are indications that we'll remain a top advertising town. A team of three Portland State University students were the grand prize winners of the 1991 Citibank/Clio College Advertising Awards. Their multi-media campaign was judged best among more than 500 entries, including entries from prominent universities with more extensive marketing programs. The winning TV spot was filmed at PSU, in campus buildings and on the park blocks. 1991 was the first year that the celebrated Clios included a student competition.

Appropriately, Portland played host to the American Advertising Federation national convention in June, 1992. Portland is also home to the American Advertising Museum, the first advertising museum in the world.

Winning Architecture

Architecturally, Portland draws praise and awards both for individual projects, and for the way the city's buildings, transit, parks and open spaces form a distinctive, harmonious whole. When the American Institute of Architects awarded its prestigious Architecture Firm Award to the Zimmer Gunsul Frasca Partnership in 1991 – honoring "a firm that has consistently produced 'distinguished architecture' for at least 10 years" – Portland basked in the glow. ZGF was "particularly recognized for its work in reshaping the city of Portland."

As in the advertising arena, the Portland list of architectural awards is long. It includes award-winning buildings that were designed by prominent architects, like A.E. Doyle, Pietro Belluschi and Michael Graves. Other architectural firms are well represented too. There are also many less famous Portland buildings that command our attention today. In their book *Frozen Music*, Gideon Bosker and Lena Lencek call Portland "an intelligently curated architectural museum." While they may not be award winners, you'll find many buildings that are wonderful examples of a variety of architectural styles that have come – and gone – in most other American cities. We'll help you locate the buildings you shouldn't miss when we look at Portland's cultural scene.

"The Best of Portland"

We'll mention one more award winner, since it is so in keeping with the theme of this section. Graphic Arts Center, a noted Portland commercial printer, won two national awards in 1991 for its promotion package, *The Best of Portland*.

Rather than a brochure or folder filled with close-ups of the printing plant and descriptions of the process, GAC produced a truly beautiful 32 page booklet with glossy, artistic photos and lovingly written descriptions of Portland. As GAC Vice President J. Droge explained, "Our goal was to dramatize to people in New York City and other major markets that coming to Graphic Arts Center and Portland is truly an exciting experience."

Indeed they did. The photographs and the printing are so fine that you are tempted to smell the full size roses or grab hold of a shiny apple. As we compiled information for this book, red pens and highlighters hovered over text, circling useful data and making notes. But the GAC brochure remains pristine; it was just too beautiful to mark up.

As for the awards: *The Best of Portland* won the Printing Industries of America "Best of Category" award, for printers self-promotion pieces, from a field of 6,800 entries. And it won the "Gold Ink Award," for special achievement in the printing industry, from *Publishing & Production Executive Magazine* and Printing Impressions.

The Best of Portland, *WW* Style

Like other newspapers, Portland's newsweekly, *Willamette Week*, does an annual "Best of Portland" issue. The intention here is not to compare their best picks to those of other cities. Rather, we list some of the winners in recent years, to give you a feel for the variety of choices in Portland, and for the newsweekly itself.

The feature includes some of the expected categories, like "Best Downtown Runner's Route" (for "running where you can be seen") and "Best Event for Kids in the Past Year" (slumber parties at selected branches of the Multnomah Public Library). But it also includes more exotic winners, like the following:

- ▸ "Best Bus Stop" (SW 6th and Jefferson, where all northbound buses stop)
- ▸ "Best Neighborhood Aroma" (baking bread near the Franz Bakery)
- ▸ "Best Tree" (a willow on Gillihan Loop Road, Sauvie Island)
- ▸ "Best Place to Absorb Poetic Vibes" (Cafe Lena)
- ▸ "Best Place to Watch Guys Take Their Shirts Off" (Wallace Park)
- ▸ "Best Bar for Meeting Pro Basketball Players" (Shanghai Lounge)
- ▸ "Best Downtown Wading Fountain" (Lovejoy Fountain)
- ▸ "Best Reason to Drink and Drive" (Motor-Moka, the drive-through espresso bar)
- ▸ "Best Way to Impress Out-of-town Guests" (plane ride into the Mount St. Helens crater)
- ▸ "Best Place to Descend into Hell" (the Chapman Square bathroom)
- ▸ "Best Place to be Embarrassed on Your Birthday" (Tequila Willies)

Look for the "Best of Portland" during July and read it yourself. This sampling doesn't come close to doing justice to the choices, and the rationales of the judges are fun too.

You Can't Win Them All

You can't be in the top ten all the time. The next section looks at some of the rankings that Portland boosters would rather forget. We could argue that many of these low scores are old scores – often dating back to the 1980s. But in the interests of fair play, we look at them anyway. As you'll see, some are amusing, and some are more serious. We'll include a few top scores to boost any lagging spirits. And if a ranking seems suspect, we'll try to add some perspective.

We're in the Money?

Money magazine is one publication that regularly rates cities without falling victim to Portland's charms. In its search for "the best places to live," the September issue annually ranks 300 metropolitan areas. Portland was number 101 in 1988, 81 in 1989, 38 in 1990, 60 in 1991, and 132 in 1992.

While Portland may not be a *Money* winner, the Northwest often does well. Bremerton was number one in 1990, and Seattle, Tacoma, Olympia, and Eugene/Springfield were among the top ten that year. In 1991, Bremerton was number two and Boise number four. 1992 wasn't a very good year for the Northwest: all of these cities dropped in the '92 rankings.

But Portland does get more than just a passing mention each year. To put together each article, *Money* surveys a sample of their subscribers to determine "what they valued in a place to live," collecting data on everything from water quality and taxes to house prices and commuting times. Then, "with the help of Fast Forward, a Portland, Ore. computer consulting firm," they match the 300 metro areas to the subscribers' priorities. But before we bemoan Portland's poor showing, we should note that most Portlanders are not typical *Money* subscribers, whose median household income in 1992 was $71,760.

Raining on Romance

Bert T. Sperling, who owns Fast Forward, was profiled in the March 31, 1989 *Oregonian*. According to Mr. Sperling, Portland is the 43rd most romantic city in the U.S. As *The Oregonian* explained, Mr. Sperling was asked by Korbel champagne "to find the nation's most romantic cities" from among 75 metro areas. Reporter Spencer Heinz summarized some of the reasons for Portland's poor showing:

> the Portland metropolitan area ranked about two-thirds down the list as far as "net marriages" – that is, marriages minus divorces; three-fifths down the list for per-capita flower sales; and, in the category of women 18 and older who received gifts of diamonds, the Portland area ranked in the bottom quarter.

Portland did very well – second and fifth respectively – in the rankings for good restaurants and movie theaters, "but the city lost ground in the categories of taking a walk on the beach and watching a sunset. It has no ocean beach. Also, sunsets require sun." The most romantic city? San Francisco, followed by Honolulu and Los Angeles.

But all is not lost for romantics in Puddletown. The February, 1992 issue of *Glamour* magazine picked The London Grill at the Benson Hotel as one of the six "most romantic restaurants" in the United States. And if you don't grow your own, you can always get a good deal on a bouquet of roses in the Rose City.

About That Sun

According to more than 40 years of National Weather Service data, Portlanders can expect 224 cloudy and 74 partly cloudy days a year. They will see precipitation of .01 inches or more on 152 days. To put that data in perspective, consider the following:

- ► Commenting on our poor showing in the romantic sunset category, Bert Sperling told *The Oregonian* that Portland has "the lowest number of sunny days...except for Seattle."
- ► In "Portland: The Most Livable City?" researchers Nancy J. Chapman and Joan Starker found that "only Cleveland, Rochester, and Buffalo" have more rainy days than Portland. And "only Akron, Anchorage, Seattle, and Pittsburgh have more cloudy days."

But despite the dreary data, Portland actually gets rather high marks for its climate. We'll give you the full weather report when we consider Portland's geography.

Crime Toppers

On a much more serious note, Portland was number 322 (out of 333 metropolitan areas) in the 1989 *Places Rated Almanac* crime rankings. Since lower rankings mean less crime, 322nd is not admirable. The *Almanac* used statistics on murder, robbery, aggravated assault, burglary, larceny theft, and motor vehicle theft to determine city scores. Chapman and Starker recommend that we "interpret the crime data with caution," since there is some evidence that Portlanders may be more likely than the residents of other cities to <u>report</u> crime.

While that argument may be valid for some crime categories, it is hard to make a convincing case for bank robberies. According to an article in the June 27, 1989 *New York Times*, Oregon "led the nation in bank robberies per capita" in 1988:

> Portland, with a population of 388,000, reported 238 bank robberies in 1988. That is 200 more than Chicago,...193 more than Atlanta...and 143 more than Detroit.

The article suggests various explanations, ranging from "user friendly" lobbies that have no armed guards or bullet proof teller enclosures to an overcrowded prison system that can't house all the convicted felons. While the Oregon bank robbery statistics improved in 1989, 1990 and 1991, rates were up again in 1992. By that year's end, 262 bank robberies had occurred in Oregon. 1993 may be no better; more than 20 robberies were reported in just the first three weeks! And most Oregon bank robberies take place in or near Portland.

Stressed Out?

Zero Population Growth, Inc. has conducted three "stress tests" in the past few years, "to examine how cities are coping with the environmental, economic and social stresses that can result from uncontrolled population growth." Their analysis considers "population change, crowding, education, violent crime, births, community economics, individual economics, hazardous wastes, sewage, water, and air quality."

Portland doesn't score very well. Portland's 3.1 overall rating in 1985 was closer to 3, which means "warning" than 4, for "danger." Our 3.2 in 1988 was not much better. A "spinoff" study looked at environmental indicators, but Portland's 3.0 rating was still nothing to write home about: of the 204 cities rated, 79 did better than Portland, 38 received equivalent scores, and 87 did worse.

We could question the results. In the water category, for example, Portland received a rating of 4. ZPG admits that the water data was incomplete, as "the status of renewable water supplies" was unavailable. The April, 1991 *ZPG Reporter* even notes that "no city qualified for a 'best' rating, in which the area's water would be of high quality and in abundant supply to serve the city's present population." Portland is served by the Bull Run Watershed, which has long been considered a particularly high quality and abundant water source. The abundance has been questioned lately, in view of the droughts of 1991 and 1992, and the area's population growth. But a "danger" rating seems a bit exaggerated. We'll look again at the ZPG analysis when we consider Portland's environment.

Gridlock

According to an Associated Press report in *The Oregonian*, Portland was ranked 14th in the nation for gridlock. Using 1988 data, a study at the Texas A & M University rated traffic in 39 metro areas. Los Angeles, in first-place, was the worst, followed by a second place tie between Washington, D.C. and San Francisco. Seattle shared its fourth place ranking with Miami and Chicago. Portland has apparently lost ground; it was in 17th place the last time around.

Everyone in the Pool!

Given the next statistic, people are probably not driving to the swimming pool. According to Portland Future Focus's *Environmental Scan*, which was done in 1990, Portland has far fewer public indoor swimming pools per capita than cities of comparable size. Portland has three pools, or roughly one pool for every 140,000 residents. Other U.S. cities, like Denver, Seattle, and Minneapolis/St. Paul have one pool for about every 60,000 people.

The "Sneeze Capital"

Oregon magazine called the Willamette Valley "the Sneeze Capital of the country." The April, 1986 issue quotes Dr. Emil Dardana, an allergy specialist, who claims that "the Willamette Valley has more grass pollen than anywhere in the world."

More recently, the July 20, 1992 *Oregonian* called 1992 "the Year of Endless Allergies." And to many allergy sufferers it truly was. The mild winter allowed trees to flower early. With the persistent drought, the normal air-cleansing rains never materialized. The result was more people suffering, for longer than usual.

Tax Town

Some have suggested that we add Tax Town to the city nicknames list. According to the June/July, 1992 issue of *Your Taxes*, a newsletter published by Oregon Tax Research, Portland's tax burden in 1990 was the worst of 51 U.S. cities. The data comes from a study by the District of Columbia. It cites the example of a family of four who paid "an estimated average of $3,457 in state and local taxes" on their $25,000 income.

We could, of course, question the study's methodology, or speculate on the tax burden for a retired couple or a family with a different income. Such a review might change the results to some degree, but the sad truth is that taxes in Portland are high. And the topic is hot. We'll have lots more to say when we devote a chapter or two to the saga of taxes in Portland.

The 85th Healthiest City?

According to John Tepper Marlin's *The Livable Cities Almanac*, the healthiest city in the U.S. is Honolulu. Portland weighs in at a dismal 85th out of 100 metro areas. But his thesis is built on an interesting premise, for Marlin equates the healthiest cities with those where "people live the longest." He uses death rates in 1987 as his "overall measure of city health." While the rates are adjusted for "what we might expect based on the area's median age," is it really valid to use death rates as the main indicator of city health?

Perhaps a city's morbidity statistics – its data on illness – are better indicators of its healthiness. Locale is certainly a contributing factor in some deaths. But so are genetics, ethnicity, employment, life experiences, and lifestyle, to name just a few. Many of those who now consider themselves Portlanders spent much of their lives elsewhere. According to the 1990 census, about 14% of the people in Multnomah County moved to Oregon between 1985 and 1990. And analysts at Portland State University found that 72% of those who moved to Oregon between 1980 and 1990 were 65 or older.

So don't be overly alarmed. Indeed, we're reminded of Mark Twain's famous line, "The report of my death was an exaggeration."

Over the past few years, Portland has won much praise, and has developed an international reputation for its livability. But as this section shows, the Rose City isn't Paradise. We've seen what everyone else is saying about our city. What do Portlanders think?

What Do Portlanders Think?

What do Portlanders think about their city? Nancy J. Chapman and Joan Starker surveyed members of the City Club of Portland to determine "what Portland residents think is unique about their city, and also what aspects most contribute to, or detract from its livability."

Although their sample is small – 40 of the 50 people surveyed responded – the researchers "tap a particularly knowledgeable and well-travelled group." The following excerpt is from their article, "Portland: The Most Livable City?":

> ...Portland's physical environment generated the most positive comments -- the diversity of its surrounding environment; its size, reflecting the amenities of a large city as well as a small town atmosphere; its scenic setting. In the social environment the strongest impression is of the honest, open political climate and the informal, slow-paced ambience of the city. The negatives center on the poor economic conditions in recent years [the early 1980s], the provincial populace, and the wet climate.
>
> A number of aspects that constitute the uniqueness of Portland are not captured by the objective data....Several themes appeared that cut across a number of categories. The first of these is moderation. Portland was described as moderate in size, climate, political activity, and in the pace of life.
>
> The second recurring theme is of accessibility. The accessibility of natural beauty and recreational opportunities in the mountains, the seashore, and the desert was mentioned often. But Portland is also seen as a city in which people can easily become involved in social and civic affairs. The social, political, and business worlds are all described as "open". This accessibility extends to the transportation system; the city is easy to get around in both by car and on foot.

These paragraphs were published in 1987, but they still ring true in the 1990s. Chapman and Starker reported that "Portland's physical environment generated the most positive comments." We look next at those aspects of our city.

At the

Confluence

of Two Rivers

A Look at the Landscape

Is It Still Raining?

A Bird's Eye View

River City Bridges

What About Earthquakes?

A Look at the Landscape

...Portland has been a city built by gravity; goods from the forests, farms, mines and rivers have flowed to its wharves and warehouses. Nearby farmers and loggers harvested wheat and lumber, and the city's early artists gleaned scenes of land and water. Paintings of sweeping landscapes and novels about men and women taming the forests, settling the rich valley floors and coaxing crops from the dry Columbia basin to the east were standard for the first fifty years. Even today, in every art form from sculpture to music, nature maintains its invigorating, sometimes overpowering, inspirational power.

> Chet Orloff, "Starting With Art: Portland's Climb (and Claim) to Higher Culture," *ARTWORKS in Portland, Oregon*, 1984.

Writing about the beginnings of culture in Portland, historian Chet Orloff began with the land and the water. Although his subject is history of the arts, his words are also an appropriate beginning to our look at geology, geography, topography and climate.

Natural, physical features and climactic forces have considerable impact on the city itself, and on living in the city. In Portland, this impact is underlined by an active awareness on the part of the people who live here. Whether they are newcomers, immigrants of many years, or natives, Portlanders really notice, and are in part defined, by their natural surroundings.

For example, while Portlanders are rarely troubled by the rain, they appreciate, even delight, in the sunshine. Newcomers are heard to comment repeatedly on how green it all is. It is not uncommon for conversations to pause while participants – newcomers, immigrants and natives alike – stop to watch the sunset. And everyone loves the all too infrequent clear days when we can see Mt. Hood, Mt. St. Helens and Mt. Adams. So before we consider Portlanders, let's describe the physical landscape of their city, and the climate they find so dear. The following maps can help you locate the features we'll mention as we describe the lay of the land. The map on pages 44-45 is a state map; the map on pages 46-47 shows the northwest corner of Oregon in greater detail. Map credits are on page 78.

COLUMBIA
PORTLAND
COAST RANGE
WILLAMETTE VALLEY
CASCADE RANGE
KLAMATH MOUNTAINS
HIGH
Nehalem
Wilson
Trask
Tualatin
Sandy
Clackamas
Pudding R.
Santiam
Yaquina R.
Marys R.
Alsea
Calapooia
McKenzie
M. Fork Willamette
Coast Fork
Umpqua
Calapooya
Coos
Waldo Lake
Deschutes
L. Deschutes
Crater Lake
White
Warm Springs R.
Crooked
Fifteenmile Cr.
Summer Lake
Williamson
Sprague
Upper Klamath Lake
Klamath
Evans
Applegate
Sixes R.
Pistol R.
Chetco

Oregon Landforms Map

| |------------------------| |
0   miles   50

Landform Map of Oregon

by Erwin Raisz

Scale 0 ▭▭▭▭ 50 Miles

Geologically Speaking

While Portland is often characterized in placid terms, its geologic history is not. In his article "Portland's Landscape Setting," PSU Professor Larry W. Price summarizes the events that created the Portland landscape:

> ...Portland has been the scene of a series of spectacular geologic events. It began with huge lava floods issuing intermittently from eastern Oregon through the Columbia Gorge to inundate the area. Over time these flows were folded, faulted, buried under sediments, penetrated by local volcanoes, weathered and eroded. Most recently, another series of floods originated to the east of the mountains, this time consisting of vast amounts of water choked with rock debris and ice; these torrents surged through the Portland area, cutting and filling to create the terraced landscape we now see.

We'll "see" this "terraced landscape" when we get a bird's eye view of Portland, later in this section.

Geographically Speaking

The rivers and Portland's proximity to the ocean are important parts of the landscape. Here are the specifics:

- Portland is located about 65 miles east of the Pacific Ocean, in the Willamette Valley.
- Flowing through the valley, the Willamette River bisects Portland into east and west halves. The west side is hillier than the east.
- The confluence of the Willamette and Columbia Rivers is just north of the city, with the Columbia River forming the border between Oregon and Washington.
- To the west of the Willamette Valley is the Coast Range.
- About 30 miles east of Portland are the Cascade Mountains.
- Crossing the Cascades on its way to the Pacific Ocean,

the Columbia River flows through the spectacular Columbia River Gorge just east of the city.

▸ Visible on clear days and easily accessible from Portland stands 11,235 foot Mt. Hood, a peak of the Cascades.

▸ Portland has a latitude of 45 degrees North and a longitude of 122 degrees West.

▸ And for those who measure by distances to other places, Portland is 173 miles south of Seattle, and 639 miles north of San Francisco.

Blame It On the Mountains

The mountains provide impressive views and serve as an awesome reminder of the natural environment beyond the city; a reminder that mountains, forests and beaches are only an hour's drive. But more critical to this discussion is that the mountains, along with Portland's latitude and the proximity of the Pacific Ocean, determine the climate. Before we look at the weather from day to day, it's helpful to consider some of the factors that create the weather:

▸ Air that crosses the Coast Range cools as it moves east, dropping considerable amounts of precipitation on the coastal mountains.

▸ As a result, the air that reaches Portland is drier than the air that originally moved in from the ocean.

▸ The storm systems that reach Portland don't often make it over the Cascades, remaining instead on the west side of the state, and nourishing the conifer forests that flourish here.

▸ During the summertime, the Coast Range is a barrier to cool, damp, ocean air.

▸ Similarly, the Cascades shield Portland from weather systems that form in the interior of the U.S., so that the city rarely experiences the extreme hot and cold temperatures that are recorded in east and central Oregon.

While the mountains usually keep Portland temperate, Portland still has a few days of extreme weather each year, when we have low temperatures, high winds, ice storms or snow.

Extremes: Storms and the Gorge Effect

We experience the extremes because of the interaction between physical and climactic factors. First, the Rose City is subject to what has been called "the gorge effect." Here's what happens:

► Cold easterly winds sweep up the Columbia Gorge, which acts like a hugh wind funnel.
► Conditions in the city become colder and windier.
► When winds in the Gorge collide with warm, moist air moving in from the coast, rain turns to freezing rain.
► Freezing rain results in what is called "black ice," a treacherous layer of ice that covers roads, trees, sidewalks, power lines – indeed anything to which ice can cling.

And although Portland has relatively few hurricanes, tornados or thunderstorms, the city does experience what meteorologists call "mid-latitude cyclonic storms." Portlanders still talk about the 1962 Columbus Day storm, when winds in the city topped 100 miles per hour, resulting in millions of dollars of damage.

How does all this translate into the weather on a day-to-day basis? Put more simply, just when do you need an umbrella? The next section sheds some light (rain?) on that question.

Is It Still Raining?

Many complaints are heard about the rain, but these are countered by reminders that Portland's yearly average of 37 inches of precipitation is below that of many other cities. It just seems as though Portland gets more because it takes longer to fall....

> Christine A. Tripp, "Reopening the Oregon Trail," *World*, Winter, 1988.

There's an old wive's tale that a wet climate is good for your skin. Those of you who have read the *We're Number One* section know that the Collagen Commission for the Study of Beauty found that Portland tops the list of cities that are easiest on the complexion. So perhaps the tale is true.

Be that as it may, the fact is that Portland gets a lot of rain. And while sun worshippers may have a hard time adjusting to the weather, the other notable fact here is that Portland actually gets high marks for its climate. In the 1989 *Places Rated Almanac*, Portland was ranked 16th out of 333 metro areas. There must be a lot of folks out there who believe that they won't, like the witch in the Wizard of Oz, melt if they get wet.

The Daily Weather Count

Here's the data from the National Oceanic and Atmospheric Administration (NOAA). The first number is the figure for 1990; the number in parenthesis reflects the number of days as a mean calculated from at least 40 years of data. Each year, Portland has (drumroll, please):

- 63 clear days (mean = 68)
- 82 partly cloudy days (mean = 73)
- 220 cloudy days (mean = 224)
- 165 days with at least .01 inches of precipitation (mean = 152)
- 20 days with temperatures of 90 degrees or more (mean = 11)
- 33 days with temperatures of 32 degrees or below (mean = 43)
- 7 days with thunderstorms (mean = 7)

Taking Portland's Temperature

Next are the NOAA figures for temperature and rainfall. They reflect statistics that were recorded and averaged over a 30 year period.

Month:	Temperatures High:	Low:	Monthly Average:	Normal Rainfall:
January	44.3	33.5	38.9	6.16"
February	50.4	36.0	43.2	3.93"
March	54.5	37.4	45.9	3.61"
April	60.2	40.6	50.4	2.31"
May	66.9	46.4	56.7	2.08"
June	72.7	52.2	62.5	1.47"
July	79.5	55.8	67.7	0.46"
August	78.6	55.8	67.3	1.13"
September	74.2	51.1	62.7	1.61"
October	63.9	44.6	54.3	3.05"
November	52.3	38.6	45.5	5.17"
December	46.4	35.4	40.9	6.41"

Precipitating

Putting it all together, winters tend to be mild and rainy. Portland's 32.86" of rain in 1990 was 4.53" less than our "normal" 37.39". July and August are the driest months; November, December and January are the rainiest. According to NOAA, Portland gets about 88% of its yearly precipitation between October and May. But we are not immune to droughts. With little precipitation in the previous months, the 1992 water shortage was quite serious and water use had to be restricted.

Wonderful Winter

Snowfall averages only about seven inches per year, and there are usually no more than five days of measurable snow. Snowstorms normally bring only a few inches of snow, but it can stop the city cold – schools close, and lots of people just take the day off. Depending on the accumulation, it is not uncommon for the public schools to open two hours late, for conditions improve quite quickly as the temperature warms up.

Winters can also bring a few storms with freezing rain. The resulting "black ice" can be extremely treacherous. Portlanders either chain up their tires, or stay home. We can also get hail. Many a jogger has wished for a hat when hail falls, unexpectedly, from the sky. And it can get foggy, usually in the fall or early winter.

Spring, Summer and Fall

Summers are mild and dry. It rains very rarely, and the humidity is usually quite low. The *Placed Rated Almanac* calls the spring and fall "transitional." Perhaps you can best understand that by just reviewing the high and low temperatures, and the rainfall, on the chart. Gardeners might be interested to know that the first frost usually occurs around November 7; the last frost is April 3. NOAA also indicates that the airflow is typically northwesterly in the spring and summer, and southeasterly during the fall and winter months.

Variable Forecasts

As PSU Professor Daniel M. Johnson explains in his article "Weather and Climate of Portland," we must consider Portland's location and the varied topography in the Portland area in any discussion of weather. Portland is, in Johnson's words, "a fascinating mosaic of microclimates." For example:

- ▸ The West Hills may experience a significant snowfall that brings only trace amounts of snow to other areas.
- ▸ The east side is often colder than the west, even at similar elevations.
- ▸ Fog also varies by location. It can be sunny in higher elevations, while areas in the valley are fogged in.

The last element that must be mentioned, and that doesn't really come through the statistics, is the changeable nature of the weather in Portland. It is true that it can rain all day. But variable weather is far more common. As the realtors tell newcomers, if you don't like the weather, just wait a few minutes.

How Portland Compares

For those who are still worrying about the weather, a few more statistics. They are from *The Book of American City Rankings*, by John Tepper Marlin and James S. Avery with Stephen T. Collins:

- 34 U.S. cities get more rain than Portland.
- 53 cities have worse humidity.
- 57 cities are windier.
- 71 cities have more days with temperatures over 90 degrees.
- And Portland doesn't even show up on the list of the country's coldest cities.

A Dearth of Umbrellas

Like many Oregonians, I often shun raincoat and umbrella even during heavy showers, preferring to sprint or pretend it's not happening. However, this time, the umbrella....I raised the umbrella and popped it open. In a flash I was covered with sand. The umbrella had last been used...in a fort-building project at the beach on Sauvie Island.

Catherine Windus, "Kids and Teens," *The First Portland Catalog*, 1987.

When we first saw Portland, it reminded us of the French city of Lyons. Lyons is also a city of bridges. Part of Lyons is built into hills; other areas are flat. And both cities are temperate, and rather rainy. But Lyons has many umbrella stores. Umbrella makers can be found who will fix a broken favorite, and one can choose from a large variety of styles, fabrics and sizes. One can certainly buy an umbrella in Portland. But the accessory counters at our department stores are no match to Lyons's umbrella stores. And the yellow pages list only three umbrella shops in Portland, one of which sells blinds and awnings!

A Bird's Eye View

Just as topography, climate and natural surroundings have shaped Portland and Portlanders, men and women have, over the years, made decisions that affected geographic, physical and spatial realities in the city. Some, like platting the downtown into relatively short blocks, were made when Portland was just a struggling townsite. Others, like the crazy quilt of service districts that provide for schools, water and sewers, came about as the city grew and developed. Still other efforts, like the development of a regional light rail line, were made only a few years ago.

If we were to fly low over the city of Portland – like the lucky people at Bergman Photographic Services, Inc., who took the aerial photo on pages xii-xiii – what combination of "people-made" and natural features would we see? We'll consider many of these features in detail in later sections. In the meantime, let's take a tour in our mind's eye, for a panoramic view can teach us a great deal about the Portland metro area.

Setting the Scene

Our guide might begin the tour with the description PSU Professor Larry W. Price uses in his article "Portland's Landscape Setting." He describes the Portland landscape as "a broad valley floor, the confluence of two rivers, a longitudinally elongated ridge of hills, and a spattering of extinct volcanoes."

Most trips begin with a look at the map, and ours is no different. The shaded relief map on pages 56-57, which was prepared by Metro's Data Resource Center, nicely illustrates Price's description. The shading on the map darkens as the elevation gets higher. Have a look, and off we go.

Up, Up and Away

Let's begin near the Willamette River, which divides the city into east and west sections:

▸ Beginning with areas closest to the river, we'd see commercial, industrial, retail and residential buildings on both the east and west sides. Our guide could tell us about the successful

Shaded Relief Map
Terrain Data

Source: Soil Conservation
    Service
Map Accuracy: Control point
    positional accuracy is plus
    or minus 40′
Data collection scale: 1"=2,000′

Map by Metro, March, 1993

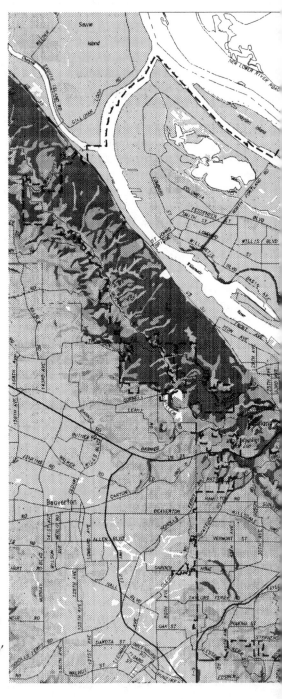

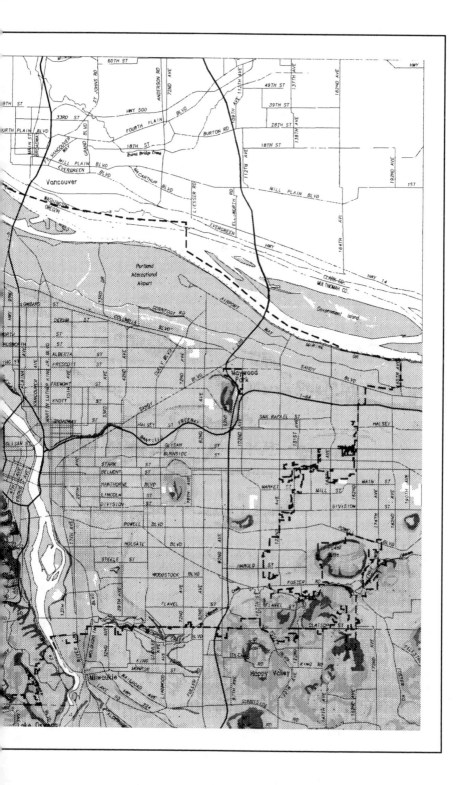

urban renewal and redevelopment programs that have, since the 1970s, focused primarily on the west side's downtown.

▸ Flying over the east side, we'd admire the "Twin Peaks" of the new Convention Center and the new home of the Oregon Museum of Science and Industry. Our guide would talk about recent east side development projects and future plans, including the new Trail Blazers arena and a convention center hotel.

▸ A similar flight, a few years from now, would show us the full implementation of east side development plans. City planners hope to tie the east and west into a unified whole, by developing a center city that truly spans both sides of the river. Plans also include redeveloping the east side riverfront. A variety of plans for that are on the drawing board.

▸ We'd count ten bridges spanning the river. We wouldn't see any toll takers, since crossing the river does not cost money. We also wouldn't see any ferries. South of downtown we would see Ross Island, which is actually a group of four islands that together measure about 300 acres. Most of the land is owned by the Ross Island Sand and Gravel Company.

▸ Heading north, we'd see the busy Port of Portland, and the warehouses in northwest Portland. We'd also see the northernmost tip of the city, which is where the Willamette and Columbia Rivers meet.

West Side Wonders

▸ Next we could circle over the west side. We'd find 4,600 acre Forest Park an amazing sight. It's the largest park within a city in the U.S. We could circle over Council Crest Park, the highest spot in the city, with an elevation of 1,040 feet. Our guide would explain that Portland has about 280 parks within the city limits.

▸ We'd notice that the west side is hillier than the east. The "ridge of hills" Professor Price describes are on the west side, where they run roughly parallel to the Willamette River.

▶ Before heading east, let's imagine we stood on one of these hills. Our guide could again quote Professor Price, who describes the view:

> If one were to stand on a prominence in the Portland Hills and look eastward over the city, the general impression would be that of a low plain rising gently to the east occasionally interrupted by isolated conical hills. These are ancient volcanoes that erupted locally...from six million to perhaps a few hundred thousand years ago.

East Side Enticements

▶ Heading southeast, we would see Mt. Tabor. Professor Price explains that a Mt. Tabor sign "states that Portland is the only city in the United States with a volcano within its limits." East of Mt. Tabor, we'd see more of the "conical hills" including Kelly Butte, and then Powell Butte, one of the newest parks in Portland. Looking north we'd spot Rocky Butte. Professor Price calls Rocky Butte "perhaps the best place in Portland to have a 360 degree panorama of the city."

▶ Focusing next on east side greenspaces, our guide could point out the Johnson Creek corridor, in southeast, and the Columbia Slough, which runs parallel to the Columbia River. Looking west from the Columbia Slough, we'd see Smith and Bybee Lakes, which are just south of the confluence of the two rivers. Many other parks and greenspaces dot the landscape.

▶ As we head back downtown, our guide could talk of the Forty Mile Loop, a 1904 plan to ring the city with interconnected parks, trails, and greenways. It remains unfinished, but plans now envision a loop of about 140 miles. We'd learn about Metropolitan Greenspaces, a group that has mapped the region's remaining greenspaces, and seeks to acquire as many as possible, to protect and preserve them for all to enjoy.

▶ Before leaving the east side, our guide would point out Lloyd Center, one of the nation's first shopping malls. Lloyd Center was somewhat unusual in that it was located close to downtown; within, not outside, the city.

Downtown Delights

▸ Focusing on downtown, we'd see city blocks that seem particularly short. Indeed they are; they measure only 200 feet. The first city blocks were platted by Lovejoy and Pettygrove – the New Englanders who tossed a coin to name Portland. Short blocks were used in some New England cities, for two important reasons. They were quicker to clear of timber, and they provided more valuable corner lots.

▸ Today's pedestrians find the city very walkable, in part because of the short blocks. They allow a greater choice of routes, and enable the wanderer to easily get his or her bearings. Writing in the 1991 *Portland Metropolitan Office Guide*, Doug Bean cites another reason. "The perceptual space – the distance that occupies peoples' attention – is about 100 to 150 feet ahead....In Portland, pedestrians are never farther than 100 feet from an intersection, meaning they are always within their perceptual space."

▸ We'd spot handsome downtown buildings, in different architectural styles, but we wouldn't see many skyscrapers. We might actually recognize some buildings, that are famous for their design or architectural features.

▸ Our guide would fill us in on the building ordinances that limit the height of new buildings, protecting our views of the mountains, and allowing ample light to reach the city streets. We'd hear that new Portland buildings must have retail space at the street level, providing more services to everyone, and making walks through town all the more appealing.

▸ Our guide might mention the 200 foot blocks again at this point. It is easier to build single buildings on short blocks, and their design can be better appreciated when they stand alone.

▸ If we took a walking tour once we were back on the ground, we'd see that all these factors work to eliminate the "canyon" feel of some cities, where towering skyscrapers block the light and present only concrete walls to the passersby. We'd also see the drinking fountains, sidewalk sculpture, seating areas and flowers that rejuvenate and amuse Portland pedestrians as they walk the city.

▸ From the air, we'd quickly spot Pioneer Courthouse Square, which has been called the city's "living room." Pioneer Courthouse Square was built on the site of the old Portland Hotel. To the chagrin of many, the hotel was torn down in 1951 to make way for a parking lot. But by the early 1980s, Portlanders saw the error of their ways, and Pioneer Courthouse Square replaced the parking lot, as part of Portland's conscious efforts to reclaim the city (and its air) from the reign of the automobile.

Getting Around

▸ We'd see MAX, the light rail system that connects east side suburban areas with the central city. We'd also spot lots of buses. MAX and the buses are part of the award-winning TRI-MET transportation system, that allows a whopping 43% of all downtown commuters to leave their cars at home, minimizing traffic congestion and air pollution in the city.

▸ We'd notice the downtown transit mall, and our guide would describe "fare-less square," the downtown zone in which anyone can ride TRI-MET for free.

▸ Our guide might discuss the plans to extend the light rail line out to west side suburban areas. Federal money will be available, routes have been determined, work is in progress.

▸ Despite the successful efforts to foster public transportation solutions, we'd see that busy freeways and interstates surround the center city and cross the region. The freeways came before the light rail and the award-winning buses. They were important to the city's development, connecting Portland with other west coast locations, and with the suburbs that grew up around the city of Portland.

▸ Our guide might reminisce about the decision, back in the 1970s, to destroy a perfectly good highway, in order to build Waterfront Park on the west side riverfront. We might also hear that in the early 1990s the City Council voted down a similar plan to move the east side freeway that runs along the river.

At this point in our trip, we should land, since there are critical things that a bird's eye view cannot make clear. We need to look at some good maps, like the ones that follow.

Mapping Portland

The maps on the following pages provide current, graphic information on the various jurisdictions that divide the natural topography. They also locate some of the features that we mentioned as we flew over the city:

▸ As the map on page 63 shows, there are five counties in the regional area: Multnomah, Clackamas, Washington and Yamhill Counties in Oregon, and Clark County in Washington. The Census Bureau refers to these counties as the Portland Consolidated Metropolitan Statistical Area, or the Portland CMSA. While almost all of Portland is in Multnomah County, there are small sections of the city that are in Washington or Clackamas Counties.

▸ The map on pages 64-65 shows the Portland metro area. The approximate Portland boundary is drawn in a bold black line in the center section of the map. This map locates many of the smaller cities and towns in the metro area, including Beaverton, Hillsboro, Tigard, Tualatin, Lake Oswego, West Linn, Oregon City, Milwaukie, Gresham, Troutdale, Wood Village, and Vancouver.

▸ The next map, on pages 66-67, focuses on Portland and its closer suburbs. Major streets are identifiable.

▸ The map on pages 68-69 shows the freeways that ring the downtown and radiate out to the suburbs. It also shows some of the city parks.

▸ Finally, the map on pages 70-71 focuses on downtown. It locates all the streets, and many of the sights, parks, and places of interest that are found downtown. The map also shows the boundaries for TRI-MET's fare-less square.

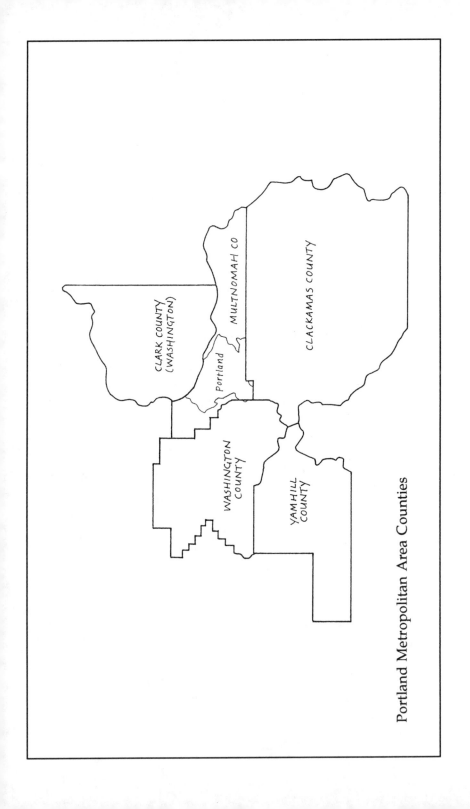

Portland Metropolitan Area Counties

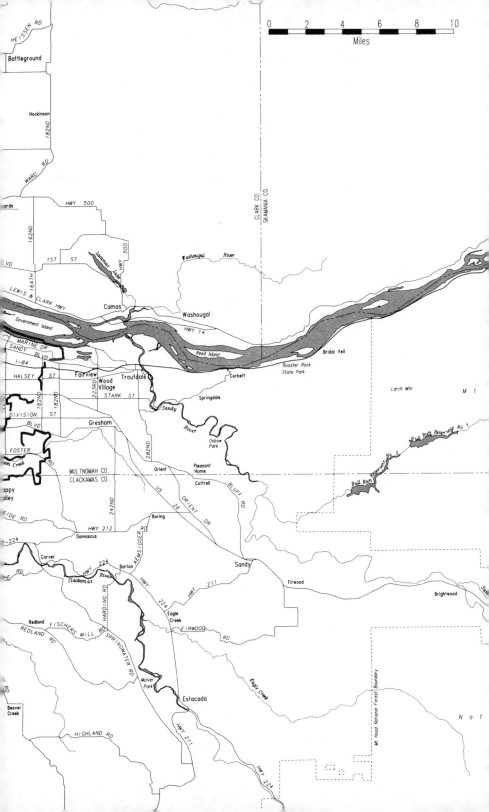

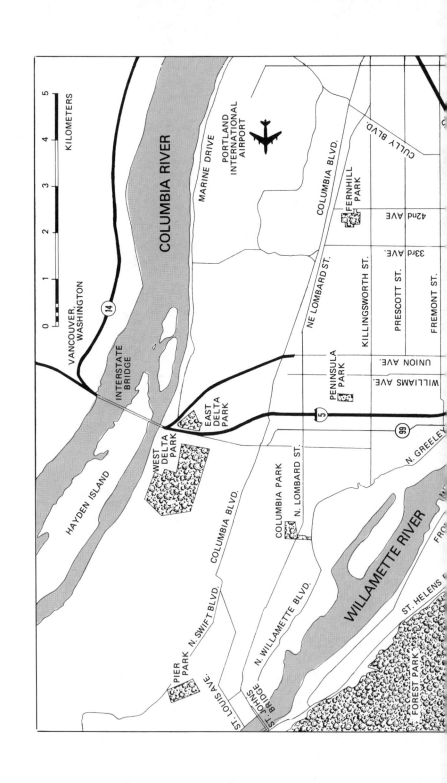

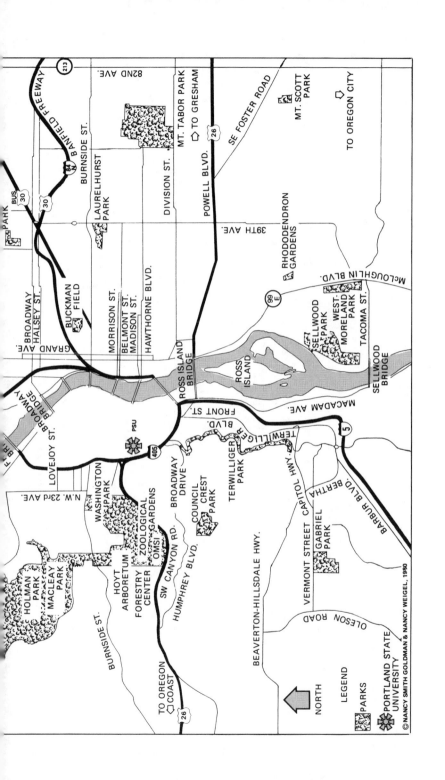

© NANCY SMITH GOLDMAN & NANCY WEIGEL, 1990

LEGEND

PARKS

PORTLAND STATE
UNIVERSITY

NORTH

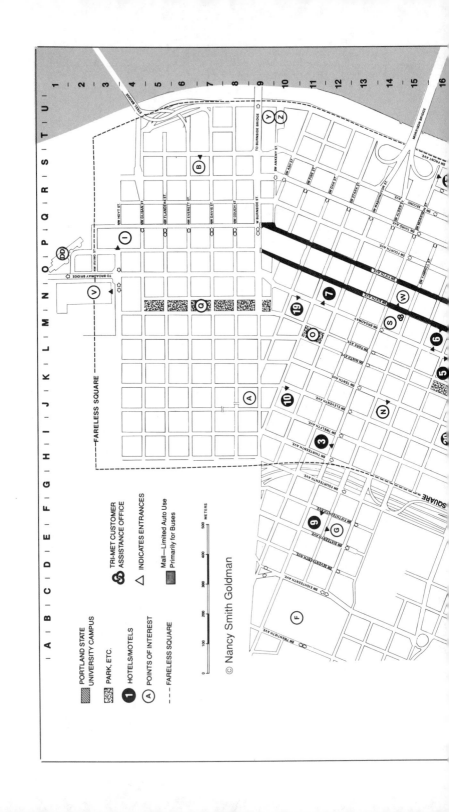

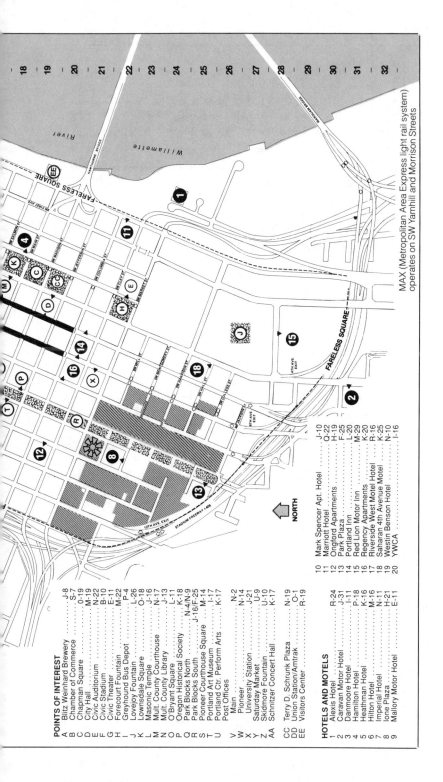

MAX (Metropolitan Area Express light rail system) operates on SW Yamhill and Morrison Streets

POINTS OF INTEREST

A	Blitz Weinhard Brewery	J-8
B	Chamber of Commerce	S-7
C	Chapman Square	O-19
D	City Hall	M-19
E	Civic Auditorium	N-22
F	Civic Stadium	B-10
G	Civic Theater	E-11
H	Forecourt Fountain	M-22
I	Greyhound Bus Depot	P-4
J	Lovejoy Fountain	L-26
K	Lownsdale Square	O-18
L	Masonic Temple	J-16
M	Mult. County Courthouse	N-17
N	Mult. County Library	J-13
O	O'Bryant Square	L-11
P	Oregon Historical Society	N-4/N-9
Q	Park Blocks North	K-18
R	Park Blocks South	J-16/F-25
S	Pioneer Courthouse Square	M-14
T	Portland Art Museum	I-17
U	Portland Ctr. Perform Arts	K-17
	Post Offices	
V	Main	N-2
W	Pioneer	N-14
X	University Station	J-21
Y	Saturday Market	U-9
Z	Skidmore Fountain	U-10
AA	Schnitzer Concert Hall	K-17
CC	Terry D. Schrunk Plaza	N-19
DD	Union Station/Amtrak	O-1
EE	Visitors Center	R-19

HOTELS AND MOTELS

1	Alexis Hotel	R-24
2	Caravan Motor Hotel	J-31
3	Danmoore Hotel	I-11
4	Hamilton Hotel	P-18
5	Heathman Hotel	K-16
6	Hilton Hotel	M-16
7	Imperial Hotel	N-11
8	Ione Plaza	H-21
9	Mallory Motor Hotel	E-11
10	Mark Spencer Apt. Hotel	J-10
11	Marriott Hotel	Q-22
12	Ongford Apartments	H-19
13	Park Plaza	F-25
14	Portland Inn	L-20
15	Red Lion Motor Inn	M-29
16	Regency Apartments	K-20
17	Riverside West Motel Hotel	R-16
18	Saharan 4th Avenue Motel	K-25
19	Westin Benson Hotel	N-10
20	YWCA	I-16

East Side, West Side

The city is usually divided into five sections. Going clockwise from the top, they are North Portland, Northeast Portland, Southeast Portland, Southwest Portland, and Northwest Portland. The Willamette River is the east-west divider, and Burnside Street is the north-south divider. North Portland is that wedge of the city that is east of the river, and west of Vancouver Street.

Addresses always include the N, NE, NW, SE or SW designations, and Portlanders use them easily in conversation when describing locations. They are often used in place of or along with neighborhood names.

Counting Heads and Miles

Finally, a few numbers to go along with the maps:

▸ Roughly 75% of Portland's residents live on the east side of the river.
▸ Portland is not large; it measures only 132 square miles.
▸ Of the almost 1.5 million people in the metro area, only about 438,000 live within the Portland city limits.
▸ About 238,000 people in the the metro area are Washington state residents.
▸ As in many other metro areas, people often live, vote and pay taxes in one place, and work, play, shop, or go to school in another.

Crossing Borders

In addition to city and county jurisdictions, the region is divided into a veritable crazy quilt of oddly overlapping service districts. According to an article by James Mayer in the April 8, 1991 *Oregonian*, the metro area has 220 local governments, and "the typical suburban resident may be governed by as many as a dozen local governments with more than 50 elected and 15 appointed officials."

It is common to find that your water district boundary is different from the school district; that the fire and rescue district lines have no relation to the parks district, and so on. The

Garden Home neighborhood is a prime example. Most people consider Garden Home to be in southwest Portland. But many Garden Home locations are actually in an unincorporated area of Washington County. It gets even more complicated: residents have a Portland mailing address, their children attend Beaverton schools, and their taxes help support the Tualatin Valley systems for parks, recreation, fire and rescue.

Some like the current system, for they believe that local service districts are more responsive to their needs. Others see inefficiencies and wasteful duplication. As the region grapples with tax cuts, water shortages, public school reforms, growth, and budget shortfalls, consolidation of services has become a hot topic – which bring us to the Metropolitan Service District.

A Must Mention for Metro

Before we close, we must mention Metro. Most Portland metropolitan area residents who live in Oregon live within the Metropolitan Service District. Metro is the name of the regional government for the district. *The 1992-93 Metro Guidebook* explains: "Most people know us as the agency that runs the Oregon Convention Center, the Metro Washington Park Zoo and solid waste disposal and recycling programs....[Other] programs touch on core quality-of-life issues such as transportation, urban growth, water quality, parks and recreation, the arts and sports/spectator facilities. We also operate the ever-popular Metro Recycling Information service, coordinate a regionwide Metropolitan Greenspaces program and have launched a 50-year planning effort known as Region 2040."

The map on the pages 74-75 shows the Metro boundaries. Just about all the locations we've mentioned in this chapter are within those boundaries. The map on pages 76-77 shows the Urban Growth Boundary, or the UGB, which is another important line around Portland. We'll explain it in detail on page 164, in the section on planning. We include it here to make it easier to compare the two. Have a quick look now. We'll refer you back to it when we discuss the UGB a little later.

On any tour, we develop a sense of place, but not an in-depth understanding. Later sections will fill in the gaps. But first, two more geographic/geologic topics: bridges and earthquakes.

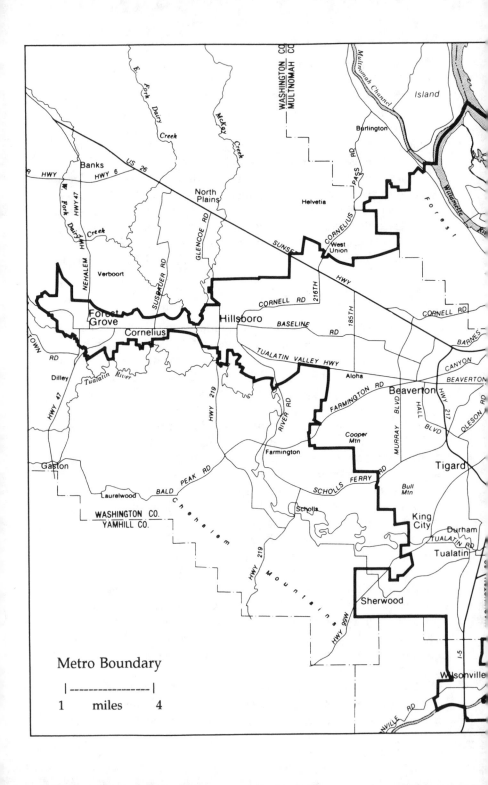

Metro Boundary

|------------------|
1   miles   4

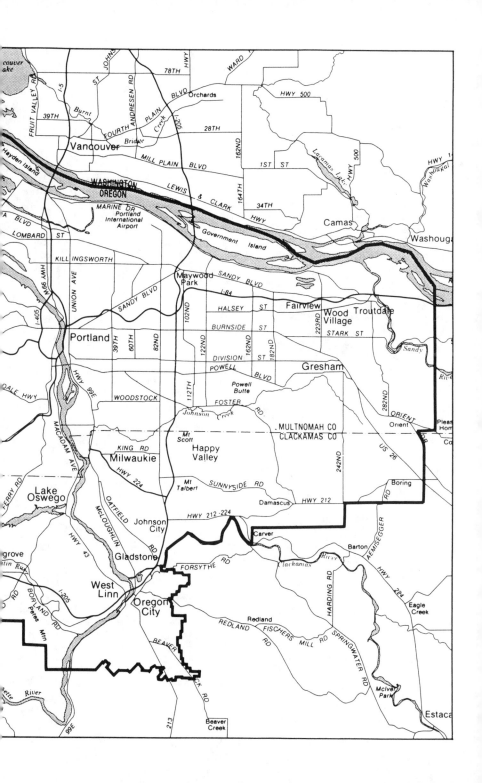

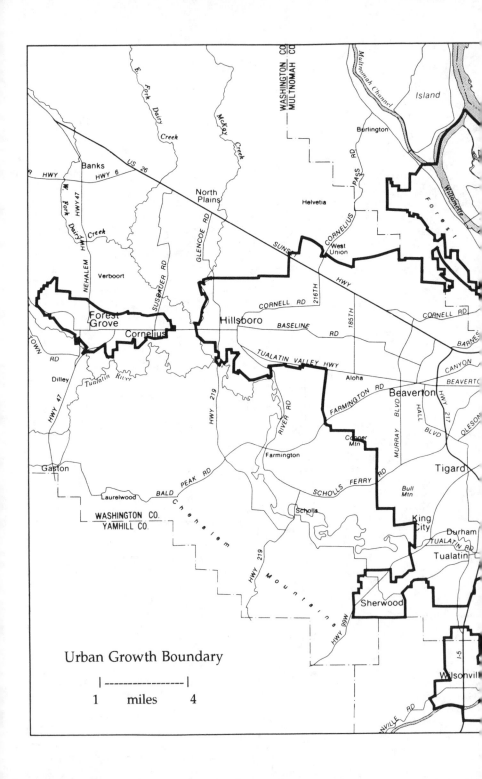

Urban Growth Boundary

1   miles   4

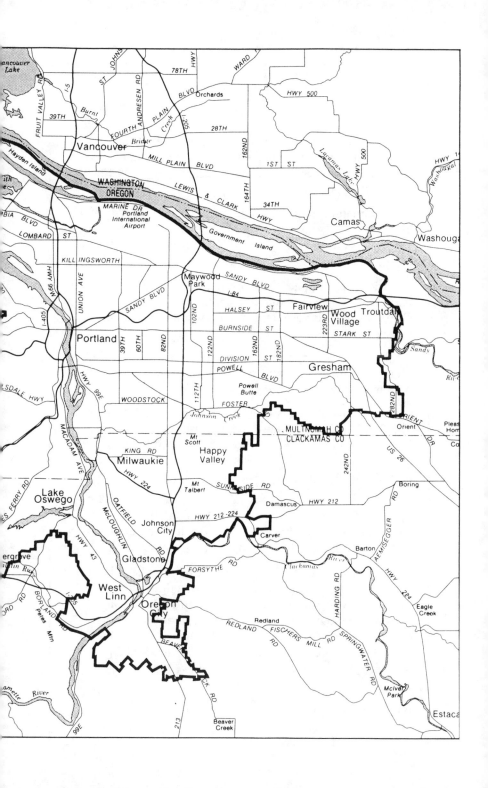

Map Credits

The map on pages 44-45 is a 75% black and white reduction of a color landform map that appeared in the *Oregon Environmental Atlas,* which was produced jointly in 1988 by the Oregon Department of Environmental Quality and the Portland State University Geography Department Cartographic Center.

The map on pages 46-47 is the northwest quarter of Erwin Raisz's Landform Map of Oregon. It was drawn in 1941, and is used with the permission of Raisz Landform Maps.

The map on pages 56-57 is an enlargement of a shaded relief map which was drawn by Metro's Data Resource Center in 1993. It uses terrain data from the Soil Conservation Service.

The map on page 63 was drawn for this book in 1992. The approximate Portland boundary was based on information obtained from the City of Portland.

The maps on pages 64-65 and 66-67 are Metro maps. The first is Metro's Major Arterial Map, dated 1990. Judy Horowitz added the approximate Portland boundary, based on information provided by the city. The second is Metro's All Arterial Map, also dated 1990.

The maps on pages 68-69 and 70-71 are from the 1993 Portland State University Summer Session Catalog. They were modified slightly, and are used with the permission of Nancy Goldman, PSU School of Extended Studies.

The map on pages 74-75 is a Metro map of the Metropolitan Service District Boundary. It was drawn in 1987. The map on pages 76-77 is Metro's map of the Urban Growth Boundary. It was drawn the same year. Slight changes have been made in these boundaries since 1987, but, since a larger scale map is necessary to identify them, Metro continues to distribute the 1987 version in this scale.

Metro and State of Oregon maps are government documents. As such, they are in the public domain.

River City Bridges

Within the Portland city limits, ten bridges span the Willamette. But, as Sharon Wood points out in *The Portland Bridge Book*, we should also count the two bridges that cross the Willamette just south of the city, as well as the two that cross the Columbia to connect Portland with Vancouver. That brings the bridge total to fourteen. Three railroad bridges complete the picture. Wood's book describes each bridge in detail. Here's a few of the highlights she mentions on the topic of Portland's river bridges:

▸ Portland can claim "the world's only telescoping double-deck vertical lift bridge" (the Steel Bridge), "the world's oldest lift bridge" (the Hawthorne), and "North America's longest tied-arch bridge" (the Fremont).

▸ The city's first bridge was the Morrison, which opened in 1887. It was replaced twice; in 1905 and again in 1958.

▸ The Burnside Bridge is close to the river's narrowest down-town spot, which measures about 900 feet across.

▸ The Hawthorne bridges the river's widest downtown spot, which measures roughly 1,200 feet.

▸ MAX crosses the river on the Steel Bridge, which opened initially in 1888 to serve the railroad.

▸ The Ross Island Bridge has water pipes "suspended from the bridge's roadway," to carry water from the Bull Run Watershed to the west side.

▸ Multnomah County officials believe "that Portland bridges are healthier than their Midwest and East Coast counterparts...." They cite a few reasons, including the fact that the area's environment is "less damaging," we have no acid rain, and salt is not used on roadways during the winter months.

▸ But bird droppings – from the thousands of pigeons and starlings that roost on the bridges – are a problem. Rain turns the droppings acidic, so "they deteriorate protective coating and corrode steel."

▸ At the time of the book's publication in 1989, Wood reported "the Average Daily Traffic (ADT) for the fourteen vehicle bridges" to be "500,000 and growing."

The following bridge facts are from Karl Klooster's "River City" columns, which were published initially in *This Week* magazine and later compiled in Klooster's *Round the Roses: Portland Past Perspectives*.

▸ The Morrison was originally a toll bridge. The owners charged people, sheep and hogs five cents each; horses and cattle could cross for 10 cents. The toll for two horses and a driver was 20 cents. When the city bought the bridge in 1895, they did away with the toll.

▸ The St. John's Bridge was designed by D. B. Steinman. He is probably more famous for another bridge he designed – San Francisco's Golden Gate. But "Steinman considered this Gothic towered beauty, dedicated in June 1931 during Rose Festival, to be his masterpiece."

Perhaps that will be a comfort to Californians in our midst. The following section, on earthquakes, may not be!

What About Earthquakes?

On March 3, 1993, geologists announced that a new study verifies the existence of two earthquake faults that run under the city of Portland. The same study also provided indications of a third fault. Scientists had suspected their existence for years. Although the story was reported by the media, not much attention was paid by very many Portlanders.

But at 5:34AM on March 25, 1993, the wake-up call came. An earthquake measuring 5.6 on the Richter scale rocked parts of Oregon and Washington. It was the third largest recorded quake in Oregon's history. Fortunately, there were no casualties, and damages were limited. But it was not the newly identified faults that were at fault; the quake's epicenter was located about 30 miles south of Portland. As *The Oregonian* explained the following day, "geophysicists think the quake was caused by a shift in the Earth's crust along the Mount Angel fault."

The quake was felt for hundreds of miles, and it focused considerable attention on our need to prepare. As Ian P. Madin, who is a seismic hazard expert at the Oregon Department of Geology and Mineral Industries, explained to *The Oregonian*, "If this had been 20 miles closer to Portland, you'd be out on the street looking for broken glass from buildings....There's no particular reason to believe that the next one isn't going to be closer to home."

And The Big One?

The faults under the Rose City are not the only reason that some Portlanders are suddenly considering earthquake insurance. Those in the know describe various earthquake scenarios, that point to faults located off the Oregon Coast, local faults in the Portland area, and plate collisions. Oregon sits on the North American Plate, and the San de Fuca Plate lies off the Oregon Coast. These plates are located in what is known as the Cascadia Subduction Zone. Here's how the experts explain the various possibilities:

> There have been no big earthquakes in Oregon's brief history and there is no question that damaging earthquakes have been far less frequent in Oregon than in

California or Washington. However, geologic research tells scientists that Oregon will someday experience big earthquakes, and because we are poorly prepared, the damage could be great. We are faced with a small chance of a great disaster....

Geologic research in the last few years has shown that Oregon and Washington have probably been shaken by numerous <u>subduction zone earthquakes</u> during the last several thousand years. Subduction zone earthquakes occur when two great crustal plates slide past each other beneath the coast of Oregon and Washington. These earthquakes occur, on average, every 500-600 years, and the most recent was about 300 years ago. The subduction zone earthquakes were probably centered along the coast of Oregon and Washington and may have been as large as Magnitude 8 to Magnitude 9. Such earthquakes would cause significant shaking and damage in much of western Oregon. Scientists cannot predict whether the next such event might occur in 2 years or 200 years.

> "Earthquake Hazards in Western Oregon,"
> State of Oregon Department of Geology and
> Mineral Industries, July 9, 1990.

Based on evidence from local faulting, many experts believe an earthquake of magnitude 6.0 to 6.5 is possible with a frequency of about 500 years. While this size of quake is nothing to take lightly, it's just a vibration compared to a magnitude 8.0 to 9.5 quake that some researchers are predicting could occur due to the subduction zone movement associated with tectonic plates off the Oregon coast.

> John W. Ferguson, *The Oregonian*, May 10,
> 1991.

"We now realize," the [New York] Times quoted Dr. Thomas Heaton, a seismologist at the United States Geologic Survey office in Pasadena, "that the most dangerous fault in the United States lies off the Pacific Northwest."

The Times cited an article in the new issue of Science magazine suggesting that the conditions could create an earthquake measuring 9.5 on the Richter scale. "Such an earthquake," the newspaper explained helpfully, "would cause most of the buildings in a city like Portland, Ore. to collapse."

David Sarasohn, *The Oregonian*, April 14, 1991.

Research on buried coast marshes by Curt Peterson, assistant professor of geology at Portland State University, has found that large earthquakes have occurred on the Oregon Coast during the last 2,000 years. They recur about every 340 to 380 years, with the last quake in 1690.

Testifying in support of the [building] code change, Peterson said that using a 370-year recurrence interval, there is a 20 percent probability of a subduction zone quake striking Oregon within the next 50 years.

James Bela, *The Oregonian*, July 23, 1992.

Risk Management, 101

Although the March 25th quake surely served as a wake-up call for many, some Portlanders were already aware of the risk and promoting preparedness. Both city and state building codes have being updated, to ensure that new buildings will be more able to withstand earthquakes. The Marquam Bridge, which carries more than 100,000 vehicles a day, was renovated in 1992 and 1993. Renovations included measures to help it withstand an earthquake. And in July, 1992, the City Council authorized a study of potential earthquake effects on the Bull Run dams. (They came through fine on March 25.)

As for locating the fault line nearest your house, the Oregon Department of Geology and Mineral Industries, in cooperation with Metro, has prepared a map of earthquake susceptibilities. It was scheduled for release just days after the March quake hit. It should be available by the time you read this section. If you would like a copy, give either agency a call. Talk about a successful advertising campaign!

With a sense of the physical landscape, and a feel for the city that has been created on that landscape, let us now consider the people of the city of Portland.

Settlers

and

Wannabes

"Respectable Emigrants"

So who are these Portlanders, anyway? Before looking at today's demographics, it helps to look at the past. Portland is only 150 years old, and as with all places, those who came before set the stage for those today.

The Very First Settlers

Who was here? Writing an article in the Fall, 1979 *Oregon Historical Quarterly*, Paul G. Merriam notes that the land that would become Portland was "inhabited only occasionally by wandering Indians and itinerant trappers and traders...." But the land that would be Oregon had been inhabited for thousands of years. *The First Oregonians*, a 1991 collection of essays compiled by the Oregon Council for the Humanities, notes that Indian settlements could even go back "15 thousand years or more." And they were diverse, for "...Oregon was home to dozens of individual bands, all with their own traditions, language peculiarities, and ways of life."

The future site of Portland may have been nothing more than a rest stop for the "Indians and itinerant trappers and traders" that Merriam describes, but there were hundreds of Indian villages throughout the state. Stephen Dow Beckham explains in *The Indians of Western Oregon*:

> Along a bay they might have as many as twenty different settlements, each with its own name and each containing from twenty to as many as eighty people. In the valleys these villages were often at the meeting points of streams or near the riverbanks. These were the first towns of Oregon....

But they would not to survive the arrival of the white settlers. Beckham writes of that "tragic chapter in American history" in his article in *The First Oregonians*.

"To Oregon"

The discoveries of Lewis and Clark and the opening of the Oregon Trail brought new groups of people to the Pacific

Northwest, who would build their own towns. E. Kimbark MacColl quotes Peter H. Burnett, California's first governor, who described early Oregon settlers:

> [They] were all honest, because there was nothing to steal; they were all sober, because there was no liquor to drink; there were no misers, because there was no money to hoard; and they were all industrious, because it was work or starve.

Writing in *Merchants, Money and Power: The Portland Establishment 1843-1913*, MacColl continues:

> Most Oregon settlers were plain, respectable, reasonably well educated white people of moderate circumstances. The typical immigrant seemed far more a home seeker and builder than an explorer, gold seeker or land speculator. Land speculation, however, did consume the attention of countless new residents.

Terence O'Donnell and Thomas Vaughan also consider the question in *Portland: an Informal History & Guide*:

> Dorothy Johansen, a distinguished historian at Reed College, has written on this influence of people on a place, and particularly with respect to Oregon and Portland. Her theory is the straightforward one that as birds of a feather flock together so do people of like mind, and further that these people, creating a community in their own image, perpetuate it by those whom they welcome as well as those whom they do not.
>
> Why, historian Johansen asks, did people come to Oregon in the first place – those immigrants of the middle 1800s – and why did they not go to California instead? The answer, she suggests, is that Oregon even in this early period had a reputation different from that of California's and thus drew a different kind of people....
>
> She cites the well-known story of the branch in the Oregon Trail, the route south to California marked by a heap of gold quartz, the one north by a sign lettered "To Oregon." Those who could read came here.

O'Donnell and Vaughan cite passages from pioneer writings that bolster this argument, including a letter from one Jesse Applegate, who told his brother that

> almost all the respectable portion of the California emigrants are going on the new road to Oregon – and nearly all the respectable emigrants that went last year to California came this spring to Oregon.

And, in a passage that seems almost prophetic, they quote another pioneer, whose reasons were a little different:

> "The health of the pine forests and limpid streams took my fancy," wrote William Rector. "I had lost much of my ambitions for wealth or society. And often I indulged in visions of a happy retreat from the ague and fever and from the toils and vexations of a business life."

Speaking at a lecture on May 2, 1991, historian David Johnson explained that individual young men went to California – by the thousands – during the 1840s and 1850s, seeking the quick riches that gold might bring. But those who came to Oregon – by the hundreds – were primarily family men. They came to claim, under the Donation Land Law, one free square mile of land, on which to start or settle a family. By 1855, the entire Willamette Valley had been claimed. These early settlers, according to Johnson, passed their land, and their vision, to their children, and the continuing presence of these old families today attests to the continuity of that vision, which helped shape the growth and character of both Portland and Oregon.

Numbers and Home Towns

Where did all these folks of good character come from? And just how many were there?

- ▸ In 1850, census takers counted just over 800 white people in Portland. Oregon's population that year was 11,873.
- ▸ About 75% were male; about 50 individuals were foreign born. Gordon DeMarco's *A Short History of*

Portland reports that there were 54 blacks in Oregon in 1850.

▶ Historians estimate that about one quarter of the earliest Portland settlers hailed from either New England or New York.

The city grew moderately, as the following chart shows:

Year:	Population:
1860	2,874
1870	8,293
1880	17,577
1890	46,385
1900	90,426

The people who settled in Portland had diverse backgrounds. Merriam provides some details:

▶ More than one fourth of Portland's population in 1860 was foreign born.

▶ From 1860 to 1910, Irish, German, Chinese, British, Scandinavian and Canadian immigrants arrived in the greatest numbers.

▶ By 1870, approximately 50% of the people in Portland were either foreign born, or had at least one immigrant parent. By 1890, that figure grew to 59%.

▶ In 1890, about 10% of the city's population couldn't speak English.

▶ According to Carl Abbott's *Portland: Gateway to the Northwest*, Portland's Chinatown was home to 7,800 people by 1900.

Into the Twentieth Century

The population of Portland more than doubled between 1900 and 1910. The Lewis and Clark Exposition had introduced many visitors to the city, and land claims were soon being subdivided as the area experienced a real estate boom. The population then increased by 25% between 1910 and 1920, and by almost 17% from 1920 to 1930. Other west coast cities experienced similar growth. With railroad connections, streetcar lines, paved roads and electric lights, these young cities were becoming "civilized" and livable to even those who might lack a pioneering spirit. Here's how the city grew:

Year:	Population:
1910	207,214
1920	258,288
1930	301,815
1940	305,394
1950	373,628

Historians tell us about the people behind the numbers:

▸ According to DeMarco, Scandinavians were the "largest ethnic group" in Portland by 1910. He notes, though, that most hailed from the American midwest – Wisconsin, Minnesota, and Iowa – rather than Scandinavia.

▸ During the first two decades of the 20th century, Portland's Italian population increased from under 1,000 to about 10,000. Many lived in what was called South Portland, a neighborhood between Harrison and Curry, from the river to Fifth.

▸ German Jews came to Portland as early as the 1840s. Eastern European Jews arrived at the end of the century, settling also in South Portland. The Jewish community flourished there from the late 1890s until the 1920s, when some residents began to move out of the central city. By 1940, there were about 8,000 Jews in Portland.

▸ The big jump from 1940 to 1950 hints at what was a significant population rise during the war years. According to Abbott, thousands of people came to Portland to work in the shipbuilding yards, and the metropolitan area's population grew from about 500,000 in 1940 to over 660,000 in 1944.

Unfortunately, newcomers were not always welcomed. The histories recount prejudice and violence against the Chinese, exclusions laws aimed at Blacks, clubs that were closed to Jews, Ku Klux Klan attacks on Catholics, and antipathy toward the poor migrants and Blacks who came to work in the wartime shipyards. It is not a element of Portland's history of which we can be proud.

The Post-War Years

The postwar years were not a time of great growth for the city of Portland:

Year:	Population:
1960	372,676
1970	379,967
1980	368,139
1990	437,319

Like many other American cities, Portland's population actually fell between 1970 and 1980. Even the apparent jump of about 69,000 from 1980 to 1990 is misleading, for around 66,000 is attributable to annexation. In other words, the city's population increased only because people living in areas around the city were now counted as official Portlanders, since the city had annexed the land on which they lived.

But the years after the war were nevertheless a time of expansion. Thanks to cars and freeways, families could live further away from the center part of the city. One of the reasons for the drop from 1970 to 1980 was that the suburbs became home to many. In Portland, the metro area – including Multnomah, Washington, and Clackamas Counties in Oregon and Clark County in Washington state – grew substantially:

Year:	Population:
1950	620,000
1960	822,000
1970	1,007,000
1980	1,245,000
1990	1,478,000

Which brings us, finally, to the 1990s.

Counting Portlanders

Let's begin with a quick look at Oregonians. The 1990 census counted 2,842,231 Oregonians. That's up 209,075 - or 7.94% - from the 1980 count of 2,633,156. Given all the hoopla about growth and newcomers, that doesn't seem too bad, especially when compared with the national growth rate of 9.8%. But the numbers are deceiving for a few reasons.

First, the 36 counties in Oregon had very different experiences. Twelve Oregon counties saw a net drop in their population since 1980. Nineteen counties experienced a growth rate of between .1% and 15%. And five counties grew more than 15%. Secondly, most of the population growth in the state took place in the late 1980s. The state actually lost population during the recession in the early 1980s.

Finally, the state is currently growing faster than the national average of about 1% per year. For the last few years, Oregon has grown about 2% to 3% a year. The fastest growing counties in the state are in the Portland metropolitan area and the vicinity of Bend, in central Oregon.

Portland and the CMSA

For the 1990 census, the Portland metropolitan area includes Multnomah, Washington, Clackamas and Yamhill Counties in Oregon, and Clark County in Washington. It's officially called the Portland/Vancouver Consolidated Metropolitan Statistical Area, or the Portland/Vancouver CMSA. Here are the overall numbers:

- ▸ Portland's population in 1990 was 437,319, making it the 30th largest city in the U.S.
- ▸ With a population of 1,477,895, the Portland/Vancouver metro area is the 27th largest in the nation.
- ▸ About 75% of the people who live in Multnomah County live in the city of Portland.
- ▸ About 44% of all Oregonians live in the Portland metro area.

Here are the county breakdowns:

County:	Population:
Multnomah	583,887
Washington	311,554
Clackamas	278,850
Yamhill	65,551
Clark	238,053

And here are the population figures for the other cities in the metro area:

City:	Population:
Beaverton	53,310
Forest Grove	13,559
Gladstone	10,152
Gresham	68,235
Hillsboro	37,520
Lake Oswego	30,576
Milwaukie	18,692
Oregon City	14,678
Tigard	29,334
Troutdale	7,852
Tualatin	15,013
Vancouver	46,380
West Linn	16,367

The metro area grew significantly:

▸ Overall, the CMSA population went from 1,300,927 in 1980 to 1,477,895 in 1990, an increase of almost 14%.
▸ Washington state's Clark County had a huge growth rate of almost 24%.
▸ The Oregon counties in the CMSA experienced an overall growth rate of just over 12%. Most of that growth was in the suburbs, as the next numbers show.
▸ Washington County led with a population increase of 65,694 people, a growth rate of 26.7%.
▸ Yamhill, with growth of 10,219 people, was up 18.5%.

- ► Clackamas County, with 36,939 more people, had a growth rate of 15.3%.
- ► But Multnomah County, with an increase of 21,240 people, had a growth rate of only 3.8%.

Making Babies

While the metropolitan area has seen significant growth, not all of it can be attributed to disillusioned Californians, people escaping growth in Seattle, or easterners who have discovered the joys of the Northwest. Some of it is called natural increase, and it's our own fault: we've been having babies, and we're doing so at a rate higher than the death rate. And as the timber industry experienced cutbacks and people moved in search of jobs, there was also some migration between counties.

Portland State University's Center for Population Research and Census estimates that, for the last decade, Washington County's natural increase was roughly 28,000 people. Washington County's net migration was about 38,000. Clackamas County, with a natural increase of about 16,000 and net migration of roughly 21,000, had similar proportions. But in Multnomah County, growth was due to a natural increase of about 32,600. Multnomah actually had a negative net migration of

---

Following the Harvest

Oregon is an agricultural state, and each year migrant farm workers help harvest everything from strawberries to Christmas trees. Metropolitan area counties are home – either temporarily or permanently – to some of these workers.

According to Oregon State University Professor Bob Mason, who was quoted in the December 30, 1990 *Oregonian*, more than 121,000 workers harvest Oregon's crops. About 66,000 are from other countries, and approximately 29,000 are American citizens who move around the country, following the harvest. About 25,000 workers are Oregonians, and about half of those Oregonians are children.

approximately 11,700 people in the last decade. People left the county for a variety of reasons. Some, for example, just moved to the suburbs, while others left the state when the recession hit in the early 1980s.

Now that we have a sense of the numbers, let's look at what the 1990 census can tell us about the people behind the numbers.

"Generally Speaking"

Generally speaking, the population of the PMA [Portland metropolitan area] is more affluent, better educated, more racially and ethnically diverse, more likely to speak a foreign language, and more geographically mobile than the population residing outside the PMA....

> Governor's Commission on Higher Education in the Portland Metropolitan Area, *Working Together*, November 15, 1990.

The 1990 census provides a wealth of information on characteristics of the population. We'll delve into it in the next section.

A Portland Profile

What can the 1990 census tell us about the people it counts? While the census doesn't look at all aspects of our lives, every American is counted every ten years. Census takers strive to collect data from all households on age, sex, household composition, race, ethnicity, and housing. One in six households is asked to complete a longer questionnaire, which includes questions in other areas, like education, jobs, income, and specific housing characteristics. Here's some of the information the census takers found when they tallied the forms for all Portlanders:

437,319	people live in Portland.
211,914	are men.
225,405	are women.
159,815	are between the ages of 25 and 44. (That's 36.5% of the population.)
34.5	is the median age in Portland.
21.9%	of the people in Portland are under age 18.
14.6%	are 65 years or older.
187,268	households make up the city.
103,967	of the households are family households.
32.0%	of the family households are married couple families with related children.
84.6%	of Portlanders are white. (That's the highest proportion among the 50 biggest U.S. cities.)
7.7%	are black.
1.2%	are Native American.
5.3%	are Asian or Pacific Islander.
3.2%	are of Hispanic origin.
198,368	housing units are in Portland.
53.0%	of the housing units are owner-occupied.
44.9%	of the housing units in Portland are owner-occupied one-family homes.
$340	is the median rent paid in the city.
69.2%	of renters pay rent of $250-$499 per month.

If you would like to see how Portland compares with Multnomah, Clackamas and Washington Counties, take a look at the chart on page 102. It provides the very same information as we reported on the previous page for those three counties.

Were You Born in Oregon?

We can sketch a more detailed picture of the people in the Portland area from the data collected on the longer questionnaires. The charts on pages 100 and 101 include selected information from that survey, including information on place of birth. Page 100 provides data for the city of Portland; page 101 has the same information for the Portland/Vancouver CMSA. That's the area that includes Multnomah, Clackamas, Washington and Yamhill Counties in Oregon, and Clark County in Washington state.

Married With Children?

While the numbers can be interesting in and of themselves, they are even more revealing when we look at them in comparison to other data. Here are a few examples of how Portland compares with national census data:

▸ About 36% of the family households in the U.S. are households that include a married couple and related children. The comparable Portland figure is 32.0%. The county proportions are higher. In Multnomah County, 34.1% of the family households are married couple families with children. Clackamas reports 40.8%; Washington County almost 42%. So if you're wondering about neighborhoods, there's a better chance you'll find couples with kids in Washington or Clackamas County than in Portland. You'll beat the national odds in both suburban counties.

▸ A good chunk of those families will include a working mom. Both the Portland and the CMSA proportions are quite close to the national average for working women with children under the age of six. Almost 60% of these women work nationwide, compared to 61.7% in Portland and 60.0% in the metro area.

▸ Slightly less than 8% of the U.S. population was born in a foreign country. 7.7% of Portland's residents were born outside the U.S., but only 5.9% of the metro population was born in another country.

▸ When the census was taken, the median rent in Portland was $340 per month. The county medians were a bit higher: Multnomah reported $347, Clackamas $404, and Washington $429. But all four were less than the national median of $437 per month.

▸ The median age in Multnomah County – 34.2 years old – is close to the state median age of 34.5. In 1980, the statewide median was 30.2 years. But we can't blame the rise entirely on the baby-boomers, who are now thirty and fortysomethings. For Oregon has become a popular state among older Americans, who like the temperate climate and the affordable real estate. Some have actually followed their baby-boomer children, who had already found their way to Oregon.

Making Sense of the Census

The 1990 census was taken in April of 1990. Preliminary population counts were available in August. By February, 1991, more detailed census data was released for counties, cities and metro areas. Information from the long questionnaire became available in 1992. Census data will continue to be "news" in 1993 and 1994, for it literally takes years for the Census Bureau to analyze and report on the information that is gathered.

Here in Portland, census data is available at the Center for Population Research and Census (CPRC) at Portland State University. The CPRC also does regular population projections and estimates that supplement census information. We have used quite a bit of information in this book that was made available by the Center. The staff there are knowledgeable and tremendously helpful. If you are in the market for census data or population projections that go beyond what you read in the newspaper, give them a call.

Within the Portland City Limits

51.8%	of the people who lived in Portland when the census was taken were born in the state of Oregon.
7.7%	were born in another country.
39.4%	of those age 5 and older lived in Oregon in 1985.
45.9%	of those age 5 and older still lived in the same Portland house as they did in 1985.
58,962	young Portlanders were enrolled in elementary or high school.
10.9%	of them were in a private school.
37,610	Portlanders were attending college.
7,749	Portland children were getting a good start in a preschool.
82.9%	were at least high school graduates.
25.9%	had at least a bachelor's degree.
66.7%	of the Portlanders age 16 or older were in the labor force.
61.7%	of Portland women with children under the age of 6 were in the labor force.
79.8%	of Portland women with children between 6 and 17 were in the labor force.
65.0%	of Portland's workforce drove to work alone in their cars.
12.9%	carpooled.
11.0%	used TRI-MET.
9.0%	walked or worked at home.
20.3 min.	was the mean travel time to work for Portland commuters.
$25,592	was the median household income in Portland in 1989.
$32,424	was the median family income in Portland in 1989.
$14,478	was the per capita income in Portland in 1989.
14.5%	of the people in Portland were below the poverty level in 1989.

In the Portland/Vancouver Metro Area

49.2%	of the people who lived in the CMSA were born in the same state they lived in.
5.9%	were born in another country.
38.1%	of those 5 and older lived in the same state in 1985.
46.3%	of those age 5 and older still lived in the same house as they did in 1985.

243,198	metro area children were enrolled in elementary or high school.
8.2%	of them were in a private school.
102,088	metro area residents were attending college.
29,234	metro area children were getting a good start in a pre-school.

84.5%	were at least high school graduates.
23.6%	had at least a bachelor's degree.

68.6%	of metro area residents who were age 16 or older were in the labor force.
60.0%	of metro area women with children under the age of 6 were in the labor force.
77.6%	of metro area women with children between 6 and 17 were in the labor force.

73.8%	of the metro area's workforce drove to work alone in their cars.
12.3%	carpooled.
5.4%	used public transportation
7.0%	walked or worked at home.
21.7 min.	was the mean travel time to work for metro area commuters.

$31,071	was the median household income in the metro area in 1989.
$36,768	was the median family income in 1989.
$15,078	was the per capita income in 1989.
9.9%	of the people in the metro area were below the poverty level in 1989.

Demographic Characteristics
of the Metropolitan Area Counties

	Mult.	Wash.	Clack.
Population:			
Total	583,887	311,554	278,850
Men	283,849	152,313	136,996
Women	300,038	159,241	141,854
Age Data:			
Median age	34.2	32.7	35.1
Age 25-44	36.1%	36.8%	33.5%
Under age 18	23.1%	26.8%	26.7%
65 and older	13.6%	10.1%	11.5%
Household Data:			
Total households	242,140	118,997	103,530
Family households	143,137	83,098	76,704
Married-couple families			
with related children	34.1%	41.9%	40.8%
Race, Hispanic Origin:			
White	86.9%	91.9%	96.3%
Black	6.0%	0.7%	0.4%
Native American	1.2%	0.6%	0.7%
Asian, Pacific Islander	4.7%	4.3%	1.7%
Hispanic origin	3.1%	4.6%	2.6%
Housing Units:			
Total housing units	255,751	124,716	109,003
% that are owner-			
occupied	55.3%	60.8%	71.7%
% that are owner-occu-			
pied one-family homes	45.9%	48.1%	51.7%
Renters:			
Median rent	$347	$429	$404
Those paying rent of			
$250-$499/month	69.9%	63.4%	59.1%

Peoria of the Northwest?

The 1990 census data sketches a picture of people in Portland. But it remains an outline only. We can add color, texture, and depth to our developing picture with data from another source: the advertising and marketing industry. Portland has actually been a favorite among test marketers. According to Saatchi & Saatchi, a New York advertising agency, Portland was the second most popular test market in the United States in the late 1980s.

Both the September, 1989 issue of *Pacific Northwest* magazine and a November 20, 1989 advertising supplement to *Advertising Age* reported Saatchi & Saatchi's rankings, which found Minneapolis to be the number one test market. Why did Portland do so well? For a few reasons:

▸ Our demographic characteristics made us appear to be pretty average folks.

▸ Advertising is not too expensive here.

▸ We're fairly isolated from other markets; in other words, we don't see Seattle commercials here.

▸ And, as Saatchi's Ira Weinblatt explained to *Pacific Northwest*, "People pick test markets in parts of the country that they like to visit."

But even average people have their peculiarities. The following tidbits on the lifestyles and buying habits of Portlanders appeared in articles or graphics in the *Advertising Age* supplement. Market research firms and individual authors are mentioned to give credit when credit is due. We'll start with a look at leisure.

Portlanders at Play

According to the Lifestyle Market Analyst, National Demographics & Lifestyles, of Denver, the leisure time activities of Portlanders do not always reflect national norms:

▸ Portlanders do more camping, hiking, snow skiing, and gardening than most other Americans. In fact, Portland is among the top 30 (of 212) markets for these activities.

▸ Portland is also in the top 30 for a few other "leisure time interests" including:

- ▸ use of RVs and four-wheel drive vehicles
- ▸ hunting and shooting
- ▸ motorcycles
- ▸ fishing
- ▸ sewing
- ▸ wildlife and environmental interests
- ▸ and pets.

It appears from the above that we really like outdoor activities. But as Susan Hauser points out in her article on Portlander habits, we also get high scores for some indoor interests:

- ▸ Portlanders like to read. Ms. Hauser notes that Portland is "the No. 2 reading-est town in the country, after Seattle, according to *The Oregonian.*"
- ▸ 71% of us go to movies frequently. That may or may not be the same 71% of us who have bought lawn or garden supplies during the last year.
- ▸ We really do like to garden, and we are the number two city where people say their favorite hobby is gardening.
- ▸ We also go shopping, downtown or at one of the five area malls; and drink beer, often of the microbrewed variety.
- ▸ We apparently like to vacation close to home. As Ms. Hauser explains, "The most frequent travel destinations for Portlanders are the Oregon coast (46%) and Central Oregon (18%)."

To Market, To Market

While we may be average, we have some buying habits that set us apart a bit from other Americans. Using data from Arbitron/SAMI that ranks 54 major markets in the U.S., Alan B. Miller Jr.'s article offers a peek into our shopping carts. It's a good bet that he'll find some cat food there:

▸ Arbitron/SAMI found that Portland was the number one market for canned chili, dry cat food, and non-dairy creamer.

▸ We were number two for fruit pectin, ripe olives, and coffee filters.

▸ Portland was third for natural cheese, grape juice, disposable lighters, fireplace logs and non-chocolate candy bars.

▸ Perhaps because we can get it fresh, we ranked 54th – or last place – for canned salmon. Refrigerated orange juice (also 54th) and butter/margarine blends (52nd) were not very popular either.

Finding It At Freddy's

As for favorite department stores, Julie Tripp's article reports results from a Belden Associates' 1989 Trade Area Profile, including the following:

▸ 75% of the people surveyed were Meier & Frank shoppers.

▸ 44% shopped at Nordstrom.

▸ and an impressive 88% had been to a Fred Meyer during the past 30 days.

Birkenstocks, Latte and Unlisted Phone Numbers

Let's embellish the picture with a few reasonable speculations. Although we haven't seen any hard data, Portland is rumored to be among the top cities for espresso consumption, Birkenstock sandal purchases, and unlisted telephone numbers. Despite the climate, we are not very high on the list of umbrella-buying cities. But – and this was confirmed by the company – we do buy a lot of Subaru cars. A local Subaru dealer was the top volume Subaru seller in the U.S. in 1992.

The Peoria of the 90s

It appears, from a recent article in *American Demographics*, that we may be losing our test market aura. According to the January 1992 issue, 1990 census data indicates that Tulsa,

Oklahoma is "the city that most closely matches U.S. demographics." As for metropolitan areas, the Detroit metro area is "closest to matching the demographics of the nation as a whole." Neither Portland nor the Portland metro area made the *American Demographics* top 20. So we may find fewer free samples in our mailboxes and fewer test products at the grocery store.

In the mean time, if you're driving your RV to the coast to go camping – or maybe it's your four-wheel drive Subaru for skiing in Bend – don't forget your book, the candy bars or the beer. Remind your neighbor to check the cat. And next weekend you can shop, take in a film, putter around the garden, and put up some preserves.

Taking the Trail Today

Nearly half of those surveyed last year believed the county, one of California's richest, will be a worse place in which to live in the future. About 40 percent say they are interested in moving out of the county. Of those, two out of three said they might leave Southern California.

> "Angeleno Lifestyle Begins To Unravel," an article that originally appeared in *The Economist* and was reprinted in *The Oregonian*, November 7, 1990.

...a 27-year-old Oregonian who moved to Los Angeles seven years ago...was looking to leave when his boss announced he needed volunteers for a new office in Portland last year. "I knocked people down in the hallway getting to his door," he said. By May 1990 he was gone, buying a house in Portland that he could never afford in Los Angeles and thinking about getting married and having children. As he put it, "I can't even imagine raising kids in L.A."

> Robert Reinhold, "Once a Mecca, California Begins to Lose Its Allure," *The New York Times*, October 16, 1991.

"I got one call from one guy in New Jersey," Auerbach said. "He said he wanted to buy a Portland house in the $200,000 to $250,000 range. I asked him if he wanted a view."

"He told me a view of the ocean would be great."

> Jack Auerbach, as quoted in *The Oregonian*, May 6, 1990.

"Well, it might be nice to live in Washington."

> A native New Yorker responding to news that her husband had a job interview in Portland.

Apparently some folks on the east coast aren't very smart – or at least they didn't deserve to pass geography. But the truth is that most of the people who move to the Portland area come because they know just where Portland is, and they know it to be a very livable place. And although we all know someone who came from back east, the south or the midwest, most of the people who come hail from California or Washington.

May I See Your Driver's License?

Statistics from the Oregon Department of Motor Vehicles (DMV) are often used to determine where people are – literally – coming from. The DMV counts out-of-state licenses that are surrendered in exchange for Oregon licenses. They don't break down the figures by city or county, so it's hard to know how many of these people are actually moving to the Portland area. But as we've seen, the 1990 census confirms that a good number of those moving to Oregon are settling in and around Portland.

Since we looked at the 1990 census data, let's take a parallel look at the 1990 DMV data. In all, 74,239 out-of-state licenses were surrendered to the DMV in 1990. They tell us quite a bit about who is on the Oregon Trail today:

State of Origin:	Number of People Surrendering Licenses:
California	30,855
Washington	11,069
Arizona	2,959
Idaho	2,672
Texas	2,219
Colorado	2,016
Alaska	1,795
Nevada	1,682
Montana	1,273
Utah	1,172

As we've all speculated, Californians head the list by a long shot. California's 30,855 total accounted for 41.6% of the surrendered licenses. Demographers believe that 1.5 people actually move for every license that is surrendered. By that estimate, 48,283 Californians followed the Oregon Trail in 1990.

With only 339 surrendered licenses, New Jersey didn't even make it into the top ten. (Maybe that's a good thing. Beachfront property is hard to find in Portland.) The five places at the bottom of the list are Delaware, West Virginia, Vermont, Rhode Island and the District of Columbia. They average under ten surrendered licenses each month, and often number only one or two.

Of course, some Oregonians leave. In 1990, 49,110 Oregon licenses were surrendered to other states. Ironically, it appears from the DMV figures that Oregonians tend to go to the same states that send people to Oregon. California, Washington, Arizona and Idaho are high up on this list too. You'll remember that 30,855 Californians applied for Oregon licenses in 1990. The number of Oregonians surrendering their driver's licenses to California authorities was 16,424, or roughly half. So for every two driving Californians who come to Oregon, about one driving Oregonian goes to California.

As for how 1990 compares with other years, the 1990 total of 74,239 surrendered out-of-state licenses was higher than both the 1989 and 1991 totals, but not by much:

Year:	Licenses Surrendered:
1989	72,717
1990	74,239
1991	72,617

While the sagging economy of the early 90s may slow the migration a little, preliminary figures for 1992 suggest that the final 1992 numbers could match the 1990 count.

"Visit But Don't Stay..."

According to an editorial in the July 15, 1991 *Oregonian*, the same states account for a large number of the tourists who come to Oregon. The editorial indicates that most of our tourists hail from California or Washington. Texans and folks from Arizona represent another large component. Looking at the data, it's a safe bet that some of these tourists will be back, and they'll soon be on line at the DMV. In the 1970s, Oregon Governor Tom McCall became infamous for his "visit but don't stay" remarks. Clearly, he knew what he was up against.

Movers and Shakers

Moving companies are another source of information on the 1990s version of the Oregon Trail. Oregon made *USA Today* headlines in January, 1990 when both Allied and United Van Lines announced their 1989 "magnet" states, or those states that "had the highest ratio of people moving in to people moving out." Oregon was number one for United Van Lines. And, in a tie with Rhode Island, we were Allied's number two destination. We've remained high on their lists. In 1991, Oregon was again number one for United and number two for Allied. Data from Allied confirms the DMV statistics, for about 40% of those inbound Oregon moves were from California.

Doing It Yourself

Not everybody hires a moving company. According to a Ryder Truck Rental study, only 23% of those who moved in 1990 used a van line. 28% rent a vehicle from a do-it-yourself truck rental company, and 49% borrow a truck or van, or use one they own.

Another Ryder Truck Rental study of the first six months of 1991 offers information on city-to-city moves. Using government sources, plus data collected when people inquired about rental rates and truck availability, Ryder confirmed that, like Oregon, Portland is a "net inbound market." The study found that for every 100 Portland households that left, 109 households moved in.

But California did not get top billing. Ryder found that "Seattle is the primary source of people relocating to Portland." And Seattle is the top destination for Portlanders who leave. Perhaps people are more likely to choose a van line when the move is long distance, while those moving only 175 miles "just do it" themselves.

Here are the Ryder findings on the top five city "comings and goings" for Portland. People are:

Moving to Portland from:	Moving from Portland to:
1. Seattle	1. Seattle
2. San Francisco-Oakland	2. Los Angeles
3. Eugene	3. San Francisco-Oakland
4. Los Angeles	4. Eugene and Bend (a tie)
5. Sacramento	5. Medford

Moving to a "net inbound market" can have its disadvantages. On August 28, 1992, *The Oregonian* reported that it is far more expensive to rent a do-it-yourself truck if you are driving to Portland. The article quoted rates that compared truck rentals for Portland and LA destinations. The Portland rates were five to twelve times higher!

Beaverton, Anyone?

Finally, the 1990 census can tell us a bit about where all these new immigrants are settling. Census takers gathered information on interstate moves, so we know the percentage of the population that moved to Oregon between 1985 and 1990. County and city breakdowns are available. Here are some of the figures:

Place:	Moved To Oregon Between 1985-1990:
Oregon	15.3%
Multnomah County	13.9%
Clackamas County	12.7%
Washington County	17.4%
Portland	14.6%
Gresham	12.7%
Beaverton	23.0%

Beaverton, in Washington County, is clearly a popular destination for many on today's Oregon Trail. The numbers above are quite consistent with growth figures presented in the *Counting Portlanders* section. As we saw, Washington County, with a growth rate of 26.7%, led the metro area in population growth from 1980 to 1990.

Just what kind of reception are these new immigrants getting? Are Portlanders open and welcoming, or has California bashing become a new sport? We'll take a look at that in the next section.

California Steaming

Thousands of Jaycees were assembled from all parts of the country at Portland's Civic Auditorium on a June morning in 1971. They were listening to what seemed a whimsical welcoming message from the Governor of Oregon, chuckling along with the warmth of the words and the usual one-liners. "We want you to visit our State of Excitement often," I said. "Come again and again. But, for heaven's sake, don't move here to live." I got stares of disbelief and a moment of silence. Then, the delegates burst into a clap of laughter.

To ease any tensions, I added a softener: "Or, if you do have to move in to live, don't tell any of your neighbors where you are going."

Tom McCall, *Tom McCall, Maverick*, 1977.

Population paranoia meets the Welcome Wagon: Californiaphobia.

Headline in *The Oregonian*, April 8, 1990.

"Visit, but Don't Stay" and "Don't Californicate Oregon" were once popular Oregon slogans. Today, some Portlanders fear that growth will "Los Angelize" Portland, and newspapers coin new words like "Californiaphobia." It is true that Portland topped Marjabelle Young Stewart's list of polite cities in 1989 and 1990. But even polite Portlanders have been heard grumbling about the "equity refugees" who bring big bucks to Portland, driving up real estate prices and crowding the schools.

California Bashing

Californians who make the move north typically come to escape smog, traffic, crowds, earthquakes, gangs, the drought, economic woes, and the generally faltering "California Dream." And while they – for the most part – happily adjust to their adopted state, they are not immune to the grumbling. Some claim they are victims of what the press likes to call California bashing.

It is hard to determine just how extensive such bashing may be. Much of the debate seems to take place in *The Oregonian*. A look at that paper turns up some evidence – mostly anecdotal – to suggest that we are not particularly welcoming. Columnists, for example, recount the negative experiences of newcomers, and letters to the editor report various types of rather unfriendly behavior. Unfortunately, the paper seems to be fanning the flames.

For example, under the headline "Californoids Invade!" the December 29, 1991 *Oregonian* offered "wacko predictions" for the future. The article included a total of twelve California bashing comments, with all references to California and Californians helpfully highlighted. A few weeks later, a "Fun Facts" feature in the February 2, 1992 *Oregonian* asked readers to send in funny slogans to describe migrating Californians. Some people did, but, to our good credit, many wrote to criticize the paper for such "xenophobic" behavior.

"Bashing Back"

Californians are reacting to it all, and there are lots of rebuttals in the air. We've dubbed the phenomenon California steaming; others, as we'll see, have coined different phrases. Here's a selection of Californian reactions that have shown up recently on the pages of *The Oregonian*:

> ...our treatment of Californians has become so widely noted there's even an official name for it. Zeke Wigglesworth, Travel editor of the San Jose Mercury News calls it "the Oregon syndrome."
>
> "The usual symptoms are well-known," Zeke wrote recently, "things such as signs saying 'Keep Oregon Green – Go Home' and local laws prohibiting anyone from California from buying land or houses within 400 miles of Portland."
>
> Which, of course, is not true. But we all know Zeke's not an investigative reporter lost in the tangle of Oregon land-use regulations.
>
> He's a Californian bashing back.
>
> Margie Boulé, *The Oregonian*, August 27, 1992.

...I am a native Californian. Unlike the popular opinion here in Oregon, all of California is not like Los Angeles. In fact, if you talk to Californians in any city, I think you'll find that Los Angeles is the black eye of the state. Remember, though, that it is as much of a melting pot as any large city in the world. And how can an entire state be judged by one city?...

Instead of wasting time blaming Californians, maybe Oregonians should realize that growth is going to happen, whether they like it or not. Oregon is not an island unto itself, a victim of Californication. It's a beautiful state that people identify with and move to in order to enjoy and be a part of.

> Randy Schroeder, in a letter to the Editor of *The Oregonian*, November 1, 1991.

"Tired of all the fulsome praise about the Great Northwest? So are we, which is why it's a relief to hear from Peter Heimlich and Karen Schulman, suffering ex-San Franciscans exiled in Portland. Their postcard: 'In San Francisco, tourists are the worst-dressed people. In Portland, they're the best-dressed.' There!"

> *San Francisco Chronicle* columnist Herb Caen, as quoted by Jonathan Nicholas, *The Oregonian*, September 24, 1991.

P.S. Don't worry. We are not another California family moving to Oregon. Your basketball team is not good enough. It rains too much. Your politicians are not goofy enough. Your people are too civilized. You read too much. You expect too much of your children and politicians. You are too concerned about the environment. You have too much oxygen in your air because of the trees.

You are too far away from the mainstream and cutting edge of our society's evolution. More people would rather live in Greece or Spain than Switzerland; the same with California than Oregon.

> Roy A. Fassel, in a letter to the Editor of *The Oregonian*, December 4, 1991.

Sarah and her husband have made a few friends since they relocated, "but they're all just like us. Transplants. There's a real 'them and us' mentality going on here, and it's not healthy. After all, except for the Native Americans, nearly everybody or their parents came here from somewhere else, not very long ago."

As quoted by Margie Boulé, *The Oregonian*, May 22, 1990.

A Well-Kept Secret . . . or a Smoke Screen?

Is it really that bad? Has the most polite city turned hostile? Maybe. But some new residents say that although they are reluctant to admit that they are from California, the response is rarely negative. Some even describe receptions like those in Alfred J. Zangara's article in the September 16, 1992 *Oregonian*:

Recently, my family and I relocated from – dare I say it? – California ("the C-word," as my wife says)....

The first bloodcurdling event to befall us in this new wilderness came at the hands of our new neighbors in Portland.

On our first day, we were presented with fresh-baked bread, still warm from the oven; a home-made Bavarianstyle chocolate cake; a huge basket overflowing with fresh fruit.

With nary a California basher in sight, the Zangara family's good fortune continued. The article ends with sentiments that seem to be the norm among our newest immigrants:

All in all, we're very happy with our move to the City of Roses, but don't let the word get out too much – we wouldn't want a bunch o' crazy Californians movin' up here.

500,000 and Counting

Will Portland continue to grow? It sure looks that way. Projections are not certainties, but barring a catastrophe – like a severe depression or a serious earthquake in the Northwest – those in the know are anticipating and planning for continued growth.

The Regional Forecast: Population, Housing and Employment Forecast to 1995 and 2010, a Metropolitan Service District publication, is a good source of information on the topic. The *Forecast* makes the following projections for the Portland metropolitan area:

Year:	Population:
1987	1,303,427
1995	1,489,844
2010	1,789,428

That that amounts to 486,001 more men, women and children in the year 2010 than were here in 1987. In general, two numbers are repeatedly mentioned when the topic is growth: 50,000 more people in the state each year, and 500,000 more people in the metro area in the next 20 years.

Most of these new residents will live outside the Portland city limits. According to Metro estimates, the population in the four-county area will rise as follows:

County:	Population in 1987:	Population in 2010:	Percent Change:
Multnomah	562,997	629,102	+ 11.7%
Clackamas	253,404	367,907	+ 45.2%
Washington	278,307	439,352	+ 57.9%
Clark	208,697	353,067	+ 69.2%

While Clark County in Washington state will see the largest percent increase, Washington County, with 161,045 more residents in 2010, will see the most new faces. And although Oregonians are quick to blame the growing population figures on immigrants from other states, a significant number are actually new little natives. In other words, the population rises from what demographers call "natural increase" – or babies born here. With the burgeoning population will come more jobs. Metro expects a 46% increase in employment in Washington, Clackamas, Multnomah and Clark Counties by the year 2010.

The Growth Dilemma

As we've seen in the *California Steaming* section, all this growth has people nervous. Portlanders worry that the quality of life they enjoy – like clean air, brief commutes, uncrowded facilities, natural areas and a high level of civility among people – will be sacrificed to the influx of new residents. Government officials are pondering the price tag, and whether revenues are adequate to fund the costs associated with growth. Planners are searching for strategies that will maintain the quality of life in the face of more people.

These concerns are quite real. But some Portlanders believe that well-managed growth can bring real benefits to Portland. Carl Abbott, a PSU professor who studies urban planning and Portland history, considered the question in 1985 in *Portland: Gateway to the Northwest*. The emphasis is his:

> ...In fact, a city is truly livable only if it is *big enough*. To give all its residents the opportunity to realize and utilize their abilities, a city must offer an adequate base of public and private resources. Residents benefit by the opportunity to interact with others of different backgrounds and cultures. A city needs to be a certain size to be able to provide support for higher education and the arts. It also needs to be large enough to offer a variety of jobs and to develop the sophisticated business services that promote economic innovation and spinoff industries.
>
> The threshold population for a truly livable metropolitan area is a million or two – the size range of Denver, San Diego, Seattle, Minneapolis, or Vancouver, British Columbia....Subdivision sprawl and rush-hour traffic tie-ups are the obvious signs of...[Portland's] increase in population. Just as significant is a new sophistication about everything from music and theater to city planning and politics.

While growth may indeed provide the Portland metro area with enough people to support the jobs, restaurants, parks, theaters and universities that ultimately make it so livable, not everyone sees it that way. Many Portlanders think that growth is undesirable but inevitable, so we might as well try to deal with it. Still others believe that we can limit growth by passing along more of its costs to developers and new home buyers. We'll look at growth and planning issues when we consider the local government in *By the People, For the People,* our next section.

Two Million and Counting?

If the demographic experts are right, we can expect the metro area population to level off at just under two million people. That's because the baby boomers are getting older, and they are having fewer children than their parents did.

Projections for 2040 place the area's population at about 1.9 million. Is that big? It's a matter of opinion. The Denver-Boulder, Colorado CMSA had a population of about 1,848,000 in 1990. The Phoenix, Arizona area came in at 2,122,000. And metro Seattle, which will grow to about 2,630,000 in 2040, had a population of 2,559,000 in 1990.

Now that we know who came, who's here now, and who is on the way, let's look at some of the mechanics of running the Rose City.

By the People,

For the People

Running the Rose City

The City Livability Award from the U.S. Conference of Mayors. The Planning Implementation Award from the American Planning Association. High grades on *Financial World* magazine's city "report cards." Praise from CEOs who were surveyed on the best business cities. As we saw in *Winning on the Willamette,* Portland is considered a well run, financially solvent city by a variety of analysts.

Not all Portlanders sing the praises of City Hall. They want more police on the streets and more equitable arrangements for sewer installation fees. They worry about gangs and they question budget priorities. But even the critics acknowledge that – given the neglect, decay and budget crises facing so many of America's cities – Portland deserves praise. So let's look at our city's government and at agencies and programs within its jurisdiction.

Who's the Boss?

Rumor has it that the five gargoyle heads on the fountain in Pioneer Courthouse Square represent the mayor and the four city commissioners. According to the *Oregon Bluebook,* Portland is the only city among the 242 in the state to use the commission form of government. As the *Bluebook* explains, "elected commissioners, who function collectively as the city council, also serve as administrators of city departments."

The Portland City Council is composed of four commissioners and the mayor. They are elected on a non-partisan basis, and serve four year terms. Terms are staggered so no more than two commissioners and the mayor will be up for election in any given year.

Portland is also a bit unusual in that elections are often decided in the May primary. Candidates can avoid a run-off election in November if they can pull at least 51% of the primary vote. In 1992, City Commissioner Earl Blumenauer and State Representative Vera Katz were the main contenders in the primary, but neither won 51% of the vote. In their usual familiar way, Portlanders referred to the candidates as Vera and Earl while they tried to decide between the two. Vera won in November, pulling in 60% of the vote.

Madame Mayor and Mr. Commissioner

After the election, many believed that Portland was the true winner. For Vera Katz would be Portland's 46th mayor – the third woman, if you prefer to count it that way – and Earl Blumenauer would remain on the City Council. As *Willamette Week* wrote in its October 1992 endorsement of Vera Katz:

> Rarely does a city electorate face a choice between two visionary thinkers who are at once competent, articulate and wholly committed to the future of this community. Vera Katz and Earl Blumenauer have both been exemplary public servants, and both would make good mayors. In our primary endorsement, we said that although Blumenauer is arguably the most qualified and technically proficient mayoral candidate in recent history, the city would be better off with the kind of energetic verve Katz would bring to City Hall.

Whose On First?

The city government is divided into five departments. The four commissioners and the mayor each head one. When she took office in January 1993, Vera left the assignments as they had been, with new Commissioner Charlie Hales replacing the out-going Dick Bogle, and Vera replacing Mayor Bud Clark. She anticipated changes by the spring, but she began like this:

Vera Katz	Commissioner of Finance and Administration
Mike Lindberg	Commissioner of Public Affairs
Earl Blumenauer	Commissioner of Public Works
Gretchen Kafoury	Commissioner of Public Utilities
Charlie Hales	Commissioner of Public Safety

According to Jonathan Nicholas's November 8, 1992 *Oregonian* column, they are "the best we have mustered in 50 years."

On April 26, 1993, Vera shuffled the assignments. The chart on the next page lists the assignments as they were at the end of April, along with an outline of the main bureaus and offices within each department. For the latest on the commissioners and their doings, and info on any changes in assignments, check *The Oregonian* or *Willamette Week*. Or just call City Hall.

Main Departmental Responsibilities, April 26, 1993

- ▸ Vera Katz, Commissioner of Finance and Administration

    - ▸ Bureau of Police
    - ▸ Office of Finance and Administration
    - ▸ Office of Government Relations
    - ▸ Office of International Relations/Sister Cities
    - ▸ Office of the City Attorney
    - ▸ Portland Development Commission

- ▸ Mike Lindberg, Commissioner of Public Utilities

    - ▸ Bureau of Water Works
    - ▸ Bureau of Environmental Services
    - ▸ Bureau of Hydroelectric Power
    - ▸ Portland Energy Office
    - ▸ Metropolitan Arts Commission

- ▸ Earl Blumenauer, Commissioner of Public Works

    - ▸ Bureau of Emergency Communications
    - ▸ Office of Transportation
    - ▸ Office of Cable Communications and Franchise Management
    - ▸ Bureau of Purchases and Stores

- ▸ Gretchen Kafoury, Commissioner of Public Affairs

    - ▸ Bureau of General Services
    - ▸ Bureau of Buildings
    - ▸ Bureau of Housing and Community Development
    - ▸ Bureau of Licenses
    - ▸ Metropolitan Human Rights Commission

- ▸ Charlie Hales, Commissioner of Public Safety

    - ▸ Bureau of Fire, Rescue and Emergency Services
    - ▸ Bureau of Parks and Recreation
    - ▸ Bureau of Planning
    - ▸ Office of Neighborhood Associations
    - ▸ Public Monuments and Drinking Fountains
    - ▸ Willamette River Development Project

In addition, the City Auditor is responsible for auditing services, contracts and disbursements, city elections, and other related activities.

Meet the Mayor

Vera Katz got her start in politics as a volunteer for Robert Kennedy's presidential primary campaign in Oregon. Soon after that, she worked, as David S. Broder wrote in the March 4, 1985 *Washington Post*, "in the burgeoning political organization that made Neil Goldschmidt a reform mayor of Portland." She was elected to the Oregon House in 1972, where she served as Speaker for three terms, and earned a reputation for her political vision and her skill as a consensus builder. Many Portlanders think it was these qualities that ultimately won the mayoral race for her. Her contagious smile and warm hugs helped too.

Vera's early years were far from easy. She was born in Germany in 1933. Recognizing that Jews were not safe there, her family fled to France when she was still a baby. They fled again, when Vera was just seven, after the Nazis invaded France. This time they walked across the Pyrenees into Spain. They eventually arrived in Manhattan. But her father never recovered from the stress of their experience, and abandoned the family when Vera was eleven. She went to public schools, and graduated from New York's Brooklyn College. She moved to Portland in 1964, which is where she got her political start in Bobby Kennedy's campaign.

Many Portlanders have wonderful things to say about Vera Katz. We'll include just two. The first is a favorite because it's familiar, direct, and comes from another visionary leader. It appeared as a photo caption in "The Politics of Vera Katz," a *This Week* magazine profile from September 11, 1991:

> This Week magazine writer Susan Hereford made numerous attempts to reach former Gov. Neil Goldschmidt. Several weeks into a game of phone tag, a final message was relayed to her office: "This is Neil. I'm out of the country in two hours. I love Vera. That's my quote."

The second is from a June 21, 1990 *Oregonian* column by Steve Duin:

> Through years of pain and loss, her mother made sure her daughter never forgot the Jewish tradition of returning something to her community.
>
> Oregon should be grateful that when Katz finally put the wars behind her, and made her truest peace, this was the land beneath her feet.

We benefited greatly from Vera's stint in the legislature. In all probability, we'll benefit from her presence in the mayor's chair too. Let's hope she keeps on smiling. Before we take a look at the city agencies she administers and the problems she'll tackle, we'd like to mention two of her predecessors: Bud Clark and Neil Goldschmidt.

Portland's Citizen Mayor

In 1984, Portlanders elected J.E. Bud Clark to the office of mayor. His resume was not typical. His experience included tending the bar at his tavern, the Goose Hollow Inn; neighborhood activism; interests in photography and canoeing; and a revealing pose in the famous *Expose Yourself to Art* poster. Biking to work with a rose in his lapel, his bike helmet firmly clasped around his full beard, he grabbed the fancy of many in the Rose City. His exclamation "Whoop, whoop!" became about as famous as his flasher poster pose.

Portlanders liked Clark well enough to return him to office for a second term, and his bio lists many accomplishments that happened on his watch. They include construction of the Oregon Convention Center, the introduction of community policing, the Neighborhood Revitalization Program, and a variety of planning processes including Portland Future Focus and the Central City Plan of 1988. And the city won a host of awards in the late '80s and early '90s, including two from Clark's peers on the U.S. Council of Mayors.

But the blush on the rose was beginning to fade. Clark announced that he would not run again, and some criticized his leadership. While we may have been ready for Vera Katz, many people remained quite fond of Clark. When columnist Phil Stanford came up with the "Bucks for Bud" plan – in which Stanford asked *Oregonian* readers to send a dollar to the mayor to help him retire campaign debts – hundreds responded. Even *The New York Times* noticed, reporting on February 14, 1992 that Clark had received almost $30,000 to date. And sales of *Expose Yourself to Art* were on the rise.

Clark may yet return to politics. He'd like to see some consolidation between the city and the county. As he told Barnes C. Ellis for a January 6, 1992 *Oregonian* article, "Maybe I'll run for county commissioner....I'd eliminate the job."

Good as Gold...schmidt

It is true that his years as mayor date back to 1972-1979. We mention him now because his vision and his ability to get things done helped create the award-winning, livable city that we enjoy today. Whether you consider public transit, land use, neighborhoods, the riverfront, or the vibrant downtown – to name just a few of the things that set this city apart – you will find evidence of Neil Goldschmidt's vision, energy and implementation skills.

He went on to serve as Transportation Secretary in the Carter Administration and as Governor of the state of Oregon. He's back in town now, and he's still trying to make Portland a better place. Along with the law firm of Ater Wynne Hewitt Dodson & Skerritt, he started the non-profit Oregon Children's Foundation. The foundation's SMART program – for Start Making A Reader Today – connects volunteer tutors with Oregon schoolchildren who need a little extra attention. Corporate sponsors are encouraged to adopt a school. Sponsors help provide funding, and they give employees that volunteer time off each week to read with "their" children. Plans are in the works for other foundation projects that will address problems like child abuse and teen pregnancy. Goldschmidt's focus may be different, but his vision for a better future is as strong as ever.

We need one more detour – to the Oregon System – before we look at city agencies. That's the system that allows Oregonians to put measures on the ballot. As you'll see, ballot measures have great impact on life and politics in the city.

The Oregon System

We've tried to limit our scope to Portland. But some topics demand broader explanations. As citizens of the state of Oregon, we are of course subject to state laws. So we need to look at what became known as the Oregon System, a process that enables citizens to draft and vote on ballot measures that – if passed – have the force of law.

Progressive Politics

The Oregon System has two components: the initiative and the referendum. An initiative allows Oregonians to propose a new law or a constitutional change by placing a measure on the ballot during a general election. A referendum enables a citizen to refer a legislative or administrative act to a vote of the people. Both require their sponsors to obtain a requisite number of signatures before they can appear on the ballot.

Since the system of initiative and referendum was implemented in 1902, it has been used more than 350 times at the state level. According to the *Oregon Bluebook*, "the adoption of these popular legislative tools put Oregon in the vanguard of progressive and enlightened politics."

The initiative and referendum system can be used in city politics too. Registered voters may start a petition drive to refer a non-emergency ordinance to the electorate before it actually becomes law. Alternatively, they can sponsor an initiative drive to repeal an existing ordinance, or to propose a new one.

But most of the attention gets focused on statewide ballot measures, like Measure 5, the property tax limitation plan that lowered property taxes and reorganized public school funding. Measure 5 was narrowly approved by the voters in 1990. More recently, Oregonians defeated Measure 9, a 1992 initiative that sought to declare homosexuality "abnormal, wrong, unnatural and perverse." To their good credit, 57% of the electorate felt that it was the ballot measure that was perverse.

Problematic Progressive Politics

While the Oregon System gives the electorate considerable power to make and change law, it also brings high uncertainty to government. Even before the 1992 election, there was little doubt that the Oregon Citizens Alliance, the group that sponsored the anti-gay measure, would try again if they lost. Similarly, should the state revamp the tax structure, anyone can use the initiative system to raise the question again.

It won't be very difficult. To place a constitutional amendment initiative on the ballot, supporters need to gather only 89,028 signatures – enough to equal 8% of the votes cast for governor in the last general election. New law initiatives require signatures that equal just 6% of the gubernatorial votes cast. Most other states that allow citizen initiatives have more stringent requirements.

Critics also complain that the system provides little protection from poorly worded, confusing ballot measures. Although a passed measure has the force of law, initiatives rarely get the kind of scrutiny and analysis that is normally given to bills in the Legislature. During most ballot measure campaigns, the electorate must try to sort out the wildly conflicting claims of the proponents and opponents. That was the case for both Measure 5 and Measure 9.

Finally, there is concern that initiatives have become the tool of special interest groups. Ironically, the initiative system was first introduced because those with special interests had great power in the Legislature. Today, with big budgets, these groups easily collect the required signatures. A public discussion of the issues – as was perhaps envisioned in 1902 – gets obscured in savvy advertising campaigns and manipulative sound bites. For these reasons, many would like to see initiative reform.

Back to Portland

Ballot measure campaigns – particularly for highly charged issues – have great impact on Portland. And because the Portland metro area is home to about 44% of the state's citizens, it is often Portland area voters who ultimately decide an election. Both 1990's Measure 5 and 1992's Measure 9 split urban and rural voters. Enough urban voters sought tax relief to pass Measure 5. Two years later, it was the metro area voters who defeated Measure 9. With that background in place, let's return to Portland. Just what do Portlanders think about city services in our award-winning burg?

How Is Portland Doing?

New York's Mayor Ed Koch was known for his trademark "How am I doing?" He clearly liked asking New Yorkers – even those he waved to from atop a camel in Egypt – for a little feedback. Bud Clark, who served as Portland's mayor from 1985-1992, was more apt to shout his famous "Whoop, whoop!" Which does not necessarily mean that Ed Koch was any more or less successful than Bud Clark.

In a poll conducted by Griggs-Anderson Research for *The Oregonian* in April, 1992, 400 Portlanders were asked if Portland was "better off, worse off, or about the same after Bud Clark's eight years as mayor." The paper reported these results on April 14:

- ▸ 25% of those polled saw the city as better off.
- ▸ 20% felt it was worse off.
- ▸ and 46% felt that things were about the same.

Only 34% believed that, were he running, Clark would deserve to win again. The survey also included questions on city government and priorities:

- ▸ 59% of the respondents believed that city government was "on the right track."
- ▸ 57% picked "taxes and government spending" as "the most important issue facing the city."
- ▸ 34% saw "crime and drugs" as the most critical issue,
- ▸ and 23% selected "crime" as the main issue for the city.

A City Report Card

Another way to evaluate how Portland is doing is to look at Portland's first annual performance report, which was issued by City Auditor Barbara Clark in March, 1992. *City of Portland Service Efforts and Accomplishment: 1990-91* includes information and performance measures for the city's six main public services: fire, police, parks and recreation, street maintenance, sewers, and water.

In addition, the report includes comparison data for six cities: Charlotte, Cincinnati, Denver, Kansas City, Sacramento, and Seattle. They were selected for their "similar populations, service area densities and costs of living...." It also includes the results of a survey of more than 4,500 city residents – about 50% of the more than 9,000 people who were randomly solicited by mail.

The report is loaded with facts and figures. We can learn, for example, that:

- ▸ Portland's 1.88 police officers per 1,000 residents is less than the six-city average of 2.4 per 1,000 people.
- ▸ We have 39 on-duty fire department staff per 100,000 residents, 2 less than the 41 per 100,000 six-city average.
- ▸ With the exception of Seattle and Sacramento, we spend more per capita on parks than the other cities.
- ▸ And, per capita, we spend the least of all on street maintenance.

But perhaps the most interesting figures are those from the citizen survey. As we'd expect, results vary by neighborhood, and those who seek specifics should call the City Auditor's Office for a copy of the 70 page report. In the meantime, here are some city-wide highlights:

77%   of Portland's citizens feel safe or very safe walking alone in their neighborhood during the day.

57%   feel safe or very safe walking alone during the day in the park nearest their home, and

57%   feel safe or very safe walking alone downtown in the daytime.

34%   feel safe or very safe walking in their neighborhood at night.

27%   feel unsafe.

24%   apparently fall in between, reporting that they feel neither safe nor unsafe on a walk in their neighborhood at night.

10%   of those surveyed experienced a break-in or burglary in their home in 1991.

76%   reported it to the police.

92%   of those who used fire or rescue services rated that service as good or very good.

93%   of Portland homes have working smoke detectors.

60%   of Portland's citizens rated police services as good or very good.

88%   rated fire services as good or very good.

82%   found parks services to be good or very good. But then the percentages drop.

68%   rated water services as good or very good.

59%   found recreation activities to be good or very good.

45%   rated street maintenance as good or very good.

38%   found sewer services to be good or very good, and only

33%   rated storm drainage as good or very good. (We'll see why when we look at sewage overflows in *Down the Drain,* a chapter in the book's environmental section.)

Community Policing

Before we move on, we must mention community policing. As the auditor's report explains, "the Bureau is in the second year of a five-year transition to community policing. Community policing requires a fundamental shift in how the community and police work to improve community livability and decrease crime. This approach requires a shared responsibility between the police and the community for addressing the underlying problems that contribute to crime and the fear of crime."

Under the direction of Portland Police Chief Tom Potter, a strong advocate of community policing, the police department has implemented new strategies that regularly bring police officers into the community to work with citizens. Before community policing, officers typically interacted with community residents only when they arrived in response to 911 call – after a crime had been committed. The new strategy puts officers onto the street and into the community – so they can act as deterrents, develop trust, and deal with problems before they escalate. Officers work together with other city bureaus and service agencies, to empower citizens and help solve problems.

Not everyone likes community policing. But the city has gotten national and international recognition for its innovations in this area. One weakness can be traced to budgetary considerations, for the city has not been able to hire all the officers necessary if community policing is to be more than a slogan. Hiring more police officers was a major issue in the November, 1992 elections. Vera Katz is committed to community policing, and ran on a platform of cutting in other areas – like the Sister Cities program and city car usage – to hire more police. The next auditor's report will include performance measures and other data to help determine the success of community policing.

Looking at the issues presented in the 1992 mayoral campaign, *The Oregonian* survey and the auditor's performance report, a few emerge as critical. Portlanders are most concerned about crime and the interrelated issues of taxes and government spending. They are next up on our agenda.

Making Smokey Proud

According to a July, 1992 report by the TriData Corporation for the City of Portland, the Fire Bureau is doing "a very good job." The independent consultants had especially high praise for the fire prevention and public education programs, calling them "among the best in the nation." According to TriData, "Portland emphasizes prevention more than virtually any other major U.S. city."

The TriData report also commented on a topic that was a 1992 mayoral campaign issue: should four-person crews remain the norm, or should Portland consider cutting back to just three firefighters per engine, the norm in many other cities? Vera was committed to four-person crews, while Earl wanted to consider the options before making any commitments. TriData endorsed the four-person crews as "the preferred minimum." Given Vera's win, it's a good bet we'll keep the larger size, at least for now.

Mean Streets?

Murders, drive-by shootings, rapes, gay-bashing, hate crimes. Are these simply crimes that happen in a city, or are they worthy of attention in a book such as this one? Portlanders have become accustomed to the frequent articles on their city's livability, and nod knowingly when the city wins one more award. But they also believe that crime is one of the city's most critical problems, and they are not surprised when Portland is criticized for its crime rate. From the most bank robberies per capita since 1988 to the skinhead recruiting efforts that led to the murder of Mulugeta Seraw, Portland is, unfortunately, known for its crimes. The subject is worthy of our attention.

Counting Crime

So it should come as no surprise that a headline in the August 11, 1991 *Oregonian* read "Portland 18th in rate of crime." According to the article, Portland occupied 18th place when compared with other American cities with populations over 300,000. The ranking was based on data in the FBI's *Crime in the United States for 1990*. It considered each city's "overall rate of crime - murder, rape, robbery, aggravated assault, burglary, larceny-theft, and motor vehicle theft."

As one might expect, cities like Detroit, Atlanta and Miami also placed in the top 20 for crime. What's more interesting is that Portland was not the only "livable" city to grace the list. Seattle and Minneapolis were there too, as numbers 7 and 15 respectively. The article noted that Portland did a little better than in the previous two years: the Rose City had been third in 1988, and eighth in 1989. Portland's rankings are only as accurate as the reporting statistics are, and as we'll see a bit later, they may be debatable. But it cannot be denied that the metro area – particularly Portland – has a crime problem.

Mapping the Problem

As we all know, neighborhoods are not created equal, and as we'd expect, the incidence of crime varies by neighborhood. Crime statistics for each of the city's neighborhoods are available from the Portland Police Bureau. They appear each year in the Bureau's *Annual Report*, or are available upon request from the Bureau's Public Information Office. We requested them twice; once to get the rates initially, and then a second time to make sure we had the latest numbers available. Both times the information we sought arrived only a day or so after we phoned in our request. We don't have the space to include all the neighborhood data here, but if you want the scoop on a particular neighborhood, just give them a call. You should have no trouble obtaining the information.

Using the crime statistics for each neighborhood, the police are able to track crime for the city's nine geographical areas. The maps on pages 138 and 139, reprinted from the *Police Bureau 1990 Annual Report*, show both the neighborhood and the area boundaries. We'll look first at the overall crime rate – which includes crimes of all types, from bike theft and vandalism to murder and rape – in the nine areas. The second chart focuses on residential burglaries in particular.

All Around the Town

While there is some variation, the picture is really quite similar from year to year, and the statistics fall easily into subgroups, as the charts show:

Portland Crime Rates Per 1,000 People

1989:		1990:		1991:	
Southwest	64.0	Southwest	64.7	Southwest	70.7
Outer SE	105.8	Outer SE	93.1	Outer SE	100.3
Central NE	106.4	Central NE	97.1	Central NE	106.3
Outer NE	105.6	Outer NE	108.2	Outer NE	122.9
North	140.9	North	129.3	North	132.4
Inner SE	147.1	Inner SE	139.0	Inner SE	134.9
Inner NE	202.7	Inner NE	165.1	Inner NE	173.2
Northwest	193.9	Northwest	172.1	Northwest	180.0
Downtown	802.9	Downtown	795.8	Downtown	695.7
City-wide	147.5	City-wide	133.7	City-wide	136.8

We are looking at rates, so a low number is better than a high one. Southwest Portland (excluding downtown) is consistently the area with the lowest rate. Downtown, including the Burnside area, always has the highest rate.

It is important to note that there is considerable variation within each of the nine areas of the city. But even the variations look consistent from year to year. For example, the crime rate in the Irvington neighborhood, 93.3 in 1991, is always much lower than the rates for the adjoining neighborhoods of inner northeast Portland. The Lloyd neighborhood, 2672.5 in 1991, is consistently the highest in inner northeast. Both are in stark contrast to the overall rate for all of inner northeast, which was 173.2 for 1991.

The same situation is seen in northwest Portland. For example, Hillside's crime rate in 1991 was 25.2, while the Northwest Industrial neighborhood's was 2072.7. Similar fluctuations are seen in these northwest neighborhoods each year. And Lair Hill, 335.4 in 1991, is far above the southwest area average of 70.7, as it was for each year considered. Again, those interested in specific neighborhoods should get the data from the police. While useful for an overview of adjoining neighborhoods in broad areas of the city, the area statistics should be interpreted with care!

By Way of Explanation

Astute readers may be wondering how the Lloyd neighborhood could possibly have a crime rate of 2672.5 per 1,000 people. That's more than 2 crimes per person per year! Notes on the police statistics caution that the large work force in the Lloyd, downtown, Burnside and Northwest Industrial neighborhoods can distort the rate per 1,000 people. We are reminded that the 1,000 reflects only those who reside in the neighborhood, based on population census figures. A better indicator would factor in the thousands of people who come to those neighborhoods each day; to work, shop, or do business there.

The Business of Burglaries

Portland burglars apparently keep business hours. According to police records, most of the reported burglaries take place

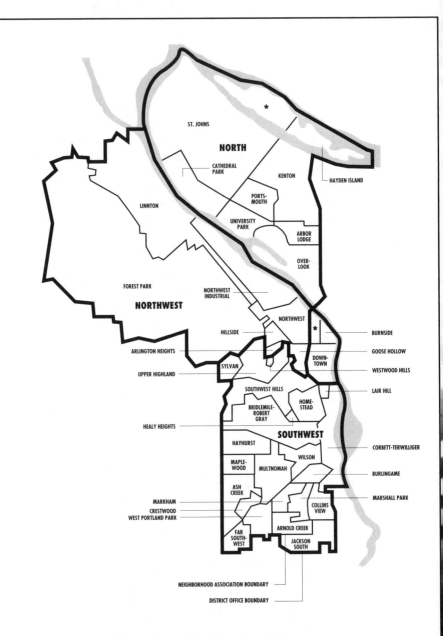

West Side Neighborhood Map

with Geographic Boundaries for Crime Statistics

* not an official neighborhood association

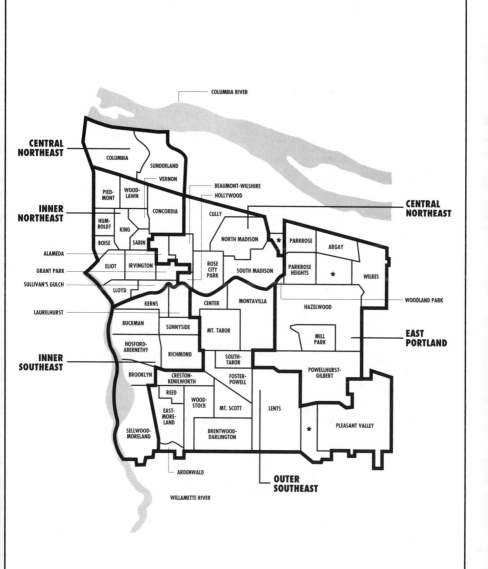

COLUMBIA RIVER

CENTRAL
NORTHEAST

COLUMBIA

SUNDERLAND

VERNON

BEAUMONT-WILSHIRE

HOLLYWOOD

INNER
NORTHEAST

PIED-
MONT

WOOD-
LAWN

CONCORDIA

CULLY

CENTRAL
NORTHEAST

HUM-
BOLDT

KING

SABIN

NORTH MADISON *

PARKROSE

ARGAY

BOISE

ALAMEDA

ELIOT

IRVINGTON

ROSE
CITY
PARK

SOUTH MADISON

PARKROSE
HEIGHTS

*

WILKES

GRANT PARK

SULLIVAN'S GULCH

LLOYD

WOODLAND PARK

LAURELHURST

KERNS

CENTER

MONTAVILLA

HAZELWOOD

BUCKMAN

SUNNYSIDE

MT. TABOR

EAST
PORTLAND

HOSFORD-
ABERNETHY

RICHMOND

SOUTH-
TABOR

MILL
PARK

INNER
SOUTHEAST

BROOKLYN

CRESTON-
KENILWORTH

FOSTER-
POWELL

POWELLHURST-
GILBERT

REED

WOOD-
STOCK

EAST-
MORE-
LAND

MT. SCOTT

LENTS

*

PLEASANT VALLEY

SELLWOOD-
MORELAND

BRENTWOOD-
DARLINGTON

ARDENWALD

OUTER
SOUTHEAST

WILLAMETTE RIVER

East Side Neighborhood Map

with Geographic Boundaries for Crime Statistics

* not an official neighborhood association

Monday through Friday, between 8 AM and 4 PM! Like the overall crime rate statistics, statistics on residential burglaries show similar patterns from year to year. The next chart shows the number of residential burglaries per 100 households:

Residential Burglaries Per 100 Households

1989:		1990:		1991:	
Downtown	1.66	Downtown	1.70	Downtown	1.45
Outer NE	2.78	Outer NE	1.97	Outer NE	2.22
Southwest	2.54	Southwest	2.38	Southwest	2.47
Northwest	3.00	Northwest	2.37	Northwest	2.70
Inner SE	3.60	Inner SE	2.41	Inner SE	3.30
Outer SE	4.12	Outer SE	2.68	Outer SE	2.56
Central NE	4.28	Central NE	2.72	Central NE	3.08
North	6.00	North	3.90	North	3.98
Inner NE	7.48	Inner NE	5.66	Inner NE	4.94
City-wide	4.25	City-wide	3.04	City-wide	3.12

Despite its poor showing for overall crime rate, the downtown actually has the lowest residential burglary rate each year; 1.45 per 100 households in 1991. Inner northeast has the highest each year; 4.94 per 100 household in 1991. And the other parts of the city fall between, again in clusters.

Reported Rapes

In 1991, 464 rapes were reported to law enforcement officials in Portland. That's up from 1990, when 424 rapes were reported. It is true that the city's population has grown, but that fact should not diminish the extent of the problem. Just about everyone agrees that reported rapes are only a small fraction of the total number of rapes that actually occur. National estimates indicate that only 10% of victims report this crime to authorities. Figures available from the Portland Women's Crisis Line indicate that slightly more than 8% of the women who called the crisis line planned to also call the police.

As is typical in other places, there are fewer reported rapes in the suburbs. In 1990, there were 67 rapes in Washington

County, and 88 rapes in Clackamas County. Even when the population differences are factored in, the rates are considerably lower in the suburban counties.

Hate Crimes

In 1989, the Oregon legislature passed a law that requires law enforcement agencies to report all crimes motivated by prejudice to the Law Enforcement Data System. They are cataloged, with the date, location and a description, in *Oregon Law Enforcement Agencies Annual Report of Criminal Offenses Motivated by Prejudice.* So we know that there were 488 reported hate crimes in Oregon in 1991. That's up significantly from the 343 hate crimes that were reported in 1990. Here's the 1991 breakdown for the metro counties:

Hate Crimes in the Portland Metropolitan Counties, 1991

Prejudice	Clackamas	Multnomah	Washington
Race/Color	3	185	10
Religious	0	10	3
Sexual Orientation	0	50	3
National Origin	0	43	12
Anti-Semitic	0	26	0
Other	0	5	0
Total:	5	319	28

Like the rape statistics, the numbers seem cut and dried. But if you read the descriptions, the crimes are not. The victims are male and female; black and white. They are assaulted with threats and obscenities as well as clubs, rocks and kicks. Bullets pierce windows; cars and homes are vandalized. Gays and foreigners are harassed by neighbors; white supremacist graffiti is spray-painted on buildings. And sometimes, the hate ends in murder, as it did in 1988, when Mulugeta Seraw, an Ethiopian student, was beaten to death by three skinheads.

For the victims and their families, it is little comfort that 488 reported hate crimes in a state of 2.8 million people makes for a very low rate. Sadly, the statistics that are becoming available for 1992 indicate that the number of reported hate crimes continues to rise. In the first six months of 1992, they were up 12.3% compared to the same period in 1991.

Law enforcement officials offer several explanations for the steady increase. There may indeed be an actual increase in hate crimes. Alternatively, victims may be more willing to report these crimes. A third possibility is that the police are more able to identify crimes as bias-motivated. All three may be valid. Whatever the explanation, they are not pretty figures.

Gangs and Skinheads

As we've seen, Portland is an attractive destination for many: young families, retirees, corporations in search of a new home. But the city has also attracted other groups. In the 1980s, Southern California gang members discovered Portland as a potential drug market. Skinheads saw the northwest as a place to recruit new members. And other white supremacist groups see it as a potential Aryan homeland. All have sent representative to Portland, and they have found a few Portlanders who are receptive to their ideas and lifestyles.

Indeed, it is now Portlanders, rather than out-of-state organizers, who are responsible for most of the gang and skinhead violence that does occur in the city. According to an officer from the Portland Police Bureau's Gang Enforcement Team, statistics are hard to come by. In August, 1991, he estimated that the number of gang members in Portland was close to 2,000. Most are Bloods or Crips, but there are also other active gangs here, including Asian gangs, Hispanic gangs and white supremacist groups. Another officer estimated about 120 active skinheads in Portland, who make up three separate skinhead groups. The more secretive Asian gangs are harder to count; they number perhaps 100.

Gang shootings are on the rise too. Police reported 189 gang-related shootings in 1989, and 206 in 1990. Again, these are reported shootings; police speculate that there could be a drive-by shooting – in which someone may or may not be injured – as often as every night. August, 1991 was particularly tragic, with two gang-related murders on the same day: one was a baby killed in the drive-by shooting of a Crips house, the other was the shooting death of a Bloods member.

Another troubling indicator is that gang activity is spreading. North Portland and inner northeast Portland had been the scenes of most gang activity, but gangs appear to now be active in other areas. The summer of 1991 saw skinhead violence in southeast Portland, a drive-by shooting in Beaverton, and reports of gang activity even in suburbs like Tualatin, Gresham, and Oregon City.

On the positive side, authorities were encouraged by the success of two gang summits in November, 1991. But gangs and gang violence remain a serious problem in the city, and what may become a growing problem in the suburbs.

Murder

Gang violence was responsible for 16 of the 33 murders that were committed in Portland in 1990. The 1990 murder figures were low, for the yearly total is usually about 50. The 1991 count was exactly 50. The first six months of 1992 were consistent; 24 murders were committed between January and July.

Why Portland?

Before looking at crime prevention, let's review some of the current theories about why Portland is a high crime city. As you mull over the numbers, consider these explanations:

▸ The state lacks adequate jail space. Criminals are often released early simply because prisons are overcrowded, and they commit new crimes when they are released. For example, business people in Portland's Old Town claim that drug dealers who are arrested there are back on the street and in business again even before the police have finished the necessary paperwork on their arrest.

▸ Information in the *Fourth Annual Oregon Crime and Drug Report*, a May 8, 1991 report by U.S. Attorney General Charles H. Turner and Multnomah County D.A. Michael D. Schrunk, backs up what Old Town merchants claim: "The absence of adequate jail space and a court imposed prisoner cap at the Multnomah County Justice Center resulted in

40% of all arrestees in 1990 being issued a citation and released from custody with directions to appear in court on a specified date."

▸ Drug use and drug deals increase the rate of criminal activity, and Portland serves as a major drug distribution and drug manufacturing point on the west coast. According to a March, 1990 report from the Multnomah County Alcohol and Drug Program, Portland's "Pacific Rim location, access to a major waterway, and its strategic position in the middle of [the] West Coast drug pipeline are all factors that contribute to a volume of drug trafficking activity beyond that usually associated with a medium sized city and county."

An alternative explanation challenges the accuracy of the national data. In that scenario, the crime rate seems disproportionately high only because Portlanders are particularly vigilant in reporting crimes. According to Nancy J. Chapman and Joan Starker, who wrote "Portland: The Most Livable City?" in 1987, Portlanders may be more inclined to report crimes to the police than are residents of some other cities. They quote two surveys done in the 1980s. One indicates that 83% of Portland's residents believe it to be worthwhile to report a crime to the authorities; the other found that only 35% of the country's crime victims actually report the crime.

A survey for *City of Portland Service Efforts and Accomplishments, 1990-91* found that 76% of those burglarized reported the burglary to the police. That beats the national reporting rates of 50% for burglaries and 74% for burglaries with forcible entry. So it is indeed possible that what we really have in Portland is more <u>reported</u> crime.

Fighting Crime . . .

While we can speculate on these questions, perhaps the more critical ones to ask concern efforts to fight crime. How is Portland coping, and can the city point to any major successes? Are we winning or losing this battle?

Some of Portland's solutions are similar to those seen elsewhere; others are more unique. Here's a sampling:

▸ Downtown business owners pay for the uniformed Portland Guides who patrol the downtown. Their presence decreases street crime and helps make residents, shoppers, commuters and visitors feel safer on the city streets.

▸ Portland's Office of Neighborhood Associations runs an active Neighborhood Crime Prevention Program in each area of the city. In a November 13, 1992 speech to the City

---

Crime and Substance Abuse

Many experts see a connection between substance abuse and crime. As these quotes show, Portland is by no means immune:

> Substance abuse contributes to physical and mental illness, crime, violence, and a constellation of other social problems. For example, it is estimated that alcohol alone is related to 65% of all murders, 35% of all rapes, 40% of all assaults, and 30% of all suicides.
>
> Oregon Health 2000 Project Team, *Health Objectives for the Year 2000*, 1988.

> ...almost one-third of the arrestees test positive for two or more drugs. Between 33-46% test positive for cocaine; 15-21% test positive for opiates; 11-18% test positive for amphetamines.
>
> Alcohol and Drug Program of Multnomah County, "Demonstration and Assessment of Need," March, 1990.

And the September 8-11, 1991 *Willamette Week* reported a U.S. Justice Department study in which "70 percent of Portland's male criminal suspects were found to be using some type of drug at the time of their arrest." That put Portland "fifth among the 23 metropolises surveyed, behind Manhattan, San Diego, Philadelphia and Chicago." Portland had the dubious honor of being first for marijuana use, and second for methamphetamine use.

Club, Police Chief Tom Potter said that neighborhood associations were one of the best things about Portland.

▸ At the same meeting, Chief Potter described the Bureau's new Youth and Family Services Division, an effort to address the root causes of crime.

▸ The Portland Public Schools offer a variety of anti-gang programs. And, to encourage kids to stay in school and away from gangs and drugs, private donors have promised a college education to students in several elementary schools in north and northeast Portland. Efforts are underway to expand the program to include more schools.

▸ A $500,000 federal grant, announced in September, 1991, funds programs aimed at helping girls who are involved with gangs.

▸ The Portland Organizing Project, a non-profit coalition of human services groups, is also working to provide alternatives to young people, by persuading the business community to provide jobs and mentoring to youth who are at risk.

. . . and Crime Fighters

Perhaps the most interesting solution is community policing, which we described in the previous chapter. Proponents of this policing strategy point to Iris Court, a Housing Authority of Portland project in northeast Portland that is no longer "ruled" by gangs and drug dealers. They also mention some areas of Washington Park, that are no longer haunts of drug dealers. Critics point to Old Town, where the efforts to get drunks and dealers off the streets have moved more slowly.

The transition to community policing began in 1990 and will be completed by 1995. Under Chief Potter's direction, the Bureau is fully committed to the community policing model. At the City Club meeting, Potter indicated that those who do not practice community policing will not be promoted. He estimated that about one-third of the officers love community policing, about one-third are convinced it works once they try it, and about one-third don't like it and don't want to change. Potter expects that the officers in this last group will soon retire or find jobs elsewhere. Because of budgetary constraints, the Police Bureau was not able to hire all of the officers it needed for the first two years of the transition. We'll be more able to evaluate the success or failure of this strategy when it is at full staff and in full implementation.

Just days before this book went to press, Chief Potter announced his intention to retire in June, 1993. Mayor Katz is a strong supporter of community policing, so it's a good bet that Potter's replacement will carry on with its implementation. Especially because Potter will help Katz select the new chief.

Public Safety 2000

Another transition may be in the policing future, for various jurisdictions are exploring the prospect of consolidation. In the wake of Measure 5, the property tax limitation initiative that passed in 1990, budget cutting and efficiency in government have become the Holy Grail of the 1990s. In 1992, Public Safety 2000, a group of business and community leaders, considered the possibility of merging the Multnomah County Sheriff's Office with the police departments of Portland, Gresham, Fairview, Troutdale, Wood Village, and Maywood Park.

Both Portland Chief Tom Potter and Multnomah Sheriff Bob Skipper favored a merger, although each had a somewhat different plan. However, Public Safety 2000 found that, due to pay equity issues and start-up costs, a merger at this time would not generate any savings. They did note that consolidation might be more appropriate in the future, and they recommended that the police agencies consolidate major non-patrol functions, like training, recruitment, records and a few others.

Other Public Safety 2000 recommendations included the realignment of some patrol responsibilities, privatization of some functions like fleet maintenance and prisoner transportation, and using civilians for some jobs. Civilianization and privatization would free up about 70 sworn officers who could be reassigned to other critical areas. For all the details, get a copy of the 109 page report from the Citizens Crime Commission at the Portland Metropolitan Chamber of Commerce.

Protecting the Populace

Inevitably, police must sometimes meet violence with deadly force. Between 1988 and 1991, 29 suspects were shot at by police. Eleven were killed. In January, 1992, a twelve year old boy was accidentally killed by bullets aimed at the disturbed man who held him hostage. Although the police were exonerated, the child's tragic death prompted a police study.

The resulting June, 1992 report did not change any policies on the use of deadly force, but it did recommend more training in a variety of areas, including confrontation skills, hostage negotiation, and dealing with mentally and emotionally disturbed people. Officers will qualify for weapon use three times per year, and their training will include night and outdoor shooting, and shooting through glass and walls. Here are a few final facts before we leave the police:

► While there have been some charges that Portland police officers have used excessive force, the number of these complaints has decreased in recent years. A consultant who has reviewed police departments nationwide gave Portland high marks when he reviewed the Police Bureau in 1990.

► Portland police are permitted to carry semi-automatic firearms. The Special Emergency Response Team (SERT) includes automatic weapons in their arsenal. Police believe it is necessary because criminals, gangs and drug dealers are becoming increasingly well-armed.

Bad News, Good News, Bad News

In 1991, 6,593 motor vehicles were stolen in the city of Portland. 7,626 were stolen in Multnomah County. But neither the city nor the county assigns more than a handful of investigators to car theft. Which is why the recovery rate seems rather surprising: about 90% of the stolen cars are recovered each year. Unfortunately, that sounds more encouraging than it really is, since few of the cars are returned in their original condition.

A Taxing Subject

When writing about taxes in Portland, one is reminded of the tests we took in school. There's a short answer section, and an essay. We'll start with the short answers.

Ordinary Folks

▸ Just about all Oregonians with income pay state income taxes that are based on their federal taxable income. They pay at a rate of 5% to 9%. Those with taxable incomes over $10,000 pay at the 9% rate.

▸ Property owners pay local taxes on their property according to rules set out in Measure 5, the property tax limitation measure that was passed by the voters in November, 1990. Measure 5 phases in limits on local property tax rates, so that property owners can pay no more than a specific amount for each $1,000 of their property's real market value. The table shows the phased in limits:

1991-92	$25.00 per $1,000 of real market value
1992-93	$22.50 per $1,000 of real market value
1993-94	$20.00 per $1,000 of real market value
1994-95	$17.50 per $1,000 of real market value
1995-96	$15.00 per $1,000 of real market value

▸ The actual tax rate in the City of Portland for 1992-93 is $23.21. It is a little over the $22.50 limit because bonded debt is exempt from Measure 5 limits. Both homeowners and business property owners pay at these rates.

Corporate Types

▸ Corporations that are doing or are authorized to do business in Oregon pay excise tax. The Oregon Corporate Excise Tax rate is 6.6% of net Oregon income.

▸ Employers pay unemployment insurance that is 1.6% to 5.4% of the first $17,000 earned by each employee. In 1992 new employers were assigned an initial rate of 3.2%.

▶ The state collects workers' compensation fees of $ .28 per employee per work day, with employer and employee each paying $ .14. Most employers also pay a 4.5% premium assessment. Self-insured employer groups paid a 5.7% assessment in 1992.

▶ Employers in the Tri-Met transit district – read Portland metro area – pay a Transit District Tax which is .6176% of their payroll. The self-employed pay this tax too.

▶ Those who do business within the city of Portland, and have gross receipts of $10,000 or more from anywhere, must pay for a Portland Business License. They are charged 2.2% of the net income of all transactions within the city, with a $100 minimum. Portland businesses that do business outside the city may apportion their income to reduce the fee.

▶ Multnomah County levies a Business Income Tax that is 1.46% of net income on business within the county. Those businesses that are located in the county, and have gross receipts of $10,000 or more, are liable. Neither Clackamas nor Washington counties levy a business income tax.

▶ Finally, corporate types must pay corporation filing fees to the state. New domestic corporations pay $50; new foreign corporations pay $440. After the first year, the state collects annual renewal fees, which amount to $30 for domestic corporations and $220 for foreign ones.

▶ Partnerships, nonprofit corporations, coops, professional corporations, and business trusts pay slightly lower fees, as do those registering an assumed business name or trademark.

Dollars for Driving

Anyone who operates a motor vehicle pays driver license and/or vehicle fees:

▶ The initial driver license fee is $26.25. Renewals are $16.25. Licenses are valid for four years.

▸ The initial registration for standard cars is $46.50. Renewals are $30.00. Registrations are valid for two years. Those who want custom license plates pay an additional $50 each time they register or renew.

▸ Before each registration and renewal, every vehicle must pass the Department of Environmental Quality vehicle emissions test, which costs $10.00.

Free For All

Oregon boosters always mention those taxes that do not get assessed in the state. They include:

▸ sales tax
▸ real estate transfer tax
▸ business inventory tax
▸ business occupation tax
▸ inheritance tax, unless a federal estate tax return is required

▸ gift tax
▸ value added taxes
▸ worldwide unitary tax

Fees for Almost All

But there are special taxes and fees that are assessed for more particular uses. They include:

▸ new tire fees
▸ car rental tax
▸ hotel/motel tax
▸ railroad and utilities fees
▸ hazardous substance fees
▸ taxes on alcoholic beverages
▸ taxes on amusement devices
▸ taxes on cigarettes and tobacco
▸ fishing and hunting license fees
▸ timber and timber severance taxes

▸ telephone tax
▸ liquor licenses
▸ urban renewal fees

These brief tax facts are current as of November, 1992. We've made every effort to be accurate, and verified all the information with the agencies involved. But for the latest information and the all-important details that effect tax liability, readers should contact the Oregon Department of Revenue, an Oregon accountant or a tax attorney. Or all three.

With the passage of Measure 5 – the property tax reduction initiative that was on the November, 1990 ballot – the state was thrown into somewhat uncharted waters. Given the limits, how would we pay for government services? What should be eliminated? Should the state levy new taxes? Which brings us to the essay part, or the saga of Measure 5.

We're In the *Money*

"Money magazine doesn't like Oregon....its January [1990] issue carried ratings of state and local taxes that pictured Oregon second highest in the country – a veritable 'tax hell'.... This January [1992], the magazine ran the same kind of chart but included property taxes, which were omitted the first time. That didn't help Oregon. It still ranked second....

This makes wonderful fodder for those who like to yell about Oregon's being a high-tax state. But it's grossly misleading.

In both years, the rankings are based on the annual state and local tax bill for a family of four with an income equal to that of the typical Money magazine subscriber. In 1990, that was $65,119. In 1992, it was $73,782.

As Mike Martin, Oregon State University agricultural economist, said: 'Because Oregon's total tax system is progressive (people with higher incomes pay more taxes), if you happen to be in that profile, you may indeed be in tax hell. But in Oregon you're probably earning less. The average family income here is only about half that of the typical subscriber to Money.'"

The (Eugene) *Register-Guard*, as reprinted in the *Daily Journal of Commerce*, March 18, 1992.

The Saga of Measure Five

Despite all the coverage in the media, some Portlanders have lost sight of – or never really understood – the politics and problems that gave rise to the infamous Measure 5. Most newcomers and visitors know even less. With that in mind, and to give a more complete picture of the tax situation in the metropolitan area, this section reviews the scenario that gave rise to Measure 5. We'll look at the initial fallout, and the prognosis at the end of 1992, as the legislature prepares to convene in Salem in January, 1993. We'll look at property tax rates, property assessments, and plans for tax reform. Finally, we'll point out the various options that may be under discussion or in the works by the time you have this book in hand.

Setting the Stage

In November, 1990, Oregon voters chose a new governor, electing Democrat Barbara Roberts as the first woman governor in the state's history. But both columnists and politicians – who rarely agree on much – have ironically commented that the real governor of Oregon is now Measure 5. Why did Measure 5 come to be? What are its implications?

The tax structure in Oregon before the passage of Measure 5 was straightforward. Oregonians paid no sales taxes, generally high property taxes that varied by locale, and income taxes of between 5% and 9%, depending on the amount of their taxable income. Portlanders who became really frustrated with the high property taxes considered a move across the river to Washington, where they'd pay no income tax, lower property taxes, and 7% to 8.1% in state and local sales taxes. Many who actually made the move to Washington continued, of course, to shop in Portland, to save on the sales tax.

But not everyone made the move north, and Oregonians were becoming increasingly troubled by the property tax system that was in force in the state. Property taxes helped pay for local government services and the community colleges, but the largest proportion of these taxes paid for the local public schools. Some people felt that property taxes were simply too high. Others were dissatisfied with the unequal level of funding that the property tax system provided for the schools. In fact, between 1968 and 1989 Oregonians had actually considered and then rejected a total of 19 ballot measures which attempted to lower property taxes and/or revamp public school funding.

In the late 1980s and in 1990, property taxes were climbing quickly in many sections of the state. Despite problems in the timber industry, many parts of Oregon had healthy, growing economies, and property assessments in those areas were steadily rising. Measure 5 was placed on the ballot as an initiative. Facing high tax bills and increasing frustration with the mechanics and inequalities of school funding, Oregonians passed Measure 5. The vote, 574,833 (Yes) to 522,022 (No), was close, but with 52% of the voters in favor, Measure 5 became the law.

The Provisions of Measure 5

Measure 5 limits the total taxes and government charges that can be paid on a property. More specifically:

▸ Measure 5 divides property taxes into a school portion and a government services portion.
▸ Beginning with the 1991/92 fiscal year, the government services portion is limited to $10.00 for each $1,000 of a property's real market value.
▸ The school portion is also based on a property's real market value, with limits phased in over a five year period, as follows:

1991-92	$15.00 per $1,000 of real market value
1992-93	$12.50 per $1,000 of real market value
1993-94	$10.00 per $1,000 of real market value
1994-95	$7.50 per $1,000 of real market value
1995-96	$5.00 per $1,000 of real market value

▸ Real market value is defined as the minimum amount, in cash, that a seller could reasonably expect to receive from a buyer, during the period for which a property is being taxed.
▸ During the phase-in period, the state must use General Funds from the state budget to replace any school revenues that may be lost because of Measure 5's limits.

▸ The state need not replace lost government revenues.
▸ At the end of the phase-in period and thereafter, total property taxes cannot exceed $15 per $1,000, even if voters in a taxing district favor such increases.
▸ After the phase-in, the state need not replace lost school revenues.
▸ If taxes or charges on a property exceed these limits, the excess amounts are reduced proportionately to bring all property taxes down to the Measure 5 limits.

The Implications

Depending upon one's perspective, Measure 5 was either right on target, or it was badly flawed. While it stipulated that the state must replace the revenues that the school districts lost because of the new tax limits, it did not provide for any new state revenues with which to replace the lost dollars. And the local governments – cities, counties, and service districts – would not receive any replacement money for the funds they might loose. Government employees at all levels, from the smallest city to the state itself, would need to scrutinize spending and consider how else to fund the services they had to deliver.

What the Proponents Said. . .

Proponents of the measure assured voters that the state government need only to "cut the fat" and control spending increases. Given Oregon's projected population growth and anticipated growth in the state's General Fund, there would be ample funds to replace the lost school revenues. They noted that the phased-in limits and replacement school funding would allow the state adequate time to responsibly and permanently address the school finance issue. The $10 government portion limit would not even affect the majority of local taxing districts, since their tax rates were already under the $10 per $1,000 limit. As for cities that might feel Measure 5's cuts – like Portland – a lesson in budgeting might prove beneficial.

Others who supported Measure 5 did not necessarily agree with the proponents' arguments. Rather, they reluctantly voted for Measure 5 as a way to force the legislature to finally deal with the problems and inequities of the troubled school financing system.

What the Opponents Said. . .

Opponents of the measure painted a very different picture. They saw few places to "cut the fat" and they feared that using the state's General Fund to replace lost school revenues would decimate the state budget. Precious little would be left to fund other programs, like higher education, human resources, and corrections. School districts had been receiving an average of 22% of their money from the state in the form of Basic School Support grants. Measure 5 did not protect that money. If it was used to replace lost property taxes – or to fund anything else in the state budget – schools could receive far less dollars in the end.

In addition, the measure did not stipulate that lost property tax revenues must be replaced dollar for dollar. In apportioning the replacement money, the legislature would to try to equalize school spending throughout the state. The wealthier school districts, like Portland, Beaverton and Lake Oswego, would absorb big cuts, and they would not be allowed to even try to raise additional money locally.

As for the government services portion, there was grave concern among elected officials and local government employees. While some cities would not feel the impact because their taxes were below the $10 per $1,000 limit, other cities would face substantial cuts in revenues, with no provision for replacement. They could be in a double bind: first, they would collect less tax money because of the new limits; and second, they would receive less support from the financially troubled state.

So Who's Right?

In sorting out all the rhetoric, it is hard to know who to believe. Is there lots of "fat" in state spending? Will it be necessary to cut "essential" services? Perhaps part of the answer lies in the definitions. To some voters, very few services are truly essential. Police and fire protection and the protection offered by health department regulations fit the definition of essential services. To others, the availability of a good community college or a top-notch university is critical. Some believe that parks must be funded and maintained at a high level. Others think the state shouldn't be funding human welfare programs anyway so cuts in those services are not problematic.

Looking at the Numbers

In round numbers, Measure 5 takes a large bite out of the state's overall budget. (For the uninitiated, the legislature is in session every other year, so the state budget covers two year periods.) When it finally passed, the 1991-93 budget included $625 million for the state's public schools, since school districts would loose that much because of the property tax reductions. The 1993/95 budget will need to include $1.2 billion for the public schools, and the 1995-97 budget a whopping $2.9 billion.

To look at those numbers in perspective, the entire 1991/93 state budget is $5.6 billion. A quick calculation reveals the fact that the replacement money necessary for 1995-97 is more than half of the 1991-93 state budget. While the 1991 legislature was able to find the needed $625 million without completely devastating any programs, the replacement money needed for 1993-95 and 1995-97 is so high that – without some form of new taxes – wholesale program cuts may be unavoidable.

Wielding the Budget Knife

Among the cuts in the first phase were:

- ► Suspending or eliminating approximately 100 programs and 700 jobs at state colleges and universities
- ► Eliminating dental programs serving poor adults
- ► Eliminating payments to adults who can't afford health insurance, but do not qualify for Medicaid
- ► Reductions in the supervision of parolees
- ► Reductions in funding for a wide range of local programs, from the Metropolitan Arts Commission and Portland Future Focus to the Washington Park Zoo and local summer schools
- ► Reductions in hours, staff, and programs at the Multnomah County Library

Again, whether such cuts are "essential" services or "fat" is a determination each of us must make for him or herself. On the opposite side, individual state agencies sought ways to increase revenue. For example, as a consequence of the higher education cuts, tuition rose at state colleges and universities.

Business as Usual?

Some would say yes, and they would point to Portland. For the most part, local governments in the Portland area were able to weather the first round of property tax reductions, thanks to rising property values. For while Measure 5 limits the government portion of property taxes to $10 per $1,000 of assessed value, higher assessments translate into more tax dollars. And that is exactly what happened in Portland. Reflecting steadily rising property values, assessments in many areas went up significantly, and with them, the bottom line on the tax bill.

It is unclear how long Portland will be able to squeak by. Much will depend on property values. Another problem is the fate of Portland's urban renewal projects. Although government officials initially believed that increment tax funding – the mechanism that funds urban renewal – was exempt from Measure 5 limits, the Oregon Supreme Court ruled that it is not exempt. That ruling may force the city to pay $9 million in interest from its general funds, making that money unavailable for other needs. It may also delay or doom a variety of urban renewal projects. Both possibilities will have a negative impact on the quality of life in the city.

The Replacement Revenue Game

As the 1991 legislative session came to a close, a sense of relief that we made it through the first round was mixed with a sense of foreboding. Virtually all government leaders believed that some replacement revenue was essential in the future. But most legislators and local officials thought that Oregonians were simply not ready to accept any new taxes. The best strategy would be to show that the government could tighten its collective belt, and act in a fiscally responsible fashion.

After initially promising to push for a sales tax, Governor Barbara Roberts decided on a different strategy. She held a series of "conversations with Oregonians" on the state's overall tax structure. Thousands of Oregonians were asked to describe the services that were necessary and the appropriate ways to fund those services. But the tax package that she crafted after the conversations never made it to the ballot, for the legislature refused to pass it during the July, 1992 special session that was called for that purpose.

Another attempt failed in November, 1992, when voters trounced Measure 7, a plan for split-roll taxes. Proponents of split-roll taxes – which set lower tax rates for owner-occupied property – were eager to redress what they saw as a problem with Measure 5. For the unexpected winner in the Measure 5 fray was Oregon business. According to an article by Jeff Mapes in the March 17, 1991 *Oregonian*, 58% of Measure 5's tax savings were on business property. And less than half of the property taxes that are paid in Oregon are paid by individual homeowners. But Oregonians not only nixed Measure 7's split-roll plan, they rejected every measure on the 1992 ballot that might eventually raise even the possibility of new taxes.

The Replacement Revenue Game, Part 2

Governor Roberts prepared three state budgets for 1993/95. As required by law, the first was balanced, reflecting Measure 5's limits. It included about $966 million in cuts. About $520 million were cuts to K-12 education, and about $275 million was sliced from human services programs. Public safety agencies were hit too, but they were slated to get just $10 million less than they'd need to maintain current services. Community college programs would be cut by 10%. Higher education would face a 13% cut in each year of the two year budget cycle. Some programs, like the College of Veterinary Medicine, would be eliminated altogether. Tuition would rise by about 7% both years.

The other budgets suggested ways to raise revenues to offset the first budget's cuts. The second budget proposed beer, wine and cigarette tax increases. It also proposed a new health provider gross receipts tax of 1%. Revenues would be used to fund drug and alcohol treatment and health programs. Finally, the third plan called for major tax reform to restore $430 million to education programs. It was not outlined in detail, but it could include a sales tax, changes in both the personal income tax and property assessment system, and a split-roll property tax.

Early speculation was that the legislature would pass a version of the Governor's first budget. But few predicted success in raising taxes. For that prospect remained slim. The results of a poll commissioned by Associated Oregon Industries were announced in mid-November, 1992, just as Roberts was putting the finishing touches on her budgets. 53% of those polled planned to vote down any tax increase plan that might be on the ballot in the next year. Just 30% favored a tax increase, and 18% were unsure. Ironically, 58% believed that replacement money was necessary. And 52% would vote against Measure 5 if it were on the ballot again.

The Bottom Line in Portland

Before we leave Measure 5, let's look at its impact on taxes in Portland. The following chart shows the tax rates in Portland for 1990-91, 1991-92, and 1992-93. It is included as a representative sample only, for tax rates do vary by neighborhood. For example, property owners in one Portland neighborhood may pay additional taxes to their local water district; others may be assessed because they live within a special fire district. And as we saw in *A Bird's Eye View*, some Portland taxpayers live in Washington or Clackamas County. But all the tax bills show the impact of Measure 5. Here's an example:

Portland Tax Rates, Before and After Measure 5

City of Portland (001):	1990-91:	1991-92:	1992-93:
Portland School District #1	$ 16.7656	$ 13.1505	$ 10.9530
Education Service District	1.4715	1.1580	.9606
Portland Community College	.9136	.6915	.6872
Port of Portland	.3193	.2391	.1863
Metro Service District	.2710	.2115	.2064
Multnomah County	4.9655	3.6052	3.6852
City of Portland	8.7983	6.4158	6.3117
Urban Renewal	------	.9118	------
Tri-Met	------	------	.2221
Total	$33.5048	$26.3834	$23.2125

Which means that, for the 1992-93 year, a property owner would pay just over $23.21 for each $1,000 of their property's real market value. The taxes on a home assessed at $100,000 would be $2321.25. The tax rate is slightly over the $22.50 Measure 5 limit because bonded debt is exempt from Measure 5. But it is substantially less than the pre-Measure 5 rate of $33.50 per $1,000.

What's It Worth?

The last factor we need to mention is the whole issue of assessments. For while the tax rate – the amount per $1,000 – was dropping, the assessed value of most metro area properties was rising. Many people saw a conspiracy. They believed that, to circumvent Measure 5, the government was just raising assessments. Since we pay taxes based on the value of a property, high values would bring in more taxes.

If you look at the provisions of Measure 5, you'll see that properties must be assessed at their real market value. Real market value is defined as the minimum amount that a seller could reasonably expect to receive from a buyer. The Portland housing market was hot in the late 1980s and early 1990s. And because Measure 5 changed the appraisal date, the first post-Measure 5 tax bills reflected an 18 month increase (or decrease) in a property's value. The net result was that many property owners saw their assessed values skyrocket, and with the higher value came higher taxes. Specifically:

▸ On the tax bills mailed in October, 1991 – the first post-Measure 5 bill – property values in Multnomah County increased by an average of about 20%. Some residential properties went up by as much as 40% or more.

▸ Similar increases were seen in the suburbs. In the first year of Measure 5, the average home in Clackamas County rose 19% in value. And in Washington County, home values went up an average of 29%.

▸ In the second year, most Multnomah County property values went up again. But reflecting only 12 months of change and a more moderate housing market, most of the increases were between 5% and 15%. But the tax rates were now down to $22.50 per $1,000, instead of $25.00.

▸ When all the calculating was done, Multnomah County officials indicated that – despite the rising values – 68% of the county's taxpayers paid less taxes in 1992-93 than they had in 1991-92, courtesy of Measure 5.

Officials saw another dramatic increase in the first year of Measure 5. A record number of property owners – almost 17,000 in Multnomah, Washington and Clackamas Counties – appealed their 1991-92 assessments. About 60% won an adjustment. Officials anticipated a smaller number of appeals in 1992-93, because property value increases were more moderate, and most taxpayers saw their tax bills go down.

Back To The Tax Future

But it's only a guessing game when the conversation turns to 1993-94 and beyond. The only sure thing is that the tax saga will undoubtedly continue. Governor Roberts hoped that the graphic differences between her three budgets would convince Oregonians that they must find a way to replace at least some of Measure 5's losses. But in the face of the voters' continuing tax revolt, and the rather conservative composition of the 1993 state legislature, we may again face budget cuts and cries of "No new taxes!"

Which brings us back to the closing remarks of the previous section: that Measure 5 has thrown the state into somewhat uncharted waters. As we write, the state is still floundering around. If we've found our way by the time you read this, we hope this section helps put it all in context.

In the post-Measure 5 world, good planning is a necessity. For the Portland metro area, an anticipated influx of 500,000 people over the next twenty years makes the scenario even more complicated. Fortunately, Portland has a great track record in the area of planning. We look next at a variety of growth and planning issues.

Planning Par Excellence

We are entitled, in Portland, to use the terms "growth" and "planning" in the same sentence. For we are good at planning here. There are some exceptions, especially in a few of the mushrooming suburban communities. But for the most part, planners throughout the region have been successful in the past in identifying problems and creating solutions. Indeed, planners around the world look to Portland for an example of how to do it right. Donald Canty, writing for the July, 1986 issue of *Architecture* explains:

> State of the art thinking about urban planning and design goes something like this: First, the city needs a plan, preferably one taken to the third dimension. The plan needs citizen and political support and a mechanism for implementation. Optimally, this mechanism should be an agency with broad powers of land acquisition and concerns that go beyond development to historic preservation, social problems – and design. Finally, maximum use should be made of the shaping powers of transportation.
>
> This thinking has found perhaps its purest application over the past decade in Portland, Ore. – and it has worked.

Jessica Matthews, in a column in the January 22, 1991 *Oregonian*, explains some of the interrelated issues:

> Left to themselves, developers put new subdivisions where land is cheap, i.e. far from jobs, shopping and where people already are. Then, transportation agencies must build roads to serve them. Spread out, low-density development not only depends on highways, it can only be served by them. It not only starts the roads-congestion-more roads treadmill, it makes future alternatives more difficult.
>
> There is at least one American city that has untangled this knot. When Portland, Ore., designed its new light-rail transit system, it was as part of an explicit strategy to shape metropolitan growth. Oregon had a land-use planning law that made that possible. The investment has been a stunning success.

These quotes highlight some of the major issues, especially the interrelationship between land use and transportation. The issues are significant, for most of the region's new residents will settle in the suburbs – and they'll need to get around once they are there. The sections that follow consider some of the issues, problems and solutions that are currently being debated.

The Urban Growth Boundary

Most Portlanders can't point to the urban growth boundary. But this 200 mile long invisible line that encircles the Portland metro area is a significant boundary, and it is partly responsible for the quality of life in Portland. Here's why.

If developers were free to build homes wherever they chose, most would build on land that was near already established areas, that was flat, and that had good drainage. But those areas do not always have what is called "infrastructure" – sewers; power, water and telephone lines; schools; fire stations; roads; and the like. And it is costly to build infrastructure. It is also much easier to provide public transportation in more compact areas, that have a greater population density. By identifying areas that can be developed, and encouraging "infill" in areas that are already developed, more efficient use can be made of existing infrastructure and public transportation.

By law, all Oregon cities with populations above 2,500 must establish an urban growth boundary – a UGB. UGBs are designed to separate the "city" from the "country." They indicate where development can take place, and where it cannot. The result of unchecked development is urban sprawl, and the depletion of farm land, forests and other natural areas. The UGB is Oregon's weapon against unchecked development.

The Line Around Portland

The map on pages 76-77 shows the Urban Growth Boundary for the Portland metropolitan area. It was adopted in 1980, and it was designed to set aside enough land for 20 years of growth. Planners see the UGB as a line that works. They point to areas of still undeveloped land, and calculate that, given the slump in development during the recession of the early 1980s, the UGB will easily accommodate the area's burgeoning population through 2010. While exceptions have been made, development has for the most part remained within the UGB. Area planners can tell many success stories. Unlike so many other cities, mass transit works well and economically, and the city of Portland has not fallen victim to a mass exodus to the suburbs.

But there are also critics who see problems with the UGB. They agree that there is much undeveloped land within the line. But its location is not necessarily to the liking of potential buyers. If, for example, people want houses in suburbs to the west, available land in eastern Gresham will not necessarily suit the bill. Critics also point to the low-density housing – sometimes called "farmlets" – that is going up just outside the UGB. They argue that it would be better to bring these areas into the UGB now, before the land is fully developed with expensive, low-density housing. And some are betting that the line will move – including land speculators who are buying up land just over the UGB.

By law, Metro is responsible for regional planning. While the UGB has worked to date, the region has only experienced a moderate level of growth compared to the growth it will see in the next 20 years. With that and the mounting pressure on the UGB in mind, Metro is mobilizing to develop policies and update growth management plans. The Metro Council's adoption of the Regional Urban Growth Goals and Objectives in the fall of 1991 was intended to set the tone for planning in the 1990s.

The Regional Urban Growth Goals and Objectives

The Regional Urban Growth Goals and Objectives – or RUGGOs – are not an urban plan. They do not propose a new highway on the west side or a new park in the southeast. Rather, as Metro explains, they are intended to "provide a policy and process framework for guiding Metro's regional planning program (including management of the region's urban growth boundary)." Among the themes are:

- ▸ Developing consensus for growth management, including citizen participation and coordination between cities, counties and special districts.

▶ Periodic review of the urban growth boundary, both to protect agricultural and forest land outside the line from urbanization, and to identify adjacent land that is suited to development if needed.

▶ Preserving the quality of the environment, including our air and water, as well as parks, wildlife habitats, and other natural areas.

▶ Coordinating the placement and development of jobs, housing and public services like mass transit, such that they are nearby and conveniently located.

The basic themes – regulating land use to limit urban sprawl, accessible public transportation, and regional cooperation – remain prominent. On Metro's agenda for 1993 and 1994 is a project called Region 2040. Including fast-growing Clark County in the equation, Region 2040 asks the basic question: "How can our four-county metropolitan region best accommodate 700,000 more people and continue to offer a high quality of life in the year 2040?"

With the support and cooperation of the Oregon Department of Transportation, Tri-Met, Clackamas, Multnomah and Washington Counties, and the City of Portland, Project 2040 aims to inform and involve citizens in the debate on the issues and alternatives. In 1994, Metro will move into the implementation phase, which could include amendments to the urban growth boundary and changes to the existing Regional Transportation Plan.

Planning Realities

The task is not easy, and the players will come up against the realities of regional cooperation The Oregon part of the Portland metro area includes 3 counties, 24 cities and over 130 special and school districts. While everyone supports regional cooperation in theory, turf battles can erupt when the talk gets to the nitty-gritty. For example, shortly after the passage of Measure 5, Portland and Multnomah County officials met in an effort to consolidate services and eliminate duplication. Their effort fizzled when it was announced that they could come up with only $9,700 in savings for the first year, and $173,000 for the second.

Some critics argue that local control should not be sacrificed to regional planning, and they resist such comprehensive efforts. And while Portlanders may support the general idea of infill housing and higher density development, neighbors often mobilize to fight proposals for higher density housing or the development of available land in their neighborhood. Which brings us from regional planning to planning in the city of Portland. We look first at Portland's Comprehensive Plan.

Portland's Comprehensive Plan

Although it was adopted in 1980, the Comprehensive Plan still merits serious attention. It was required by state law, and, as a city ordinance, it has the force of law. The Comprehensive Plan was a joint effort involving citizens, neighborhood associations, city administrators and staff from the city's Bureau of Planning. It has been amended many times since 1980, and it continues to be the basis for all city planning.

The Comprehensive Plan has several components. Its goals are based on and consistent with state-wide goals, which were developed by the State Land Conservation and Development Commission. They address metropolitan coordination, urban development, neighborhoods, housing, economic development, transportation, energy, environment, citizen involvement and the plan's implementation and review process. The plan addresses public facilities and services, since "primary facilities, such as water and sewer service, must be planned and programmed to support the level of land use activities proposed by the Plan." A Plan Map "shows the type, location and density of land development and redevelopment permitted in the future." Although not part of the Plan itself, the Zoning Code "is the major implementation tool of the Comprehensive Plan Map."

Let's use Goal 5, Economic Development, as an example of how the components work together. Goal 5 calls for increasing "the quantity and quality of job opportunities through the creation of an environment which promotes and supports business and industry and attracts new investment." The supporting objectives get more specific. For example, one of the objectives for Goal 5 calls for "an adequate supply of commercially zoned land." After considering topography, current use, neighborhood dynamics, transportation issues, and the like, the

Plan Map shows which sections will be developed for commercial use. Primary facilities, like sewers and water lines, will be upgraded if necessary to support that use, and zoning ordinances must be adopted to provide definitions and standards for the use stipulated.

Planning Past and Future

While the Comprehensive Plan continues, successfully, to direct land use in Portland, it is not the plan that gets the most press. Perhaps that's because there are usually a number of plans vying for our attention. Portland's 1991 official entry for a U.S. Conference of Mayors City Livability Award explains some of the distinctions:

> ...The Downtown Plan of 1972 was, in reality, an economic development and architectural design plan for the downtown; the Central City Plan of 1987 extended the vision to the inner east side and was primarily a land use plan. Both efforts focused on bricks and mortar. The Civic Index of 1989 recommended some changes in the way institutions in the community conduct business, and primarily dealt with the way citizens relate to government and organizations.
>
> Building on these past efforts, Portland Future Focus is a quality of life plan. The community is beginning to focus on children, on jobs, on housing and on building a strong sense of community. The new partnerships being formed will make a difference for Portland and its people.

We can't possibly do them justice in just a few paragraphs, but here are some brief notes to provide a little context.

The Downtown Plan of 1972

Much of Portland's recent success is actually successful implementation of the Downtown Plan. As Carl Abbott explains in *Portland: Planning, Politics, and Growth in a Twentieth Century City*, "There was nothing new about the ugliness of the riverfront, the shortage of parking, the decline of bus service, or the shortage of municipal office space, but all four problems reached crises or decision points in 1968 or 1969. The planning process that produced the downtown guidelines emerged with the realization that choices on one issue could as easily hurt as help on the other problems."

The Downtown Plan successfully reclaimed the city back from the cars. The Transit Mall and MAX were components, as were strengthening the downtown as a retail, office, housing, government, and entertainment center. The plan called for and promoted historic preservation. The creation of open spaces, like Waterfront Park and Pioneer Square, became a priority. The award-winning plan was clearly a success.

The Central City Plan of 1988

The Central City Plan, which was adopted in 1988, details the next steps. According to the Portland Development Commission, it "focuses on the Willamette River as a link, rather than a barrier, unifying the east and west sides of the central city." If the planners succeed, the downtown of the 1990s will truly span the river, with two thriving areas forming one vibrant city center.

They appear to have gotten a good start. Redevelopment of Lloyd Center, the new Convention Center, and the relocation of the Oregon Museum of Science and Industry are recent changes on the east side. Plans are in the works for a new Trail Blazers Arena and entertainment complex, and a major hotel. The East Bank Esplanade, which will run along the river, will connect OMSI, the Blazers complex, and the Convention Center. Trendy stores and restaurants are moving to NE Broadway and SE Hawthorne streets. And there is even talk of water taxis to ferry commuters, shoppers and tourists back and forth across the river.

The Civic Index Project of 1989-90

On the premise that "the processes that lead to decision-making are as critical to a community as its physical and economic assets," citizen participants in the Civic Index Project looked at ten components of Portland's civic infrastructure. By civic infrastructure, they meant factors like citizen participation, civic education, volunteerism and philanthropy, community leadership, intercommunity cooperation, and the like. Their final report included recommendations on regional perspectives for planning, citizen participation, and communication.

Portland Future Focus

Bridging to the New Century: Portland Future Focus Strategic Plan was an effort to "plan for Portland's future in the face of the community's changing role in the state and region." Issued in August, 1991, it culminated a community-based strategic planning process that began in April, 1990. Its intention was to portray a vision for Portland's future, and a plan for realizing that vision.

The Portland Future Focus Policy Committee identified 25 goals, that encompass everything from a call for preserving and expanding natural areas to fostering small businesses. Noting that "many of the issues raised by rapid regional growth cross boundaries of long-established governments and service districts," the final report recommends restructuring government in the metro area, because "the Portland region needs a government that is equipped to deal with urban needs on a region-wide basis."

The report identified six critical goals as starting points. The committee's intention was not to emphasize these above the others. Rather, the six were selected because the committee felt that they were not being adequately addressed elsewhere. They are quoted below, from the city's 1991 entry to the U.S. Conference of Mayors City Livability Awards competition:

- ▸ Reduce crime, eliminate violence, and better support victims, beginning in high crime areas of the city.
- ▸ Embrace diversity and eliminate bigotry.
- ▸ Capitalize on Portland's location on the Pacific Rim and to increase trade. To seek family-wage jobs for all residents and to provide training for those who need it.
- ▸ Graduate all children from high school with the ability to read, write, compute, and reason and with the skills enabling them to succeed in the workforce or in post-secondary education.

▸ Manage regional growth to reduce the cost of public services, to slow environmental degradation, and to enhance the quality of life.

▸ Build stronger, innovative, more responsive elected and citizen leadership.

Portland Future Focus won the competition for the City Livability Award. And the final report includes detailed, concrete action plans for implementing the six goals, complete with timetables and assigned responsibilities. But the actual implementation will be the real test.

The APP Strategic Plan

The Association for Portland Progress, which promotes the growth and development of the city center, has also been considering the future. Their November, 1990 Strategic Plan sets goals and objectives for the next five years. While the APP agenda includes some of the goals we've seen in other plans, APP's focus is clearly on downtown business and retail interests. We quote their top priorities from the APP *Strategic Plan Executive Summary*:

▸ Maintain easy access to and within downtown through a balanced system of transportation and parking management.

▸ Reinforce downtown's position as the focus of Portland's quality of life.

▸ Reinforce downtown's retail growth.

The Task Force on Local Government Services

Though not a plan in the same sense as the ones above, this is an appropriate place to mention the task force appointed by Governor Roberts in June, 1992. With former Governor Neil Goldschmidt as the chair, Roberts asked the task force to look at government services in the Portland metro area, and to propose a variety of ways to increase efficiency and save money. They made many recommendations, including the following ones:

- ► Merge all the city and county police departments in Multnomah County.
- ► Establish uniform business income taxes for all jurisdictions.
- ► Create a state corporation for the delivery of tri-county mental health services.
- ► Coordinate government purchasing through a regional purchasing coop.

They also made recommendations in areas as diverse as educational service districts, road maintenance, unincorporated areas, cable regulation, and election laws. Roberts promised to give careful consideration to every proposal. There's a good chance that Vera Katz will find them on her agenda too.

The Livable City Project

The Livable City Project is an outgrowth of the various plans we've discussed. In an effort "to make sure we... accommodate growth while strengthening, not destroying, our city's neighborhoods," the Portland Planning Bureau is talking with citizens at all levels – from developers to neighborhood residents – about planning for infill housing, transit stations, vacant land, and main streets. Other city planning efforts that involve citizens are the Regional Rail Program and Reclaiming Our Streets, a traffic safety program. Mention of the Portland Planning Bureau brings us to the last piece of the planning picture: a roster of the planning agencies and a brief explanation of their functions and programs.

A Reprise for Metro

We discussed the Metropolitan Service District in *A Bird's Eye View*, but a reprise focusing on Metro's role in regional planning is useful here. In November, 1992, voters passed Measure 26-3. In doing so, they approved a variety of changes in Metro's governance, structure and responsibilities.

Among them is that regional planning is to be Metro's primary function. Metro must develop a Regional Framework Plan that addresses transportation and mass transit, the urban growth boundary, housing densities, urban design, parks, water, and interstate coordination. Within legal limits, city and county comprehensive plans and land use decisions must be consistent with the Metro plan. Other Metro functions include these regional concerns:

- ▸ the operation of Washington Park Zoo, the Oregon Convention Center, and other spectator, sports and entertainment facilities
- ▸ solid waste management (better known as recycling and garbage disposal)
- ▸ the acquisition, development and maintenance of greenspaces
- ▸ natural disaster planning
- ▸ the development of regional data such as population statistics, maps, and economic projections

In the future, regional strategies will be the solution in more and more areas. Metro will continue to be one of the most critical players.

The Portland Development Commission

Donald Canty's description of ideal urban planning, which is quoted more fully at the beginning, describes "an agency with broad powers of land acquisition and concerns that go beyond development to historic preservation, social problems – and design." As the article goes on to explain, the Portland Development Commission is just such an agency.

The Portland Development Commission, or the PDC, is a city agency that was formed in 1958. PDC goals include revitalizing the center city, improving housing city-wide, and generally advancing Portland's economic development and employment. Within the framework of the Comprehensive Plan, the Downtown Plan of 1972 and the Central City Plan of 1988, the PDC courts investors, assists corporations considering Portland as a location for their business, promotes development of specific areas and projects, and spearheads redevelopment.

The PDC has been at least partly responsible for many of the newer additions to the Portland skyline. Projects for the '90s include continued redevelopment on the east side near the Convention Center; redevelopment of the Union Station area in northwest Portland; and development adjacent to the airport, along the Columbia's south shore.

Urban Renewal Blues at the PDC

In the chapter on Measure 5, we discussed the PDC's post-Measure 5 problems with urban renewal funding. The PDC's continued success in the '90s – and the survival of the projects we mentioned above – may depend on the resolution of the urban renewal funding dilemma. Here's why.

According to a PDC brochure on urban renewal, property tax money "is used to unlock the door to much larger amounts of private investment and federal funds." Because of the PDC's urban renewal projects, "private businesses have invested more than $2 billion in downtown – about 20 times the sum City taxpayers have committed to downtown renewal." Such investment creates jobs and "adds value to the tax rolls that otherwise wouldn't be there."

Here's one final quote from the PDC brochure. It gives a nice summary of the PDC position on urban renewal, and describes the PDC's first accomplishment:

> In the three decades since PDC was established, City Council has created 16 urban renewal areas in Portland, starting with the South Auditorium Project, where on 110 acres of decayed downtown property emerged a dazzling array of new offices, shops, high-quality housing and world-class fountains and public plazas. This was the development that launched Portland's transformation. Yet only three percent of the funding came from public resources; the rest was private investment. The result: Some $394 million in new assessed property value has been added to the tax rolls.

Let's hope that Vera Katz has urban renewal on her agenda too.

Association for Portland Progress

The Association for Portland Progress is a non-profit organization of 77 downtown business leaders, who, in the words of their 1991 annual report, "are either chairman, president or the principal Oregon officer for their respective companies." This high-powered group focuses its energies on Portland's central business district, by establishing programs to foster the safety, continued growth, development, and vibrancy of the city center.

APP task forces on parking, transportation, city revenue, housing, human services, business development and retailing work to achieve the organization's goals. The APP has been responsible for several successful and innovative programs, including the creation of an Economic Improvement District.

The EID was passed by downtown property owners in 1988, as a way to pay for special programs to keep the downtown clean, safe and vibrant. By agreeing to tax themselves, property owners in the district were able to pay for the Sidewalk Cleaning Program, the Portland Guides and Patrol Officers, and a variety of marketing efforts. Most visible to residents and visitors are the friendly, green-jacketed Guides who patrol the streets. They offer information and assistance to shoppers, tourists and downtown employees, and they maintain a presence on the street that discourages criminal activity.

The EID was very successful, but the passage of Measure 5 threatened the funding. The APP solution was voluntary participation. An indicator of the district's success is that owners of 80% of the properties downtown agreed to the new voluntary program.

Not everyone supports the APP. The September 5-11, 1991 *Willamette Week* ran an article on "Coups We Could Use," and named the APP as a recommended target. WW's rationale: "Power-mad business booster group is trying to take over downtown and infuse it with all the zest and vitality of Mr. Rogers' neighborhood...." WW was also critical of the APP's role "in awarding contracts to operate [the] city's parking lots."

Portland Bureau of Planning

The city's Planning Bureau is both a player and a facilitator in the planning arena. For example, it was staff from the Planning Bureau who worked with the business community and a Citizens' Advisory Committee to develop the 1972 Downtown Plan. The 1980 Comprehensive Plan was prepared, with considerable citizen input, by the Bureau. And in its original conception, city planners were to be available to help citizens develop what would become the 1988 Central City Plan. In the end, the 1988 plan was actually completed by the Planning Bureau. The change came in part because Margaret Strachan, who conceived the project in 1984 while serving as a city commissioner, was not re-elected.

Our description of the Comprehensive Plan is also indicative of the Bureau's responsibilities. City planners are involved in developing the broad vision, such as vibrant commercial centers, as well as the implementation tools, like the zoning ordinances that allow such commercial development. Portland Future Focus is still another example. That plan recognizes that higher density housing and urban infill is necessary to maintain the urban growth boundary in the face of regional growth. It calls on the Planning Bureau to develop infill strategies for this redevelopment, without destroying the character of neighborhoods in the process.

The Institute of Portland Metropolitan Studies

This new Portland State University Institute is part of the School of Urban and Public Affairs. According to the Fall, 1992 *SUPA Report,*

> The Institute is part of the Portland Agenda, designed to assist with the implementation of PSU's urban university concept. The mission for the Institute is to bring university resources to bear on critical issues facing the five-county metropolitan area. Rather than building its own central staff, the Institute is envisioned as a new "front door" for PSU, facilitating better direct relationships between multi-disciplinary research teams drawn from throughout the university and the metropolitan community. The Institute is envisioned as a hot-house for ideas, expanding both our knowledge of metropolitan dynamics as well as inspiring the free exchange of ideas in an objective, unbiased atmosphere.
>
> ...the Institute and its Board can also provide important civic leadership for building better working relationships among local governments, civic and business organizations across the region. In this way, the Institute

will be able to make a fundamental contribution to the capacity of the metropolitan area to respond to existing and emerging challenges to quality of life.

Under the very able direction of Dr. Ethan Seltzer, who served most recently as the Land Use Supervisor for Metro, the Institute is developing workplans, programs, projects and research proposals to forward its agenda. We'll quote just one example of a possible research theme, to give you a better idea of how the Institute can convert their mission into specific projects. It is from their Draft Board Workplan of October 12, 1992:

> Many of the recent discussions regarding government structure in the metropolitan area have focused on unit costs for various services....Rather than starting with a discussion of structure and unit cost, it may be more fruitful to begin with an examination of the kind of relationship that citizens and households want to have with government and service delivery systems. In particular, the following kinds of questions might arise: What are the determinants of community quality of life? What kind of relationship do citizens want to have with government and public services? Who do they want to hold accountable, for what purposes, and when? Then...how should government be structured in response? Finally, what is or should be the relationship between quality of life and government structure?

The Institute could not have come upon the Portland scene at a better time. As we've seen, many of the same issues are raised over and over again, in the various planning groups, the reports they write, and the recommendations they offer. While it is useful to involve many citizens and organizations, a little more coordination and less duplication of effort might make for smoother, more efficient planning and implementation.

The challenges are many, but people throughout the entire metro area are mobilizing to plan our future. Let's hope all the effort brings us the bright future we seek.

A Plan For Everyone

The *Portland Future Focus Strategic Plan* is not the only plan that addresses quality of life issues. There are a variety of other plans being developed or being implemented that do just that, in areas that range from the arts and education to housing and health care. Some are statewide efforts; others focus on the metro area. Most of them are discussed in an appropriate section of this book, but here's a quick list of some of the plans and reports that were issued after 1988. The sponsoring body or appropriate agency to contact is listed in parentheses:

- Arts Plan 2000+ (Metropolitan Arts Commission)
- Health Objectives for the Year 2000: Report of the Oregon Health 2000 Project (Oregon Department of Human Resources)
- Oregon Benchmarks: Setting Measurable Standards for Progress (Report to the 1991 Legislature by the Oregon Progress Board)
- Oregon Educational Act for the 21st Century (also called the Katz Plan after Vera Katz; 1991 Oregon Legislature)
- Oregon Shines: An Economic Strategy for the Pacific Century (Oregon Economic Development Department)
- Regional Solid Waste Management Plan (Metro)
- Regional Transportation Plan, 1989 Update (Metro)
- Resolving Homelessness in Portland and Multnomah County: A Report and Planning Framework (Housing Authority of Portland)
- Working Together: A Community and Academic Partnership for Greater Portland (Report of the Governor's Commission on Higher Education in the Portland Metropolitan Area)

Sibling Rivalry, Portland Style

After our sobering look at growth and taxes, we end this section with two topics that are a bit more light-hearted: sister cities and official Portland designations.

Sister Cities, Kissin' Cousins

In fact, Portland has enough sister cities to have sibling rivalry. According to John E. Salisbury, Oregon Coordinator of Sister Cities International, and staff at Portland's International Sister Cities Office, we have a variety of active official and unofficial sister city arrangements. Many are Pacific Rim connections. Here are the matchups for cities around the metro area:

Oregon City:	Foreign Sister:
Beaverton	Birobidzhan, Russia
Beaverton	Cheonan, Korea
Beaverton	Gotemba, Japan
Beaverton	Hsinchu, Taiwan
Canby	Kurisawa, Japan
Forest Grove	Nyuzen, Japan
Gresham	Ebetsu, Japan
Gresham	Owerri, Nigeria
Gresham	Sokcho, South Korea
Hillsboro	Fukoroi, Japan
Lake Oswego	Mordialloc, Australia
Oregon City	Tateshina, Japan
Portland	Ashkelon, Israel
Portland	Corinto, Nicaragua
Portland	Guadalajara, Mexico
Portland	Kaohsiung Municipality, Taiwan
Portland	Khabarovsk, Russia
Portland	Sapporo, Japan
Portland	Suzhou, China
Portland	Ulsan, South Korea
Wilsonville	Kitakata, Japan

In addition, the Port of Portland has a sister port: the Port of Chiba, Japan. And *The Oregonian* even has a sister newspaper: the *Hokkaido Shimbun*, of Sapporo, Japan.

Sister Cities Politics

In this time of budget cutbacks, you'll hear occasional grumbling about tax dollars spent on sister cities programs. But supporters counter that – especially for the Pacific Rim cities – cultural exchanges also bring economic benefits.

Some complaints may be justified. Gresham Mayor Gussie McRobert got a lot of flack when she visited Owerri, Nigeria during the fall of 1991. For few anticipate Nigeria's participation in Oregon's economic development, and some taxpayers had a hard time with the cultural benefit arguments.

But Portlanders were justifiably proud when a delegation of environmental and emergency management experts went to help sister city Guadalajara cope with the aftermath of a huge explosion. Their request for help – and our quick response – might not have happened without an existing relationship between the two cities.

The Official City Sandal

The state of Oregon actually has an official state nut. It also has an official state motto, seal, flower, bird, insect, gemstone, tree, fish, rock, animal, and flag. It has official colors, as well as a poet, an historian, a father and a mother, and a song and a dance. Sadly, Portland is no match for the state in this arena.

Officially Portland

According to the folks at City Hall, the city of Portland has only three official symbols: a flower, a bird, and the city seal. A drum roll, please:

City Flower:	The Rose (what else?)
City Bird:	The Great Blue Heron

And the city seal looks like this:

The seal shows Lady Commerce in the center. Forests, mountains and a ship entering the port fill the background. A sheaf of grain, a cogwheel, and a sledgehammer are at her feet. According to materials from the Metropolitan Arts Commission, "these figures symbolize the origins of the city, its culture, agrarian base, and industry." Lady Commerce and the city seal were the inspiration for Raymond Kaskey's *Portlandia*, the 36 foot hammered copper sculpture that sits above the entrance to the Portland Building.

For those of you wondering about the state nut, here's a partial list of our state symbols.

State Animal:	American Beaver
State Bird:	Western Meadowlark
State Colors:	Navy Blue and Gold
State Dance:	Square Dance
State Fish:	Chinook Salmon
State Flower:	Oregon Grape
State Gemstone:	Oregon Sunstone
State Insect:	Oregon Swallowtail Butterfly
State Nut:	Hazelnut
State Rock:	Thunderegg
State Song:	"Oregon, My Oregon"
State Tree:	Douglas Fir

For the scoop – complete with pictures – on the state seal, flag, motto, father, mother, poet, and historian, check the latest edition of the Oregon *Bluebook*. Finally, it should come as no surprise that Portland is known fondly as the City of Roses, while Oregon is the Beaver State.

The City Sandal

Some of those who saw early drafts of this book were distressed to learn that Portland has only three official designations. In a civic-minded spirit, they suggested some additional, as yet unofficial, designations. At last report, they were hoping for a popular mandate. Typical Oregonians, they are currently sponsoring a petition drive to get enough signatures to put an initiative on the ballot in the next election.

Here are their proposed designations, as they will appear on the ballot if the signature drive succeeds:

City Accessory:	Bicycle Pump
City Beer:	Blue Heron Ale
City Beverage:	Latte
City Bread:	Whole Wheat Sourdough

City Chip:	Wood
City Dessert:	Frozen Yogurt
City Granola:	Honey-nut Marionberry
City Fabric:	Gore-tex
City Hobby:	Winning livability awards
City Pizza:	Smoked-salmon Artichoke
City Sandal:	Birkenstock
City Slogan:	"Expose Yourself to Art"
City Snack:	Blackberry Bran Muffin
City Sneaker:	Nikes
City Sport:	Recycling
City Toe:	Webbed

A vocal minority supported the potato chip as the proposed official city chip. Lobbyists from Washington County had suggested another possibility: the silicon chip. But after a close vote among the steering committee members, the wood chip won out.

Several designations are still open. They include the city pasta, sandwich, soup, vegetable, and toy. Not to worry: if the initiative passes, the organizers promise another petition drive as soon as appropriate designations are determined. Readers with suggestions are encouraged to forward them to: Portland Possibilities Inc., Editorial Department, 6949 SW 11th Dr., Portland, OR 97219. Winning entries and final designations will appear in the next edition of *The Facts of Life in Portland, Oregon.*

While these official diversions are fun, we must get back to the business at hand. An important area – the environment – was skipped in *By the People, For the People.* That's because environmental issues are critical enough that they rate their own section. *An Environmental Report Card* is up next.

An

Environmental

Report Card

*Drinking the Water and
Breathing the Air*

Down the Drain

Hazardous to Your Health?

Reactor Reactions

Real Recyclers

Drinking the Water and Breathing the Air

Question: How many Oregonians does it take to change a light bulb?

Answer: Three. One to change the bulb, and two to consider the environmental impact.

Or, as the *Oregon Environmental Atlas* says more seriously, "Public concern about the environment is a tradition in Oregon...." What does that mean for Portland? Does it translate into clean and plentiful water, and air that meets state and federal air quality standards? What about solid and toxic waste disposal? Are Portlanders vigilant recyclers? We'll focus on these and other questions in the sections that follow.

It's In The Air

Although various pollutants can affect air quality, it is particulate matter, ozone and carbon monoxide that tend to be the culprits in Portland.

- ▸ Particulate matter will be more familiar (but just as polluting) by its less formal names: dust and smoke.
- ▸ The *Oregon Environmental Atlas* explains that ozone, the main chemical in smog, "is formed when warm temperatures and sunlight trigger chemical reactions involving hydrocarbons and oxides of nitrogen." The *Atlas* points to cars, gas stations, dry cleaners, paint fumes and selected industrial processes as hydrocarbon producers. Automobile combustion produces nitric oxide.
- ▸ And carbon monoxide is spewed into the air as part of automobile exhaust, and in the smoke from wood stoves.

Portland has had problems with these pollutants in the past. During the early 1970s, for example, carbon monoxide standards were violated on over 100 days each year. But Portland's air quality has improved, and remains reasonably good.

Here are some numbers, from the Oregon Department of Environmental Quality's *Oregon Air Quality Annual Report* for 1991. The first set shows the number of days each year on which pollution concentrations in Portland were above national standards. That's not what we want; concentrations should be below the standards for clean air:

Number of Days Exceeding Standards in Portland

Pollutant:	1986	1987	1988	1989	1990	1991
Fine Particulate	1	0	0	0	0	4
Carbon Monoxide	1	1	1	2	1	2
Ozone	3	1	2	0	4	1

July and August were unseasonably hot in 1990, with 20 days of 90 degree temperatures during those two months. The high temperatures helped cause the most "bad ozone days" since 1981. The summer of '91 was more moderate, with only nine days of 90+ temperatures during those months. As a result, we had just one "bad ozone day." While 1991 saw two days of high carbon monoxide levels, we are still far below the 100+ exceedance days of the early 1970s. The most noticeable increase in 1991 was for fine particulate pollutants. Portland exceeded federal standards on four days.

A second way to evaluate air quality is to use the Air Pollution Index, or API. The API reflects overall the air quality every day. It is keyed to potential health effects, which can be good, moderate, unhealthful, very unhealthful or hazardous. The following chart shows the number of days Portland had in each category from 1989 to 1991. The information is from the *Oregon Air Quality Annual Reports* for those years:

Rating:	Number of Days:		
	1989	1990	1991
Good	261	235	226
Moderate	92	105	125
Unhealthful	0	4	4

(Portland experienced no very unhealthful or hazardous days.)

You may have noticed that the number of days do not total to 365. That's due to the occasional glitch or computer snafu, when readings aren't recorded. While the city's API and exceedance day scores aren't perfect, all in all it's not a bad report card. Ironically, more sophisticated monitoring may be contributing to the higher pollution scores. DEQ notes that the rise "may only be the result of more intensive monitoring efforts and do not necessarily indicate deteriorating air quality."

Improving the Air

Portland should benefit from recent federal and state legislation on air quality. For example, a 1991 state clean air law imposes industrial emissions fees, which may encourage polluters to reduce their emissions. The same law also imposes regulations on wood stoves, which should decrease the amount of pollutants going into the air.

DEQ has also developed a forecasting program that will alert Portlanders that high ozone and carbon monoxide levels are anticipated on a given day. With a little luck, at least some civic-minded Portlanders will use a bike or a bus on those days, reducing the chance of unhealthful air.

The Portland metro area is also among those places that must sell oxygenated gasoline from the beginning of November to the end of February, as mandated by the federal Clean Air Act of 1990. Preliminary estimates suggest that oxygenated gas will reduce carbon monoxide emissions by about 17%.

Water, Water Everywhere

Portland has long been known for its abundant and high quality water. But in the aftermath of the 1992 drought, Portlanders are wondering just how plentiful it is. Can we withstand droughts in the future? Will there be enough water for the 500,000 new Portlanders who will arrive in the next 20 years? And are the city's backup wells – which are tapped when the reservoirs run low – free of contamination? First, some background.

Portland gets its drinking water from the Bull Run Watershed, which is located east of Portland, on the northwest slope of Mt. Hood. It is indeed an impressive water source:

- The water is particularly soft water, and it is clear.
- The water has a pH level of 7.0, which is close to neutral.
- The reservoir capacity is 21 billion gallons.
- About 730,000 people in the region use Bull Run water.
- Together, they use 120 to 130 million gallons daily.

Even more impressive than the numbers are the findings of an independent 1989 water quality study, which are quoted in the Portland Development Commission's *Facts* brochure:

> Portlanders have such high quality water it boggles the imagination of those who see it. It's almost too good. It's almost unproductive for aquatic life. If it was degraded by several hundred percent it still would be very high quality water....

But in the summer of 1992, it was the supply – or lack of it – that boggled the mind. The previous fall and winter months had been unseasonably dry, and the city was quickly running out of water. On July 15, City Commissioner Mike Lindberg announced water restrictions. Watering of lawns and flowers was limited; cars would remain unwashed; and, more as a symbolic gesture, most fountains were turned off. We were urged to conserve water, in hopes that we would use no more than 100 million gallons a day.

Supplementing the Supply

By August we were supplementing the dwindling supply with water from Bull Run Lake. We were also tapping into three of the 22 backup wells that are located along the south shore of the Columbia River, between Troutdale and the airport. But before we were able to tap the wells, officials had to check for contamination. For a suspected carcinogen had been found on industrial property near the wells, and in May, 1991, the Water Bureau had announced that minuscule traces of tetra-chloroethylene were found in wells near Troutdale. Experts were worried that pumping the well water might draw contaminated water towards the wells.

In fact, one of the five Blue Lake Park wells to be tapped was not used in the end, for tests found traces of contamination too close to it. A second was abandoned because its manganese content was too high. But a 30 day test of the other three wells found no evidence that their use was drawing contaminated water toward the wells.

By mid-September, the shortage seemed under control. Water from the wells and Bull Run Lake was supplementing the reservoirs, and water use was down to just above the 100 million gallons a day goal. And by September 30, Commissioner Lindberg was able to lift the restrictions.

Water for the Future

But many questions remain. Can we depend on the wells in the future? Do we need another reservoir or dam at Bull Run? Should we be using Willamette, Columbia, Clackamas or Trask River water? Why weren't commercial water users – like the Port of Portland, which uses almost 1.5 millions gallons a day – forced to cut back? Are pricing schedules that reward those who conserve better than restrictions? And how will we meet the needs of 500,000 more water customers in the next 20 years if we can barely cope with a drought in the present?

Regional water planning efforts were already underway when the drought hit. Perhaps the summer of '92 was the shock we needed to convince normally "rain-drenched" Portlanders that we really must take it seriously. Finally, the concern about well contamination raised another issue. Is the water in Portland threatened by pollutants and/or toxins? We'll return to that question when we consider both sewage over-flows and hazardous waste a little later in this section.

Lots of Lead?

While Bull Run water is truly wonderful, tests have shown that some people in the metro area have too much lead and copper in the water that comes out of their tap. The culprits are their pipes. While some choose to replace pipe fittings, most experts believe that it is only a problem with water that sat in the pipes overnight. Running the water for a few moments each morning will eliminate any hazard.

Environmental Stress?

How do we rate when compared to other cities? Zero Population Growth Inc. did a study of 204 cities, in an effort to evaluate environmental factors that are linked to population. Their Environmental Stress Test looked at five indicators. They were scored on a scale of 1 to 5, with 1 the best score and 5 for the very dangerous "red zone." Portland's overall rank of 3.0 was an average of these rankings:

Score: Category:

3   Population change (Cities with stable popula-
           tions received a 1.)
3   Air quality (Based on air quality in 1988.)
4   Water (Based on quality and availability of
           ground and surface water.)
2   Sewage treatment (Using EPA data to evaluate
           wastewater treatment quality and capacity.)
3   Toxic releases (Using *Toxic Release Inventory* fig-
           ures on total releases of industrial chemicals in
           1988.)

79 cities scored above Portland; 38 cities also scored a 3; and 87 cities received a lower score. While the ZPG study provides a comparison with other American cities, we could quarrel with their results. For example, water scores did not consider renewable water supplies, so the exceptional Bull Run Watershed was not even considered when ZPG rated Portland a "4" in the water category. Our growing population was seen as a detriment for the purposes of this study. And our air quality score – a 3 for "warning" – was awarded because Portland failed to meet EPA air quality standards on three separate days in 1988.

While we may question individual scores, the study does support the theory that there is a relationship between population and environmental stress. The 25 winning cities had an average population of 201,000; the 19 losers had an average population of 706,000.

Down the Drain

While backup well contamination may indeed be a threat to our water supply, there are also other serious water issues facing Portlanders. Pollutants are being discharged into our rivers and streams. According to the Portland Future Focus *Environmental Scan*, the main sources of pollution are waste-water from homes, businesses, and storm sewers.

Portland has a serious problem with combined sewer over-flows, or CSOs, as Stuart Tomlinson explained in the March 26, 1991 *Oregonian*:

> Portland's sewer system – in place since the late 1940s – relies on sewer outfalls to handle overflows of human waste and rain runoff. Simply put, when it rains hard, rainwater and raw sewage mix and are dumped directly into the river through 54 pipes, instead of being treated at the city's Columbia Boulevard Wastewater Treatment Plant.
>
> Raw sewage is also dumped directly into the Willa-mette when pumping station computers or pumps fail. It happened during Rose Festival in 1988, when the Sullivan pump station failed and sent 2 million gallons of sewage into the river.

Tomlinson also quoted staff of Northwest Environmental Advocates, a non-profit environmental organization, who reported finding needles and other medical waste in the river and on the river bank. And Lee Siegel, writing in the September 8, 1991 *Oregonian*, quoted DEQ's Shirley Kengla, who warned Willamette River users to "try not to swallow the water. If you eat sandwiches and have your hands in the water first, wash your hands."

Mopping Up the Mess

Though there is some debate about how often the CSOs occur, the city is well aware of the problems. The Environmental Services department has done computer simulations of the CSOs. They indicated that about 4.9 billion gallons overflow into the Willamette each year, and another 1.3 billion gallons overflow into the Columbia Slough.

City officials point out that the problem is not unique to Portland. Seattle has embarked on a 20 year program to reduce their CSOs by 75%, and San Francisco is in the middle of a project that will reduce their overflows from about 80 to 8 a year. In fact, about 1,200 cities across the U.S. have sewer systems that are prone to CSOs. Portland is under orders from DEQ to reduce their overflows by 99%. But it won't happen quickly and it won't come cheap: the city expects to spend $1 billion on it, over the next 20 years.

Spendy Sewers

Before we leave the sewers, we should mention one other major sewer project now underway. Many residents in mid-Multnomah County are not connected to the city's sewers. In 1986, DEQ ordered the city hook them up to protect the ground water. But as properties were connected, the costs were rising. Facing ever-increasing sewer assessments, residents organized in 1991 to fight city hall. They were successful, and in February, 1992 the city committed to role back sewer assessments. Under the agreement, sewer assessments will average $2,200, which is a 36% reduction of the rates at the time. So if you are considering a move to mid-Multnomah County, you might want to check on sewer hookups.

The Big Green Oregonian

According to Fairness and Accuracy in Reporting, a group with its eye on the media, *The Oregonian* devotes more space to environmental issues than any other daily newspaper in the U.S.

In 1991, 4.3% of The Big O's stories were related to the environment. That's more than double the average for the other 32 metropolitan newspapers considered in the study.

Hazardous To Your Health?

A 1991 book by Benjamin A. Goldman, *The Truth About Where You Live: An Atlas for Action on Toxins and Mortality*, links information on toxins and mortality with specific counties in the United States. Multnomah County shows up among the 60 worst counties in a few analyses, including selected aspects of air quality, water quality, workplace toxins, and hazardous waste.

Before the alarm bells go off, we need to consider the data with care. For a careful reading indicates that the data is old – usually from the mid-1980s, but sometimes spanning 1968 to 1983. While the data may point to problems in the past, it does not accurately reflect conditions in the county today. Which is not to say that we don't have some toxins in our environment – we surely do. We have considered the air and the water. Now let's look at the sobering issue of hazardous waste.

Superfund Sites

According to the *Oregon Environmental Atlas*, Oregon industries produce about 20,000 tons of hazardous waste every year. The waste generation map in the *Atlas* shows that the large bulk is from businesses in or close to Portland – in Washington, Clackamas, Yamhill and Multnomah Counties. The state's only disposal facility is in eastern Oregon, near Arlington.

But haphazard or inappropriate disposal in the past haunts us today. As of October, 1992, the U.S. Environmental Protection Agency had identified nine Superfund cleanup sites in Oregon. (Superfund refers to federal legislation that mandates the cleanup of sites with uncontrolled hazardous waste or inappropriate hazardous waste disposal.) Two of the sites, Gould Battery and Allied Plating, are in Portland. A third, Northwest Pipe & Casing, is in Clackamas. And four Superfund sites – ALCOA-Vancouver, Bonneville Power Administration-Ross, Toftdahl Drums, and Vancouver Water Station #4 – are just across the river in Vancouver. If it is any consolation, Oregon has fewer Superfund sites than most other states.

There are many other potentially hazardous sites that are being investigated by the U.S. Environmental Protection Agency and/or the Oregon Department of Environmental Quality. Many will be found safe; others can be cleaned up with relative ease. But a few are quite hazardous. If you are worried about the location of your home or your child's school, you can call both the U.S. EPA and the Oregon DEQ. They can provide the latest information on both locations and cleanup. In the course of our research, both agencies were quite helpful and willing to send listings and status reports for hazardous sites. These agencies can also provide information on those local companies that are known to be currently releasing toxins into the air or water.

"Toxic Waters"

As we saw in the sections on water quality and sewage overflows, there is indeed concern about our water supply and our rivers. An excellent and comprehensive source of information is *Portland/Vancouver Toxic Waters*, a 1992 map published by Northwest Environmental Advocates. It identifies, describes and locates "more than 150 sources of pollution to the Willamette and Columbia Rivers and local tributaries."

These pollution sources include both conventional pollutants as well as toxins. Specifically, the map locates industrial dischargers, sites with contaminated ground or surface water, sewage treatment plants, combined sewage overflows, toxic landfills, and areas of extensive goundwater contamination. Interested readers can contact RiverWatch at the Northwest Environmental Advocates in Portland. The map is easy to read and understand, and sells for the bargain price of just $3.

Another map, also from Northwest Environmental Advocates, is scheduled for publication in 1993. Entitled *Columbia River: Troubled Waters*, it will be the "first-ever map of the environmental quality of the Columbia River Basin, with the Columbia River Estuary on the reverse side." Ask about that one too.

Reactor Reactions

Radiation at Reed

Until there was a problem with the nuclear reactor at Reed College in November, 1991, most Portlanders did not even know that there was a nuclear reactor in the city of Portland. Reed's small reactor is used for research at the college's southeast Portland campus.

On November 24, 1991, a minuscule amount of the isotope krypton 88 escaped through a pinhole leak in one of the fuel rods. Two student operators, who had met the same certification requirements as operators at larger commercial nuclear plants, immediately shutdown the reactor. Fortunately, the released radiation was not considered dangerous – it was less than the amount an airplane passenger is exposed to on a coast-to-coast flight. It was the first radioactive leak in the reactor's 23 year history.

Trouble at Trojan

Portlanders are much more aware of another site: the Trojan Nuclear Plant, which is located along the Columbia River, about 40 miles northwest of Portland in Rainier, Oregon. The plant, which is the only commercial nuclear power plant in Oregon, has not operated since November 9, 1992. In January 1993, Portland General Electric decided to close Trojan permanently.

Controversy has swirled around Trojan since it began operating in May 1976. Portland General Electric, 70% owner of the plant, maintained all along that the facility operated safely. But critics doubted the plant's ability to withstand earthquakes and worried about radioactive waste. They pointed to structural defects in steam generators and faulty cooling systems that forced temporary shutdowns and repairs. And they cited Nuclear Regulatory Commission statements about the plant's poor management. In fact, the plant had the worst safety record in the country in 1991.

PGE's January 1993 announcement on the permanent shutdown came as a surprise. PGE had planned to close the plant by 1996. In the fall of 1992, the utility spent millions of dollars fighting two ballot initiatives that, if passed, would have closed

Trojan immediately. During the election, Trojan critics had argued that an immediate shutdown was necessary for safety reasons, and to ensure that ratepayers would not be forced to underwrite the costs of the 1996 closure. PGE had argued that a gradual shutdown would cost less in the end, and allow time to develop alternative energy sources. PGE won.

Then, according to PGE spokesmen, the "accidental release of trace amounts of radioactive gases" on November 9 forced PGE to reevaluate. The decision was made to shut the plant permanently. Trojan opponents were skeptical. They wondered if the utility had fought the ballot measures because they wanted ratepayers to help pay the decommissioning costs. PGE officials argued that, since the fall, power needs had dropped somewhat and replacement power had become less expensive. The new problem made the plant's operation more costly, so they made the decision to pull the plug permanently.

We'll probably never know all the details. But Trojan critics are happy that the plant is finally closed. The new worries include the 450 tons of radioactive fuel rods that are left, and the economic impact of the closure on the town of Rainier and the people who worked at the plant.

Handling Hanford

The Hanford Nuclear Reservation, located about 200 miles east of Portland along the Columbia River near Richland, Washington, also has people worried. Home to nine closed nuclear reactors and more than 1,300 radioactive waste disposal sites, Hanford is believed to be one of the most polluted sites in the U.S. For many of the storage tanks that are buried underground are leaking. Other tanks could explode or catch fire. Those familiar with the problem also voice concerns about contaminated groundwater and the impact on the Columbia River.

While federal and state officials do not agree on all the details, there is agreement that the site needs massive cleanup. The U.S. Department of Energy, with a 30-year plan in hand, has budgeted almost $10 billion for cleanup costs through 1996. But the ongoing danger remains. Observers as well as officials hope the tanks will hold while the clean-up is carried out. Portlanders share the concern, for 200 miles isn't very far.

Real Recyclers

Although we are again considering waste, the picture is somewhat prettier – even award-winning. For Portlanders are very conscientious recyclers. According to the Metropolitan Service District's *Metro Recycling Level Survey* for 1991, an estimated 38% of the waste generated in the region was recycled. We recycled:

- ▸ 77% of the area's newspaper
- ▸ 65% of our magazines
- ▸ 75% of our glass
- ▸ 32% of our yard debris
- ▸ 21% of our tin cans, and 63% of our aluminum
- ▸ And 16% of our plastics.

A look at some national figures quickly shows how very impressive our statistics are. They come from the same METRO report:

Material Recycled	METRO Level	National Level
Newspaper	77%	45%
Glass	75%	17%
Plastics	16%	2%
Yard Debris	32%	3%
TOTAL	38%	17%

As the chart shows, we already surpass the 25% national goal which the Environmental Protection Agency set for 1992. Metro's Regional Solid Waste Management Plan is far more ambitious. It sets a goal of 50% by the year 2000.

Recycling Made Easy

Part of the reason for our high recycling rate is weekly curbside pickup. All Oregon municipalities with a population over 4,000 must provide curbside recycling. Here's how it works in Portland:

- ▸ Garbage collection and recycling pickups are handled by 61 garbage haulers. Each hauler holds a franchise for a specific area of the city.
- ▸ Haulers must pick up your garbage and recycling on the same day each week. They collect nine recyclables: newspaper, corrugated cardboard, glass jars and bottles, tin cans, aluminum, motor oil, scrap metals, magazines, and plastic milk jugs.
- ▸ Property owners can also arrange curbside pickup for yard debris.
- ▸ Monthly fees range from $4.25 for recyclables only to $29.25 for a 90 gallon roll cart. Weekly pickup for a 32 gallon can and recyclables costs $19.30/month. That rate includes one collection of yard debris each month.

In 1990, about 30% of the households in Portland used curbside recycling. At that time, property owners could choose their garbage collector from those operating in their neighborhood, and most recyclables were picked up monthly. In February, 1992, the city implemented the franchise system and weekly recycling. There was some confusion and complaining at the outset, but the results are indeed impressive. The number of recycling households in Portland jumped from 30% in 1990 to over 70% in 1992.

Styrocop?

In January, 1990, Portland banned the use of polystyrene foam in restaurants and by retail food vendors. The ban applies to food that is prepared on site. That's why Portlanders who don't bring their own mug get their take-out latte in a paper cup, and why there's no styrofoam plates at the salad bar. A few national magazines like *U.S. News & World Report* and *Sierra* found the ordinance intriguing, and profiled Styrocop Lee Barrett, the Bureau of Environmental Services inspector who investigates polystyrene violations. City officials report a 99% compliance rate, in part because Portlanders support the idea.

The Environmental Verdict

As we come to the end of *An Environmental Report Card*, let's review our grades. We deserve a "thumbs up" for the high quality of our drinking water, our efforts and results in the area of air quality, and our conscientious recycling. While there's clearly room for considerable improvement in the sewage system, we have at least started to clean it up. On the down side, there are many hazardous sites in the metro area. And our famous rivers are at risk because of pollutants and toxins.

We can still be proud of this record, for we enjoy an environment that is better than that in many other communities. But we must recognize that our environment is no match to the pristine and pure images some have of the Northwest. As we approach the next century, we'll need to focus on clean-up, and we'll need to act quickly and forthrightly to preserve what we have.

Finally, those interested in environmental issues may want to get a copy of *Our Green Home: The Resources of Portland, Oregon, 1992*. This detailed report, which was completed by the City of Portland Environmental Commission, compiles a wealth of environmental data, considering issues like air quality, water quality, fish and wildlife, land, vegetation, infrastructure, communications, energy, and recycling. It was to be presented to the City Council at about the same time that this book was scheduled to go to the printer, so by the time you read these words, *Our Green Home* will be available. Interested readers are encouraged to obtain a copy of the report from the Environmental Commission.

There is one more public sphere that we must consider: the public school system. For many Portlanders, school selection and neighborhood preference go hand in hand. So we focus next on school districts, neighborhoods, homes, and apartments in the Portland metropolitan area.

From

Your House

to the

Schoolhouse

Ninety Neighborhoods

"A City of Homes"

About Those Apartments. . .

Reading, Writing and 'Rithmetic

Multiple Choice School Districts

On the School Horizon

Ninety Neighborhoods

Many of the names are truly wonderful. For example, on the west side you'll find Goose Hollow, Council Crest, Lair Hill, Bridlemile, John's Landing, Multnomah, Garden Home and Terwilliger. Across the Willamette to the east are Mt. Tabor, Brooklyn, Eastmoreland, Ladd's Addition, Sullivan's Gulch, Albina, Overlook and the Alameda. Some of the names are a bit exotic; others are descriptive; and still others have Native American derivations. And the large majority – exotic name or not – are thriving.

We've mentioned only a small number of Portland neighborhoods. According to the Office of Neighborhood Associations (ONA), a city bureau that was formed in 1974, there are more than 90 neighborhood associations in Portland. A few areas don't have formal neighborhood organizations, and in other areas several neighborhoods have joined forces to form one group. Which means that there are easily more than 100 neighborhoods in the city. While we can't characterize them all, this section is for people who are curious about Portland's neighborhoods, and those who may be neighborhood shopping. We include a neighborhood association map, courtesy of ONA, on pages 210-211.

The Lay of the Land

First, a quick review of the geography for those who get lost easily or skipped *A Look at the Landscape*, this book's geography section. The city can be divided into five sections: going clockwise from the top, they are north, northeast, southeast, southwest, and northwest. The Willamette River is the east-west divider, and Burnside Street is the north-south divider. North Portland is that wedge of the city that is east of the river, and west of Vancouver Street. Portlanders use these designations routinely, in addresses and in conversation, to refer to these five parts of the city.

Portland State University Professor Carl Abbott has written extensively on the development of Portland's neighborhoods. In *Portland: Planning, Politics, and Growth in a Twentieth-Century City*, he discusses the five designations, explaining that these divisions are not sufficient:

Slicing the Portland pie into five pieces, however, ignores differences in social geography by lumping affluent East-moreland with working-class Buckman, Portland Heights with Corbett. In fact, competition for space, altitude, and prestige in twentieth-century Portland created four irregular rings around the business core of the city. The stopover neighborhoods, the everyday city, the highlands, and the automobile suburbs have each had different social standing and filled different social functions.

The First Neighborhoods

Professor Abbott explains that the "crescent of flatlands around the central business district" and close-in north and northeast neighborhoods were the areas that were settled first. They became home to most of the city's foreigners and transient workers. Much of the 19th century housing in these areas gave way to urban renewal projects, highways, and commercial uses, but some survives, in part because of the neighborhood associations that formed to try to protect the residential quality of the neighborhoods. Some of the west side "stopover neighborhood" names you'll hear are Lair Hill, Corbett, John's Landing, Goose Hollow, King's Hill and Burnside. East side "stopover neighborhoods" include Brooklyn, Albina, Boise, and Eliot.

"Streetcar Suburbs"

The "everyday city" refers to the east side, flatland neighborhoods that began as "streetcar suburbs." From 1890 to 1920, these areas were subdivided by developers. They saw "great building booms" from 1905 to 1913 and again from 1922 to 1928, when free-standing, single family homes were built to accommodate the city's growing population. Sellwood, Ladd's Addition, Irvington, Woodstock, Richmond, and Rose City Park are among the "everyday city" neighborhood names you'll hear.

To the Heights

As we'd expect, the "highlands" were settled by more affluent, upper and upper-middle class Portlanders. From their homes in the hills, they enjoyed wonderful views that were still within an easy drive of downtown. Located in the hills west and southwest of the central business district, these neighborhoods were settled for the most part between 1920 and 1940. They are still the higher status neighborhoods. Portland Heights, Willamette Heights, Arlington Heights, Council Crest, and Terwilliger are some of the west side neighborhoods in this group. There are also a few east side highland neighborhoods: Eastmoreland, Laurelhurst and Alameda were all built on rises that sat just a bit higher than other east side locations.

And the Suburbs

The "automobile suburbs" form the final "ring." Furthest from the center city, these areas were built after the second World War, and cover most of the Portland metro area. Abbott defines the east side "automobile suburbs" as those areas that "run roughly east from Ninety-second Street, which marked the approximate limit of streetcar and bus service before 1940, and south from the Multnomah-Clackamas county line." On the west side, new neighborhoods "spilled down the far slope of the West Hills onto the rolling farmland of Washington County." Most of the "automobile suburbs" are actually outside the Portland city limits.

Putting It All Together

We can draw a few conclusions that might help those unfamiliar with Portland neighborhoods:

▸ Most of the "highlands" are on the west side. As such, most of the more expensive, affluent neighborhoods are on the west side.

▸ Although some new homes have been built to fill in vacant land in the stopover, everyday and highland neighborhoods, most of the newer housing is in the suburbs. In some areas, older homes have been demolished − sometimes after protests from neighborhood residents − to make way for new homes and row houses.

▸ Many west side homes are built into the hills; a smaller number sit on stilts. A popular west side style is the daylight basement, which is built into the hill, with some rooms at street level, and others on the lower level. West side streets tend to curve around the hills, often intersecting at odd angles.

▸ East side streets are generally straight, and they tend to follow a north/south and east/west grid. A popular east side style, now known as the Old Portland, is a small bungalow home, with an open floor plan and big front porch. Many Old Portland homes were built during the building booms in the early part of the century.

If you are unsure about a neighborhood, the answers to a few questions can help you get a rough idea:

▸ How far is the neighborhood from the central business district?

▸ Is it on the east or west side?

▸ More specifically, is it in north, northeast, southeast, southwest, or northwest Portland?

▸ And finally, is it in the hills or flats?

What's Hot?

Like people, neighborhoods have personalities, and we can't really do them justice in a few paragraphs. But we can mention a few that are getting media attention lately:

▸ The Pearl District, also known as the Northwest Triangle, is just northwest of downtown. Industrial buildings and warehouses of the past are getting a new lease on life as lofts, galleries, stores and business locations. As Jonathan Nicholas put it in the July 28, 1991 *Oregonian*, the Pearl "has styled itself as the SoHo of the West Coast."

▸ The February 24, 1992 *Portland Downtowner* profiled antique stores in Sellwood; redevelopment in the Lloyd District; new stores, restaurants and theaters on Hawthorne Street; and restaurants near the new OMSI in Hosford-Abernethy.

They found four "blossoming eastside districts" and discovered "a nurturing mix of restaurants and skyscrapers, movie theaters and railway lines, and some of the most optimistic and enthusiastic retailers in the city."

▸ Northeast Broadway is, according to the March 2, 1992 *Oregonian*, "the city's newest hip strip." As the article explains, "Like Northwest 23rd Avenue and Southeast Hawthorne before it, Northeast Broadway – the part of it directly north of Lloyd Center, and south of the Irvington neighborhood – has become a trend magnet. Boutiques, restaurants and shops are elbowing their way into the core area between Northeast 12th and 24th Avenues."

▸ The July 30-August 5, 1992 *Willamette Week* named Southeast Division as "the latest site for Portland gentrification."

▸ Looking for "hidden bargains" in the home market, the October 29, 1991 *Oregonian* profiled Overlook in North Portland, Sullivan's Gulch and Concordia in northeast, Buckman in southeast, and South Burlingame in southwest. They found them "healthy and vibrant" with "character and a lively mix of residents." Other recent *Oregonian* articles have focused on St. Johns in North Portland, and Richmond and Hosford-Abernethy in southeast.

Learning the Locales

There are a few good sources for more information on neighborhoods:

▸ The map of neighborhood associations on the next page is available from Portland's Office of Neighborhood Associations. ONA can also provide sample issues of neighborhood association newsletters, and information about the different associations.

▸ Just about all the area realtors provide relocation packets that include a wealth of information about the city in general, and its various neighborhoods. They can tailor the material they include to meet specific needs. We requested

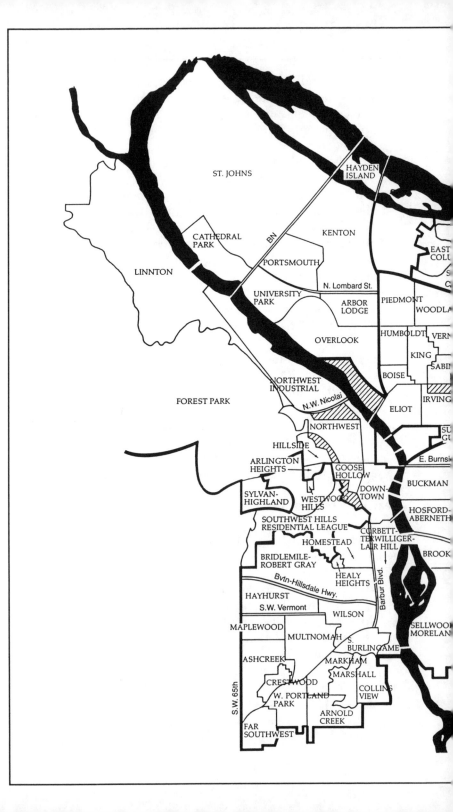

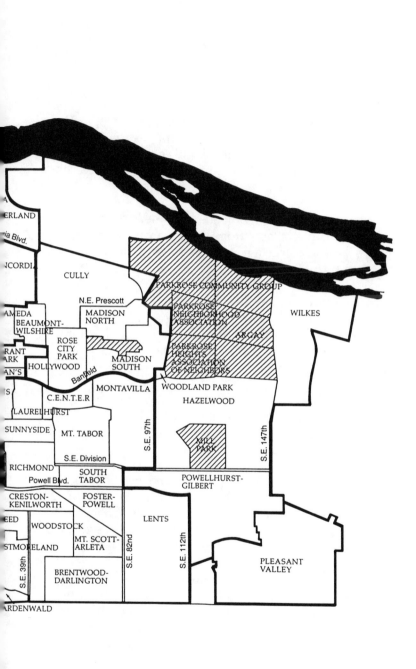

ERLAND
ia Blvd.
ICORDI
CULLY
N.E. Prescott
AMEDA
BEAUMONT-
WILSHIRE
MADISON
NORTH
RANT
ARK
ROSE
CITY
PARK
AN'S
HOLLYWOOD
Banfield
MADISON
SOUTH
PARKROSE COMMUNITY GROUP
PARKROSE
NEIGHBORHOOD
ASSOCIATION
ARGAY
WILKES
PARKROSE
HEIGHTS
ASSOCIATION
OF NEIGHBORS
S
LAURELHURST
C.E.N.T.E.R
MONTAVILLA
WOODLAND PARK
HAZELWOOD
SUNNYSIDE
MT. TABOR
S.E. 97th
S.E. 147th
S.E. Division
MILL
PARK
RICHMOND
Powell Blvd.
SOUTH
TABOR
POWELLHURST-
GILBERT
CRESTON-
KENILWORTH
FOSTER-
POWELL
EED
WOODSTOCK
LENTS
STMORELAND
MT. SCOTT-
ARLETA
S.E. 82nd
S.E. 112th
S.E. 39th
BRENTWOOD-
DARLINGTON
PLEASANT
VALLEY
ARDENWALD

Portland Neighborhood Associations

packets from many realtors while assembling this chapter, and were particularly impressed by those we received from The Hasson Group, Barbara Sue Seal Properties, and The Equity Group.

▸ Cronin & Caplan Realty Group publishes a series of neighborhood profiles and a neighborhood map. The profiles are one to two page descriptions of selected neighborhoods, and the map clearly indicates neighborhood names, neighborhood association names, and subdivision names.

▸ Those interested in neighborhoods with new construction may want a map available from Professionals 100 realtors. It locates new construction and provides information on builders and developers.

▸ Many local areas within the city have their own small newspapers. The *Portland Downtowner*, the *Southwest Neighborhood News*, and the *Northwest Examiner* are just three examples. Typically, they are available free of charge at area stores and restaurants.

▸ Some communities outside of Portland also have newspapers that are available by subscription or at the newsstand. They include the *Lake Oswego Review*, the *Gresham Outlook* and the *Hillsboro Argus*.

▸ Those who are really interested in Portland neighborhoods might enjoy *Neighborhood Accomplishments in Portland, Oregon, 1976-1983*, a history of the city's neighborhood associations, which was prepared by the Office of Neighborhood Associations.

Clearly, Portland offers many neighborhood choices, both in the city and beyond the city limits. Unlike so many other cities – where neighborhoods have been abandoned and there are few options to the "automobile suburbs" – Portland neighborhoods are vibrant, popular places to call home. And as we'll see next, the homes are actually affordable.

"A City of Homes"

Every newspaper and chamber of commerce likes to claim that its community is a "city of homes." The claim may be only wishful thinking in some communities, but it is fully justified in Portland. For the last three generations, the "Rose City" has had a higher percentage of homeownership than most other American cities....

Portland's high percentage of home ownership has also affected its physical appearance. For a century, the city has been characterized by the free-standing single-family home. Historically, residents have been opposed to apartment construction in both the city and suburbs, viewing attached or row housing as unsuitable for Portland. Thus, Portlanders have built a low-rise metropolis where residents can enjoy the advantages of both a large city and low-density neighborhoods.

Carl Abbott, *Portland: Gateway to the Northwest,* 1985.

The 1990 census figures indicate that Portland still merits its "city of homes" designation. Just over half of all the housing units in Portland are owner occupied, and 63% are detached, one-family homes. The numbers are even higher for the metro area: 61% of the housing units in Washington County and 72% of the ones in Clackamas County are detached, one-family homes.

There are a few reasons that help explain why Portland has remained a "city of homes." Since many people chose to stay in the city – rather than move to the suburbs – most Portland neighborhoods have been spared the deterioration seen in so many other cities. Federal money has helped fund housing rehabilitation programs and public transit. Residential areas that were once a 20 minute streetcar ride away from downtown are still only 20 minutes away, by MAX or TRI-MET bus.

The Bottom Line

Another critical reason is that Portland homes are affordable. Unlike many other parts of the country, the Portland housing market is still open to people who don't make six figure incomes. How does that translate into actual selling prices? The following chart provides year-to-date information on average sales prices for January through October, 1992. It is based on data courtesy of the Realtors Multiple Listing Service (RMLS™) of Portland, which appeared in their *Market Action* newsletter for October 1992.

Average Sales Prices for Portland Area Homes

January - October, 1992

North Portland	$53,600
Northeast/Southeast Portland	$85,000
West Portland	$169,300
Lake Oswego/West Linn	$197,900
Beaverton/Aloha	$112,700
Tigard/Wilsonville	$135,800
Gresham/Troutdale	$104,300
Milwaukie/Clackamas	$112,400

The RMLS™ *Market Action* newsletter for October 1992 provided the following information as well:

▸ The median sales price for metro area homes was $99,500 in October 1992. That was "the highest median price recorded in the RMLS™ system to date."

▸ Median monthly prices in 1992 varied between about $92,000 and the high of $99,500.

▸ Between January and October 1992, "the median price of a three bedroom home...was $95,000 and the average price was $107,200."

▸ The average sales price for new construction was $178,200 in October 1992; the median was $158,000.

▸ Less than 5% of the single family homes in the RMLS™ system are priced at more than $250,000.

▸ On average, it takes about 75 days on the market to sell a home. In 1992, the RMLS™ system included between about 10,200 and 11,700 active listings each month.

Values on the Rise

Portland homes appear to be good investments. During the early 1990s, prices rose at a rate that made the Portland market one of the best in the country. Since then the market has leveled off a bit. Here's a sampling of what the experts have said about the Portland housing market:

▸ In its January 1989 issue, *Changing Times* reported "what your home will be worth, by city." Using estimates by the WEFA Group, an economics consulting firm, the magazine projected that the average existing home in Portland will be worth $222,480 in 1997.

▸ According to the October 1, 1990 issue of *Newsweek*, the National Association of Realtors reported a 15.8% rise in Portland housing values, making Portland fifth among "the five hottest metropolitan areas" that year.

▸ The April 15, 1992 issue of *Smart Money* predicted a healthy real estate market for Portland, "with prices likely to rise."

▸ Comparing the second quarter of 1992 with the second quarter of 1991, the August 6, 1992 *USA Today* reported a 12.6% increase in the median price of a home in the Portland metro area.

▸ According to the August 5, 1992 *Daily Journal of Commerce*, home construction was on the rise in the Portland area during the first six months of 1992. It's important to understand the context, as the article explains:

> Through the first half of 1992, 4,022 single-family permits involving $426.4 million in construction have been granted – well ahead of 1991's 3,114 permits for $336.2 million in work. However, this year's totals [1992] are still running behind the boom year of 1990, when 4,356 new-home permits with a combined value of $456.1 million were issued.

▸ Predictions in the July 1992 issue of *Money* magazine are a little different. The magazine reported that "house prices in 19 of the 50 biggest U.S. cities won't quite keep up with inflation" in the next three years. According to *Money*, Portland will, but barely: "after subtracting 3.66% annual inflation," Portland single family homes will go up just .42% in value. The analysis was done for *Money* by the WEFA Group.

That doesn't sound like much, but it's a rosier projection than many others on the *Money* list. According to the magazine, homeowners in Los Angeles, Phoenix, Sacramento, San Diego, Minneapolis, Orlando, Boston, Tampa, New York, Salt Lake City, San Francisco, Hartford, Buffalo, Riverside (Ca.), Seattle, and selected New York and New Jersey counties will see their homes depreciate in value by up to a few percentage points.

Home-Buying California Refugees

Well-heeled newcomers from California are often attracted to "the Heights" – the close-in, older, west side neighborhoods built on the hills that overlook the central business district. Classy Dunthorpe, an enclave of large, older homes south of downtown along the river, is another area popular with "equity-rich refugees" (and a few of the Portland Trail Blazers).

But not all Californians bring lots of cash. We know one who devised a plan to sell his car so he could make a down payment on a house in Portland – which is exactly what he did to buy a home in Sellwood, a close-in southeast neighborhood near the river, which is known for its small, older homes, neighborhood shopping, tree-lined streets and antique stores.

According to William Conerly, the chief economist at First Interstate Bank, our friend may be typical of the current wave of California refugees. Conerly, who was quoted in the November 11, 1992 *Oregonian*, explained that the newest arrivals "are people in their 20s or 30s who couldn't afford a house in California and who will be looking for starter homes here."

About Those Apartments . . .

In *Portland: Gateway to the Northwest*, Carl Abbott explained that Portlanders of the past were "opposed to apartment construction in both the city and suburbs, viewing attached or row housing as unsuitable for Portland." More recently, Portland has experienced a boom in apartment construction. The Winter 1992 issue of *The Barry Apartment Report*, which is published by apartment appraisers Mark D. Barry & Associates, set the context:

> Over the last decade, the Portland area apartment market has come full circle. We had the roaring 1970's and early 1980's, the recessionary years of the early to mid-1980's, the strong comeback and expansion from 1985 to 1990, and some pullback and cooling off of the local apartment market in 1991.

That "cooling off" continued. The Fall 1992 issue of *The Barry Apartment Report* characterized 1992 as "another slow year for apartment construction in the Portland/Vancouver SMSA." What does that mean for apartment-seekers? Is the vacancy rate high? What about the rents?

"Apartment For Rent"

The McGregor Millette Report is a newsletter published by McGregor, Millette & Associates, brokers specializing in the sale of apartments. The Fall/Winter 1992 issue includes information on both rents and vacancy rates:

▸ The average monthly apartment rent in Multnomah, Washington, Clackamas and Clark counties in 1991 was $520. The 1992 average (through November 1) was $523.

▸ Looking at "seasoned" units, or apartments built before 1988, the 1992 average rent was $497.

▸ Rents for new construction, or apartments completed after 1987, are higher. The average rent for these units in 1992 was $598.

The big news, however, was that vacancy rates were down from 1991 levels. According to *The McGregor Millette Report*:

▸ The overall vacancy rate for apartments in the four county area was 4.1% for the period between January and November 1, 1992.

▸ That was down significantly from the 1991 vacancy rate of 5.5%. The 5.5% vacancy rate was the highest it had been since 1983.

The 1991 vacancy rate was high because of the 1990 apartment building boom. There were just too many new units on the market: so many that vacancy rates for new construction hit a whopping 15.9% in the spring of 1991. That pulled the overall rate for all units up to the 5.5% level. To be competitive, many apartment complexes had offered incentives, like one month free for signing a one year lease. By the fall of 1992, such incentives were only available in a few "over built" locations, like the Sunset Corridor and the Clackamas Town Center area.

What's the Rent?

We include the tables on the following page to give you an idea of actual rents and apartment availability. They list average rents and vacancy rates, for selected metro area locations, for two apartment types: a 3 bedroom/2 bath flat, and a 1 bedroom/1 bath flat. The information was collected in a November, 1992 survey by McGregor, Millette & Associates, and appeared originally in *The McGregor Millette Report*. If you need data for other areas or apartment types, it is available in the detailed tables in the report.

Rents on the Rise?

Finally, what do the experts project for the future? Noting that "the market has returned to a position of balance between supply and demand," *The McGregor Millette Report* is forecasting "a six per cent increase in rents for 1993."

Average Monthly Rent on a Three Bedroom/Two Bath Flat
November 1992

Location	"Seasoned" Rent	Vacancy	New Rent	Vacancy
Downtown/Northwest Portland	$1,015	2.8%	NA	NA
Southwest Portland	$706	9.4%	$769	0.0%
Northeast Portland	$567	3.2%	$678	6.5%
Southeast Portland	$571	1.6%	$697	5.3%
Gresham/Troutdale	$665	5.0%	$708	5.9%
Clackamas	NA	NA	$709	3.3%
Tualatin/Wilsonville	$735	8.1%	$722	3.0%
Lake Oswego/West Linn	$751	4.6%	$1,015	12.5%
Beaverton	$629	3.4%	$756	4.9%

Average Monthly Rent on a One Bedroom/One Bath Flat
November 1992

Location	"Seasoned" Rent	Vacancy	New Rent	Vacancy
Downtown/Northwest Portland	$488	4.5%	$748	19.9%
Southwest Portland	$439	3.9%	$546	4.0%
Northeast Portland	$399	2.3%	$475	0.0%
North Portland	$349	2.5%	----	----
Southeast Portland	$367	2.8%	$490	3.3%
Gresham/Troutdale	$398	2.9%	$472	3.3%
Clackamas	$401	6.5%	$485	5.6%
Tualatin/Wilsonville	$436	3.6%	$513	3.6%
Lake Oswego/West Linn	$508	5.6%	$577	3.9%
Beaverton	$438	2.3%	$512	3.4%

The old joke in real estate circles is that three things matter to those in the market for a home or an apartment – and those three things are location, location, location. Some want to be near their work or public transit; others want nearby shopping or a view. But for many, location is important for one reason only: the schools. So let's move on to *Reading, Writing and 'Rithmetic.*

Reading, Writing and 'Rithmetic

Public education was once a jewel in California's crown. But the state that was consistently in the educational Top 10 in the 1960s and early '70s has fallen to the middle or the bottom of the pack in indicators such as per-student spending and student-teacher ratio.

The precipitous decline in the last decade, experts say, is largely the result of a 1979 ballot measure that limited local property taxes, which are a major source of school financing elsewhere in the nation.

Jane Gross, "California schools bailing fast as they sink in budget morass," *The Oregonian*, April 21, 1991.

We considered calling this chapter *Reading, Writing and 'Rithmetic at Risk*. We also debated *Living with Measure Five* as a subtitle. If you skipped *The Saga of Measure Five* and are among the uninitiated, Measure 5 is a property tax limitation plan that was passed by Oregon voters in November, 1990. It radically altered the property tax system and public school financing in the state of Oregon.

Measure 5 limits the amount of money property owners can pay in property taxes. Until the passage of Measure 5, property taxes had provided an average of 57% of public school funding. Each school district was able to decide how high property taxes should be, so some schools were well supported, and others scraped by on far smaller budgets. But with the passage of Measure 5, strict limits were set on the amount of property tax that any taxing district could collect to support schools and other government services. While some school districts were within the new limits, many could no longer collect all the taxes they'd used in the past to run their schools.

Making Up the Missing Money

Measure 5 does stipulate that the state must make up the revenue that the schools lose because of the new limits. But the lost property tax money will not necessarily be replaced dollar for dollar. In replacing the lost tax revenue, the state legislature decided to move towards equalization, which means that all Oregon school districts will eventually receive roughly the same amount of money per student. For the 1991/92 school year, the state basically replaced the lost property tax revenues dollar for dollar. For the 1992/93 school year, the state developed a formula that gave every school district as least as much money as it had had for the 1991/92 year. Some poorer districts received increases of up to 25%. But given inflation and growing numbers of students, the formula meant cuts for the wealthier districts.

Measure 5 will be phased in over five years, with the tax limits dropping gradually. For that reason, the amount of money the state must find for replacement revenue goes up each year. While $625 million was the replacement bill for 1991/93, the state will need to budget about $1.2 billion in 1993/95 and $2.9 billion in 1995/97 to make up the lost property tax revenues.

Faced with these daunting numbers, the state did away with the basic school support program – state money that in previous years was distributed among Oregon school districts to supplement property tax revenues – to help come up with the replacement money. The net result is that while equalization may help some districts, there will be less overall money available for schools. As the legislature distributes the money more evenly, the richer districts will face the largest cuts, and voters in those districts will be prohibited by law from voting to tax themselves to raise operating money for their schools.

Implications for the Portland Area

The implications for the Portland metropolitan area are significant. In the past, families could choose to live in areas known for good schools and strong school support. Some people preferred the well supported Lake Oswego schools. Others avoided the financially troubled Reynolds school district. But with the passage of Measure 5, most of the school districts in the Portland metro area have had and will continue to have significant budget cuts.

Although for the most part the state squeaked through the first year of Measure 5's implementation, the traditionally richer school districts got less money. To cope, the Lake Oswego school district increased student fees, and announced cuts in driver's ed, industrial arts, foreign languages and physical education. The Portland School Board announced cuts of $5.3 million in their 1991/92 budget. A variety of administrative and support services were chopped by the budget ax, including expenses for maintenance, the central office, new equipment, and construction. Services for students at risk – like counseling and tutoring – were also cut.

If the state does not revamp the current tax system, cuts in future years will be far more severe. When Barbara Roberts submitted her 1993/95 budget in December, 1992, it included $520 million in elementary and secondary school budget cuts. That was about 10% less than what would have been needed statewide to maintain school programs at their current level. And the cuts come at a time when enrollments are growing.

Beaverton is a case in point. School administrators in Beaverton – where enrollments are soaring – were distressed by the numbers in the Roberts budget. Gail Kinsey Hill explained in the December 3, 1992 *Oregonian*:

> In Beaverton, where high growth rates are pushing up costs, the consequences could be staggering. School officials estimate that they may have to cut $24 million to $32 million from the $155 million they need next year to keep schools operating at current levels.

These figures take three factors into account: soaring enrollments, the proposed budget, and "depleted budget reserves." The impact of Roberts's proposed cuts would be severe in Beaverton. In a worst case scenario,

> ...343 teachers, almost 30 percent of the total; 69 support-staff members; and 19 administrators would lose their jobs. Athletics, elementary school band programs and driver's education also would go. Class sizes would increase to 35 to 45 students from 30 or fewer.

As for Portland, unless the legislature can come up with new revenue sources, the district could be looking at a $50.8 million cut in 1993/94.

The Bond Bandwagon

Some school districts are trying to raise additional funds by passing bond measures. For bonded indebtedness – where the money is used for construction, equipment, or maintenance – is exempt from Measure 5 limits. In some cases, districts truly need to build new schools. In others instances, districts are proposing bond measures to cover expenses that once came out of their general fund budgets. After reporting that "Oregon voters rejected nine of 19 school bond levy requests" on March 23, 1993, Bill Graves explained the strategy in the March 24, 1993 *Oregonian*:

> ...districts are turning to bonds for even small capital costs so that declining general funds can be reserved for operations....Bonds offer the only local option they have left to raise money.
>
> The Lake Oswego School District...asked to sell $4 million worth of bonds for roof repairs, computers, overhead projectors and other maintenance and equipment. The request passed 5,176 to 4,554. In previous years, the district paid for most of those expenses out of its general fund.

Passing bond levies can help, but they only serve to soften the budget cut blow. They are not the way out of the school funding crisis.

The Uncertain Future

Given the great uncertainty surrounding tax increases, bond measures and the final budget for 1993/95, it is hard to predict what the future holds. In the past, school officials have made dire predictions which did not necessarily come to pass. But few would deny that school support is at risk and in flux. What was considered a "good" Portland area school in 1990 could become a school with far more limited programs in 1995. Student/teacher ratios might go up, building maintenance might go down, and the overall educational opportunities for Portland area children may be severely diminished.

That said, readers who want the full scoop on Measure 5 should be sure to read *The Saga of Measure Five*, which starts on page 153. Others can read on, recognizing that the picture for schools could change radically, as Oregon implements Measure 5, and as Oregonians decide on new tax proposals.

Multiple Choice School Districts

In addition to the uncertainties of school funding, there is another complication in describing the public school offerings in the Portland metropolitan area. Portland is a crazy quilt of school districts. It can make for a challenging multiple choice problem for school-seeking parents:

▸ In June, 1991, the Oregon Department of Education counted 53 separate school districts in Washington, Clackamas and Multnomah counties.

▸ They include large districts, like the Portland Public Schools (PPS), which serve almost 57,000 students, as well as very small districts, like the Bonneville district, which serves only about 25 elementary students.

▸ Over the years, Portland grew by annexing adjacent unincorporated areas. For this reason, the school district lines seem oddly drawn. For example, some people who live in Portland are actually in the Beaverton school district. Other Portlanders live in the Centennial, David Douglas, Parkrose, Reynolds, Riverdale or Sauvie Island school districts.

▸ Some of the littlest districts, like Bonneville and Riverdale, only go through the eighth grade. They provide the older children with tuition vouchers that can be used to attend high school in other districts. But as we'll see, recent state legislation will encourage these small districts to merge with neighboring districts by 1996.

Making School Choices

It's best to study a bit if you want to make the right choice. There are many good sources of information for those who want to bone up on metro area schools. Since we can't describe each school, we offer the following suggestions:

▸ Just for the asking, school districts will send you a packet of materials. They typically include a detailed map, so you can determine boundary lines for each school, as well as detailed information on policies and programs.

► *A Comprehensive Guide to Family Resources and Services in Portland*, a June 1992 publication of The Family Resource Group, lists all the schools in Multnomah, Washington and Clackamas Counties. It includes an address and telephone number for each school, along with information on school size and grade levels.

► Each year, the Portland Public Schools publish a series of school profiles.

   ► The *Elementary School Profiles* include a "school-by-school report of basic skills tests results." The report also has brief data on enrollment, teacher/staff size, special programs, physical facilities, attendance, and discipline at each school.

   ► The *Middle School Profiles* present the same information for Portland's middle schools. In Portland, middle schools offer grades six through eight.

   ► The *High School Profiles* provide information on the ten high schools in the Portland School District. The report provides data for each school on enrollment, minority attendance, school personnel, facilities, special programs, graduating seniors, dropout rates, and suspensions. It also includes some descriptive information on specific school programs and alternative schools.

► Another good source on the Portland Public Schools is *The School Tool* by Donna Hughey and Karen Minkel. As they explain, "*The School Tool* is a resource that describes many of the programs and policies of the Portland School District and provides some helpful information about each school in the district." It's a good source for details on everything from the PPS absence policy and testing practices to art education and the teen parent program. School "snapshots" include a few paragraphs on each school's activities, along with relevant facts, like whether the building is wheelchair accessible and the 1991/92 enrollment figures.

The School Tool and the *Profiles* supplement each other nicely. Those who want all the available information on the PPS might want to read them in tandem. Finally, perhaps the best source for the latest school information is always other parents.

Generally Speaking

All Oregon schools must offer special programs for talented and gifted children, so you'll find TAG programs in every Portland area public school system. Standardized and achievement tests, visual and performing arts screenings, and recommendations are used to identify the top 3-5% of the students for enrollment in the TAG programs.

Kindergarten is offered by Portland area public schools, but public kindergarten programs are fairly recent additions to the mandated programs in the state of Oregon. For that reason, many pre-schools offer kindergarten classes, and a good number of children attend private kindergarten before entering first grade at public school.

So Where Are the Best Schools?

Given the uncertainties of school funding, the large number of school districts in the metro area, and the fact that such comments are inherently subjective, it is very tricky to talk about "good" schools and "problem" schools. But we'll take a stab at it anyway, and caution you to do your own checking if you happen to be school shopping. We'll start with a look at current SAT results for metro area schools.

Making Sense of the SAT

SAT scores are not necessarily the best indicator of school quality or student performance. But they are one measure, and they can help identify the schools that have a large number of college-bound students.

To determine the metro area schools with the highest SAT scores, we did an informal telephone survey. In some cases, data was available for individual high schools. In others, the data was for school districts. The chart lists metro area high schools and/or school districts with a combined average score of 900 or more. National and all-Oregon scores are also listed for comparative purposes.

1991/92 Metro Area Average SAT Scores (Above 900)

High School (HS) or School District (SD)	Verbal	Math	Total	% Tested
Portland SD	426	479	905	52%
Lincoln HS	496	526	1022	81%
Wilson HS	444	489	933	73%
Beaverton SD	450	505	955	55%
Beaverton HS	443	511	954	57%
Sunset HS	467	516	983	60%
Aloha HS	438	484	922	46%
Lake Oswego SD	460	521	981	83%
Lakeridge HS	452	518	970	86%
Lake Oswego HS	467	523	990	80%
Gladstone HS	471	492	963	34%
Hillsboro HS	437	495	932	48%
North Clackamas SD	464	504	968	NA
Oregon City HS	427	477	904	33%
Sherwood HS	445	492	937	49%
Tigard HS	446	501	947	49%
West Linn HS	460	516	976	67%
Oregon	439	486	925	55%
National	423	476	899	42%

Top Scores

Before we discuss the metro area scores, we must mention that Oregon students who took the SAT test did better than their classmates in the 23 states that use this college entrance test widely. Comparisons are a bit tricky, since states where few students take the test tend to have higher overall scores. Oregon came out on top when compared with states in which more than 40% of the seniors took the SAT. And as we've seen, 55% of Oregon's seniors took it.

The same trends are seen in the metro area scores. For example, Lincoln High posted the highest average combined score: 1022. That is especially significant because 81% of the seniors took the test. Lakeridge High had a combined average score of 970, but 86% of the Lakeridge seniors took the exam. At Sunset High School, where 60% of the seniors took the SAT, the average was 983.

One word of caution: in 1990/91, nationwide SAT scores were the lowest they'd been since the College Board began administering the test, and 1991/92 scores were the second lowest. So while some metro area schools came out on top, overall SAT performance is at a rather low level.

Testing for Everyone

What about the students who are not necessarily college-bound? How are they doing? In an effort to find out, the state began in 1991 to test all Oregon students in 3rd, 5th, 8th and 11th grade. They are tested annually in basic skills, and on a rotating basis in other subjects. We haven't the space to include all the metro area results, but include the 1992 average scores for 11th graders on the next pages.

The third column, SES, is for the school's "socioeconomic rank." An SES index for each school was determined from a combination of indicators, including the school's attendance rate, the level of parent education, whether students who enroll in the fall complete the year, and family income measures. The SES indices are then ranked in order from lowest to highest to determine each school's SES rank.

As materials from the Oregon Department of Education explain, SES ranks help schools "determine how well their students are performing compared with schools serving similar student populations." SES ranks underline the fact that "some schools may have greater obstacles to overcome in teaching more disadvantaged students than others."

Few educators are fans of standardized testing, and there are many critics of the statewide tests. As with SAT results, we caution you to consider the scores as just one indication of student performance and school success.

Metro Area Statewide Testing Scores for 11th Graders, 1992

High School	Math	Reading	SES
Portland:			
Benson HS	237	235	183
Cleveland HS	233	231	134
Franklin HS	230	228	95
Grant HS	232	232	193
Jefferson HS	227	227	29
Lincoln HS	238	236	230
Madison HS	230	227	43
Marshall HS	231	229	8
Metro Learning Center	234	236	210
Roosevelt HS	232	230	10
Wilson HS	237	235	222
Beaverton:			
Aloha HS	233	233	211
Beaverton HS	235	234	219
Sunset HS	238	237	226
Gresham:			
Gresham HS	233	232	197
Sam Barlow HS	234	234	208
Hillsboro:			
Glencoe HS	234	232	164
Hillsboro HS	235	233	203
Lake Oswego:			
Lake Oswego HS	239	237	229
Lakeridge HS	238	237	231
North Clackamas:			
Clackamas HS	237	234	216
Milwaukie HS	233	231	121
Rex Putnam HS	235	231	200

Metro Area Statewide Testing Scores for 11th Graders, 1992

High School	Math	Reading	SES
Centennial HS	233	232	136
David Douglas HS	231	230	151
Gladstone HS	233	234	192
Oregon City HS	233	232	188
Parkrose HS	231	230	107
Reynolds HS	232	232	146
Sherwood HS	233	232	199
Tigard HS	236	235	214
West Linn HS	236	234	227
Highest Possible	300	300	232
Lowest Possible	150	150	1
Oregon Average	233	233	
Oregon Midpoint			116

In the PPS, average scores at Benson, Lincoln, the Metropolitan Learning Center and Wilson surpass the statewide average of 233. The other PPS high schools match or fall under the state average. Most of the suburban high schools score above 233, while averages for the other school districts within the city of Portland tend to be 233 or just below.

"Feeder Schools"

While test scores are by no means a perfect measure, some parents consider them when selecting elementary and middle schools. For each school feeds into a specific high school. Some students are always new each year, but many come up through the same school system, and success in high school is in part tied to the basic skills that are taught in the lower grades. Based on that logic, those in search of "good" elementary and middle schools might look first in southwest Portland, Lake Oswego, West Linn, or Beaverton. More than half of the high school seniors in those areas take the SAT, and their 11th graders perform well on the statewide tests.

More Test Scores

If you want test score comparisons for the lower grades, here's where to look:

▸ Test results from the statewide testing of 3rd, 5th, and 8th graders are available both at individual schools and from the Oregon Department of Education in Salem. Usually *The Oregonian* prints summary results when they become available each August.

▸ The Portland *Profiles,* which we described above, include test results from the *Portland Achievement Levels Tests of Reading and Mathematics.* This test is given to all PPS 3rd through 8th graders in both the fall and spring of each year.

Particularly Portland: The Lower Grades

Let's take a more careful look at the Portland Public Schools. For as the test scores suggest, there is a greater difference among individual Portland schools than there is among individual schools in the suburbs. You'll find a PPS map with approximate school locations on pages 236-237. For details on specific school boundaries, check with the PPS Department of Public Information.

The *Environmental Scan,* a report prepared by Portland Future Focus in September, 1990, listed the best and worst elementary and middle schools in Portland. They used data that compared fall and spring test scores on the *Portland Achievement Levels Tests of Reading and Mathematics* over a five year period. Based on that criteria, they found that:

▸ The best elementary schools were Ainsworth, Bridlemile, Chapman, Stephenson, Smith, Hayhurst, and Alameda.
▸ The best middle schools were Markham (now called Jackson), West Sylvan, and Robert Gray.
▸ The worst elementary schools were Humboldt, James John, King, Beach, Peninsula, Ball, and Woodlawn.
▸ The worst middle schools were George, Portsmouth, and Whitaker.

For those unfamiliar with Portland or the Portland Public Schools, the results are striking. Only one school on the best list – Alameda in northeast – is on the east side. And the worst schools are all located in either inner north or northeast Portland. But not all east side schools are in trouble. Educators at two elementary schools that feed into Grant High School won national honors in 1991: the principal at Boise-Eliot received the Reader's Digest American Hero in Education Award, and a teacher at Fernwood Middle School won a Presidential Award for Excellence in Science and Mathematics Teaching.

Particularly Portland: The High Schools

The *High School Profiles* have a wealth of information. Here's a sampling from the 1990-91 edition:

▸ 35% of the city's seniors planned to go on to a four year college or university. Another 31% planned to combine a part-time job with attendance at a four year, two year or community college. (But the report cautions that "many students do not follow through on expected plans.")

▸ With 58% planning to attend a four year college or university, Lincoln High had the highest proportion of college-bound students. Wilson was next, with 51% college-bound. Grant, with 42%, was third. The other Portland high schools sent between 14% and 38% of their seniors on to four year colleges or universities.

▸ Wilson, with 1,600 students, was the biggest high school. Roosevelt, with 982, was the smallest.

▸ Benson had the highest stability index. That's the percent of students who enrolled before October 1 who were still enrolled in June. Benson's stability index was 88.9%. Wilson, at 84.5%, and Lincoln, at 80.7%, were next on the stability index list.

▸ Jefferson High headed the list for the highest percent absent.

▸ Cleveland, Madison and Roosevelt had the worst dropout rates – and thus the most dropouts. Benson had the fewest dropouts.

▸ Jefferson, Grant and Roosevelt suspended the most students. Lincoln had the fewest suspensions.

▸ 67% of the Jefferson students were from minority groups. Benson, Grant, Roosevelt and Madison each had minority populations of about 35%. Wilson and Lincoln had the lowest percentage of minority students: just about 17% of the student body. (For the purposes of the report, Native, African, Asian, and Hispanic Americans were considered minority groups.)

Particularly Portland: Alternative Programs

Finally, the Portland Public Schools offer a large range of alternative school options. One option is the magnet schools, which specialize in areas like the visual and performing arts, international studies, technical and vocational training, business, and foreign languages. Another is the immersion programs. Although there are not always enough places for all of those who apply, immersion Spanish is at taught at Ainsworth Elementary School, and immersion Japanese at Richmond Elementary. The Metropolitan Learning Center, for K-12 students, offers basic skills training along with a chance for students to pursue individual interests through independent learning. Finally, the PPS offer a variety of special programs for those who have not been successful in school, because of behavior or learning difficulties.

Multicultural Studies

In 1980, the PPS initiated the Multicultural/Multiethnic Education Project. The program has identified six ethnic or cultural groups: African-American, American Indian, Asian-American, European-American, Hispanic-American, and Pacific Island-American. Baseline Essays are being prepared to help bring teachers up to speed on the history, culture and contributions of each group. The African-American essays have received national attention. But they are controversial in both their content and their tone, and many have called for their revision. We can't review the whole debate here, but encourage interested readers to call the district's Multicultural/Multiethnic Education Office for the latest information.

Seriously Speaking

Before we move on, we need to mention two unrelated but noteworthy topics:

▸ The PPS have their own police force of about 20 officers. During the 1991/92 school year, school police confiscated about 30 guns. Although they deal with situations that range from arson and assault to suspected child abuse and drugs, the problems in Portland are less extensive than in many other urban school districts.

▸ In 1992, condoms became available at Portland high schools. They are not dispensed freely – students must meet first with health counselors. Counselors are required to ask about the student's sexual activity, urge abstinence, explain condom use, discuss sexually-transmitted diseases, and encourage that the student talk with his or her parents.

Mapping the Portland School District

The map on the following pages is from the Portland Public Schools "Directory for Schools, Support Facilities" for 1992-93. It is included to help you identify approximate school locations. As the directory emphasizes, "For specific school attendance areas, please call the Portland School District's Department of Public Information and Communication."

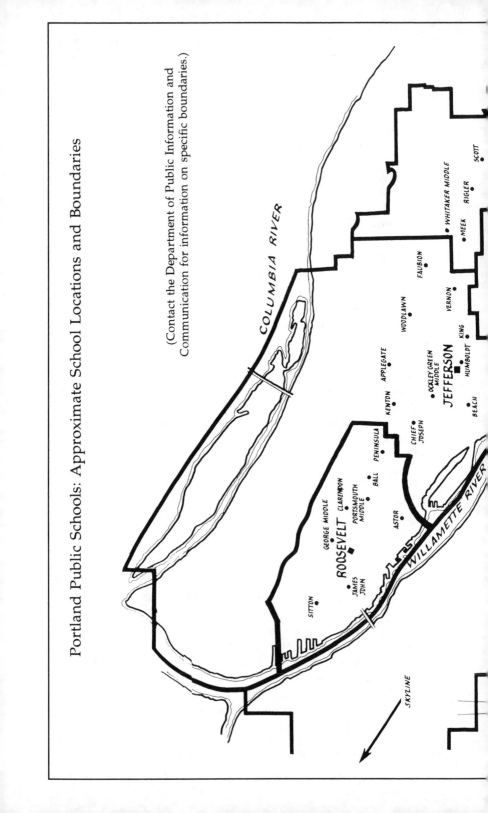

Portland Public Schools: Approximate School Locations and Boundaries

(Contact the Department of Public Information and Communication for information on specific boundaries.)

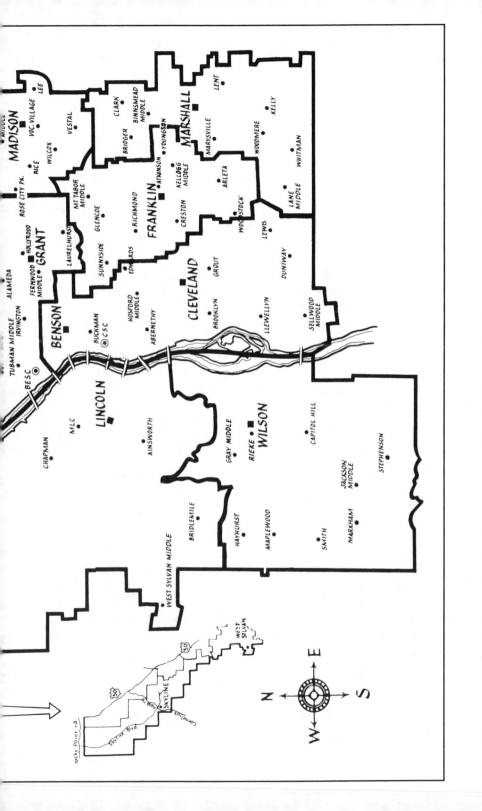

Public or Private?

What about private school options? *A Comprehensive Guide to Family Resources and Services in Portland* lists more than 150 private schools in the tri-county area, and *The School Tool* lists 42 private schools that are in Portland. But when you speak with parents of school age children, you learn that there are really only a few options for those who seek a private, secular education for their kids. That's because many of the private schools offer pre-school and kindergarten programs only, and most have a religious affiliation. For secular choices that go beyond kindergarten, the Portland area has a limited number of choices, including a Spanish immersion school, two French schools, a Waldorf school, and a few Montessori schools, as well as a handful of private day and prep schools.

Why so few choices? Perhaps because the Portland public schools compare well when matched with other urban areas. In fact, Portland is unusual among cities in terms of public school attendance. As David Sarasohn explained in the March 28, 1993 *Oregonian,* "one of the most striking things about Portland is the number of public-school kids whose parents could afford to send them someplace else." But many observers, like Sarasohn, predict that Measure 5 cuts will prompt parents to reconsider private options, and that the private school picture could change radically in the next few years. Indeed, area private schools are already reporting that applications are up and available places are limited.

Home Sweet Home

A number of metro area children attend neither public nor private school. They are the home schoolers. According to the Parents Education Association, their number is growing steadily. Staff at the association estimate that there are about 5,000 home schooled children in Oregon. The regulations here are comparatively lenient, which is one of the reasons that the state has a large contingent of home schoolers. As long as they pass an annual test, they may continue to pursue their studies at home.

Up next is a brief look at what's *On the School Horizon,* for Measure 5 isn't the only change that we must consider.

On the School Horizon

The state legislature passed two bills in 1991 that promise dramatic educational changes. One was a school consolidation bill, and the other was the Katz Plan, nicknamed for Mayor Vera Katz, who introduced the bill when she served in the Oregon House of Representatives. The Katz Plan is more formally known as HB 3565: The Oregon Educational Act for the 21st Century. Portlanders face a third change, for the Portland Public Schools hired a new superintendent in 1992. We look next at these developments.

Matchmaker, Matchmaker

The consolidation bill directs localities with separate elementary and high school districts to unify them by 1996, or lose state funding. Once implemented, the bill will decrease the number of Portland area school districts. Parents, teachers, administrators and children will need to adjust as policies, procedures, curricula, and perhaps even school locations change.

Vera's Progressive Plan

HB 3565, a controversial set of educational reforms to be phased in by the year 2010, promises to revolutionize primary and secondary education in Oregon. Its main components are:

- Head Start programs will be available for all eligible children.
- Primary schools (K-3) will be ungraded.
- Students will be assessed after grade 10, and on demonstrating their competency, will attain a Certificate of Initial Mastery (CIM).
- Students with their CIM will select either college prep programs, leading to a Certificate of Advanced Mastery (CAM), or programs geared to technical job training.
- Performance-based assessments will be developed and used to measure student progress and mastery at grades 3, 5, 8 and 10.
- Intervention strategies will assist students who need help attaining the CIM or CAM.

▸ Parents may choose a different school if their children don't make satisfactory progress in their current school.
▸ Students with their CIM may choose to attend any accredited school for 11th and 12th grade.
▸ An Oregon Report Card will measure school performance.
▸ The school year will be extended to 220 days.
▸ The business community will help design and assist with job training programs.

Progressive or Problematic?

The law has its share of supporters and critics. Proponents insist that the current system is simply not working, and that the new law is a big step in the right direction. Critics believe that the most radical component – the choice between academic and technical programs after the Certificate of Initial Mastery – is little more than tracking. Proponents see 11th and 12th graders who can move easily between the two programs. Critics see stigmatized students who may find, years later, that they lack the academic skills necessary to obtain additional education. There are many other concerns. They include the performance assessment tools; the fairness and mechanics of the school choice option and the transportation plan it might require; mandated parent involvement; and the funding – or lack of it. Given the current budget woes, proponents worry that the plan's funding will be at risk each year.

The 1991 legislature did set aside $2 million to begin implementation, and the first Oregon Report Card was released in September, 1992. In 1996, 50% of the eligible children in the state are supposed to be enrolled in Head Start, and the school year is to be lengthened from 175 to 185 days. But several groups are gearing up in an effort to amend the legislation. For example, the Oregon Education Association, which represents many of the state's teachers, does not favor lengthening the school year. The OEA also opposes the certificates of mastery components of the plan.

The Oregon Educational Act for the 21st Century has received national attention in both the press and government circles. As articles in *The New York Times* and *Education Week* attest, many besides those in Oregon will be watching.

Portland's New Superintendent

Matthew Prophet, who was Portland's successful and well-respected School Superintendent for more than ten years, retired in June, 1992. After a national search, the school board hired John E. Bierwirth, who came to Portland from New York, where he was Superintendent of the Sachem Central School District. Board members described him as a "rising star" and both community leaders and teacher organizations were enthusiastic about his selection. It's a little too soon to comment on his progress, but as we've seen, he clearly has many challenges ahead.

We've looked at the history, and the geography, and the people who are here. And we've taken a look at the government, growth and planning, environmental issues, places to live, and the schools. Clearly, they all contribute to Portland's quality of life. But they can't do it alone. We look next at some of the cultural offerings in the Rose City.

Expose Yourself

To

Portland

Not For Tourists Only

From Artquake To Zoograss

Performing Tonight. . .

Multiple Museums

Galleries Galore

In the Public Eye

Let's Get Literary

Movies 'n Music

An Architectural Antipasto

"Meet the Press"

Not For Tourists Only

If you started this book at the beginning, you already know quite a bit about Portland's livability. Portlanders can quickly commute – perhaps on non-polluting light rail – to a job downtown, while their kids enjoy an affordable home and good schools in a practically perfect neighborhood. But there's more to livability than that, and Portland has much to offer in the way of cultural activities, restaurants, parks, sports, and the other amenities that add joy, texture, depth and just plain fun to life in the Rose City.

Unlike New Yorkers, who go to the Empire State Building only when escorting out-of-town visitors, Portlanders actively partake of the city's offerings. Natives, newcomers and visitors rub shoulders at Saturday Market and in microbrew pubs, at the carousels and on the slopes of Mt. Hood, on the trails of Forest Park and at Rose Festival events. Portland guidebook writers clearly understand this. Their books are as useful to the seasoned Portlander as they are to the casual tourist. Rather than trying to repeat what the guidebooks already do so well, we refer you to a few of our favorites:

▸ *Portland Best Places* (Sasquatch Books)

The subtitle to *Portland Best Places* describes this guidebook as "a discriminating guide to Portland's restaurants, lodgings, shopping, nightlife, arts, sights, and outings." *Portland Best Places* is edited by Stephanie Irving and Kim Carlson, with an introduction by David Sarasohn. The first edition came out in 1990, and the second was published in 1992. In the words of *The Oregonian's* Jonathan Nicholas, "This is the guide that makes all the others roll over and play dead."

▸ *Portland: an Informal History & Guide* (Western Imprints, Oregon Historical Society)

We mentioned this guide by Terence O'Donnell and Robert Vaughan when we recommended history books on page 8. It was last revised in 1984 but it is well worth a read today. Architecture buffs will find it is a perfect book to take along on their meandering walks.

▸ *Portland Rainy Day Guide* (Chronicle Books)

With its 1983 publication date, Katlin Smith's *Portland Rainy Day Guide* is also an older guide, but it is still useful. For example, some of the stores on the Hawthorne Street walk may be gone, but they've been replaced by others that are equally appealing. The "puddle walks" and rainy day hikes are timeless. And you'll find that it could just as easily be called the *Portland Any Day Guide*, for the sights and suggestions will definitely be fun in the sun. This pocket-sized guidebook fits an incredible amount of information into 125 pages. Used ones do show up in the bookstores, or check the library. Just be sure you to call ahead to verify times and places.

▸ *Powell's Walking Map of Downtown Portland* (Powell's City of Books)

Powell's Walking Map of Downtown Portland is a free brochure that unfolds to a map on one side and sightseeing information on the other. The map is easy to read, with extensive information on street and building names, the MAX light rail route, store locations, parking garages, park locations and sights to see. Many Portlanders stash a Powell's map in their purse, briefcase or backpack, for easy access at any time. And for the newcomer, the info on the back provides a great introduction to the downtown.

▸ *Nancy Macklin's Map of Portland* (Nancy Macklin Maps)

This 1992 map, which is available at local bookstores, can almost take the place of a guidebook, especially for those who are familiar with the area. It is hand lettered, and shows Macklin's personal recommendations for "quality shopping, eating and sight-seeing." It includes detailed maps of downtown, Northwest, SE Hawthorne Street, Lloyd Center, and the Pearl District. It also includes day trip recommendations and some fast facts about Portland.

While we'll leave it to the maps and guidebooks to catalog all the attractions that Portland has to offer, the sections which follow include information – some brief, some more detailed – for those who seek both edifying events and frolicking fun in the Rose City.

From Artquake To Zoograss

In the course of writing this book, we collected reams of material. Many folders were literally bulging with information, but six topics weighed in with the most data. They were the files on schools, taxes, growth and planning, crime, the environment and the arts. Having addressed the more serious topics, we turn to arts and culture in the Rose City.

Perhaps we ought to rephrase that, for the arts in Portland face serious problems. When research began for this book in the fall of 1990, the arts scene here was getting rave reviews. But as we complete the final draft in late 1992 and early 1993, both artists and audiences share fears for the future.

"The Way It Was"

Let's go back briefly to the late '80s and early '90s. Portland had won the 1988 U.S. Conference of Mayors City Livability Award for development and support of the arts, and arts events were among the reasons that Portland was on so many of the best city lists. Though they wrote for different audiences – from those who read *Willamette Week* to those who prefer *Travel & Leisure* – critics and observers agreed in praising Portland for the quality, quantity and variety of cultural offerings available. Here's a sample of what was being said:

> Yes, there is a magic to Portland. Perhaps it comes from being nestled in a verdant valley at the confluence of two beautiful rivers. We do, indeed, have a superior cultural and recreational community. Our citizens have a holistic concept of "the bottom line." It includes food for the spirit as well as dollars in the bank. Our citizens don't just watch and support the arts, our citizens live the arts in our community theaters, art shows, bands, choral groups, and dance companies. We're talented, hardworking, and we're marvelous at enjoying ourselves. I can understand the rest of the country starting to sit up and take notice.
>
> Mike Lindberg, introducing the Entertainment Section of *The First Portland Catalogue*, 1987.

Word is spreading about the city's sophisticated cultural milieu, a scale and skyline that architecture critics call a singular success in American urban design, cafes, ethnic restaurants and far more galleries than a city of less than a half-million people should hope to have.

You can walk Portland end-to-end: call in at Powell's, a warehouse-size bookstore (with a cafe, for literary discussions), poke around the artists' quarter known as The Pearl, and check out the new Performing Arts Center, along with the stylish boutiques and Victorian neighborhoods....

Travel & Leisure, January, 1991.

Like George [Ziskind, a jazz pianist], most of my other friends in the Big Apple, knowing my fondness for concerts, plays, lectures and art galleries, wondered how I would survive in cultureless Oregon.

I wondered myself. But after only a few months in the Northwest, I came to see that although Portland had none of the arts superstars of New York, although Manhattan sheltered an incomparably greater density of talent, Portland was by no means a cultural Sahara. I soon found plenty to do and see, and plenty to write about.

Terry Ross, "Diary of a Culture Junkie: Partial Notes From a Year of Obsession," *Willamette Week*, September 6-12, 1990.

Warning Signs

But warning signs began to appear. Measure 5 cutbacks took their toll on public support for both the visual and performing arts community. Several theater companies regretfully went out of business, victims of long-term deficits, the recession, and a particularly tough winter in 1991, when terrible weather and the Persian Gulf war cut badly into ticket sales. And *Arts Plan 2000+: A Cultural Plan for Portland and the Surrounding Region* was completed, bringing both good news and bad. The report's first page previewed the findings:

Research – involving surveys, interviews, public meetings, and task force activities – revealed the extensive range and quality in arts and cultural offerings in the Tri-County region. It also showed that citizens' participation in the arts and their interest in cultural amenities as part of their lifestyles was equal to or greater than what can be found in many other cities. Financial support for the arts by both the public and private sectors was substantially below national norms according to several comparative indicators. This has led to severe problems for the health of the arts community including accumulated and operating deficits among major organizations.

Arts Plan 2000+

Arts Plan 2000+, or AP2+, was initiated by City Commissioner Mike Lindberg and the Metropolitan Arts Commission, and prepared by consultants from the Wolf Organization of Cambridge, Massachusetts. The result is a long-range plan for arts and culture in the Portland metropolitan area, which addresses arts organizations and agencies, human and financial resources, arts education, public involvement, cultural diversity, facilities, and public art.

While not everyone agrees with the plan's more than 60 recommendations, the report is chock full of useful information, including the results of a survey on participation in arts activities and attitudes towards arts programming. Here are some survey highlights:

- ▸ 51% of those surveyed "attended a live performing arts or entertainment event" during the past year, for which they paid an admission charge.
- ▸ 34% visited "a museum, science center or art gallery" in the past year.
- ▸ By comparison, 33% attended "a professional or semi-professional sports event" in the same period.
- ▸ 57% of those attending performing arts events were considered "heavy attenders," as they went to seven or more event a year. Portland had more heavy attenders than many other communities surveyed.
- ▸ 80% agreed with the statement "City and County government should continue to support cultural activi-

ties in our community." That included an impressive 76% of the "non-attenders."

But these encouraging statistics don't tell the full story. The report also notes that:

- ▸ Several arts and cultural organizations disbanded or went broke during the past few years.
- ▸ 11 of the 17 largest cultural organizations have serious deficit problems.
- ▸ No long-term funding plan is in place to support the operation of the Portland Center for the Performing Arts. Instead, there is a perception that this well-attended center should be self-supporting. But "no comparable facility in the U.S. operates on such a 'break even' basis and...such expectations are not realistic."
- ▸ "Portland's public art collection is something of a hodge-podge....lacking the kind of coherence and depth which normally characterizes a collection."
- ▸ Private giving to support the arts is comparatively low in Portland. While the percentage of those contributing is "within national norms," the dollar amounts contributed are comparatively low for both businesses and individuals. And big givers here give less than big givers in other comparable cities.
- ▸ Public support is comparatively low too. The report included the following figures for per capita arts expenditures in selected cities:

Atlanta, GA:	$11.80
Winston-Salem, NC	$8.54
Dallas, TX	$5.98
Portland, OR	$1.30

The report's 60 recommendations can't be summarized here. But we mention a few to indicate the directions suggested, beginning with a quote on what must come first. The emphasis is in the original report:

The consultants believe that the cultural sector's most urgent need at the present time is not more public or private funds. These are merely symptoms of a more basic requirement. The greatest need is developing a corps of active, prominent community leaders for the arts. This does not mean leaders who place the arts on a list of ten or fifteen priorities for the community. It means individuals who personally champion the arts and culture, who provide leadership through their own financial contributions, by their public statements, by their attendance, and by their willingness to articulate why the arts are critical to Portland and the region's future. **Without such leadership, the vision, the goals, and the programs identified in this plan cannot be realized and the financial resources required cannot be marshalled.**

Other recommendations include regional, rather than city or county, funding for the arts; rental subsidies for local organizations that use the Portland Center for the Performing Arts; improving the financial stability of arts groups; improving arts education; and comprehensive, regional publicity to encourage wider attendance.

The Show Must Go On

While the arts clearly face a critical juncture, our bulging files on cultural offerings in Portland nevertheless attest to the wide range of events here. There are so many we could mention, like the prestigious and well-attended Portland Arts and Lectures series and our world-class jazz concerts. James DePriest and the Oregon Symphony Orchestra at the Arlene Schnitzer Concert Hall, and the down-home Peanut Butter & Jam noon concerts in Pioneer Courthouse Square. The Portland Art Museum and all the art galleries. Chamber Music Northwest and the Portland Baroque Orchestra.

There's also the Oregon Ballet Theatre and the Oregon Children's Theatre. The Portland Gay Men's Chorus and the Tears of Joy Theatre. The authors' readings that are scheduled practically every evening of the year, and the annual poetry festival. The Portland Opera and the Oregon Shakespeare Festival/Portland. Waterfront concerts on summer weekends, and Zoograss, the Zoo's bluegrass concerts on weekday summer evenings. Artquake, September's performing and visual arts festival, and LitEruption, the spring literary festival. The list could go on and on.

What's Happening Where

While the AP2+ recommended establishing a region-wide, comprehensive source of arts information, many sources are currently available. If you're new to Portland, an easy way to get a feel for arts offerings is to pick up a copy of *Willamette Week* or the Arts and Entertainment section of Friday's *Oregonian*. The AP2+ survey found that 64% of the arts attenders used *The Oregonian* as their primary source for arts info. 12% used *Willamette Week*, and another 12% turned to the public TV and radio stations. Other sources for arts information that were mentioned by respondents were mail from arts organizations, word of mouth, and *The Portland Downtowner*. Despite the funding woes here, there's still plenty to do.

And Then There's Artquake

Another great way to learn about arts offerings in Portland is to go to Artquake. Artquake is the annual arts festival that unfolds each Labor Day weekend, on Broadway between Pioneer Courthouse Square and the Portland Center for the Performing Arts. About 200,000 attended the festival in 1992.

There's something for everyone. Artists and craftspeople display and sell their works, while their compatriots perform at scheduled, formal events or informally on the streets. Mimes mingle with jugglers, dancers peek around sculptures, authors read from their works, jazz bands play. In the children's art area, kids do improvisation while others try their hand with an airbrush or a lump of clay. Portlanders of all persuasions come out for one more outdoor festival before the summer officially ends.

Virtually all of the city's arts organizations are represented along Broadway, enabling the passersby to find out about upcoming events. It's the perfect place to get your name on the mailing list of your favorite group, pick up a schedule, or sign up to volunteer. A few hours at Artquake will introduce you to more arts offerings than you'll ever have time to enjoy.

Performing Tonight . . .

Whether your tastes run to jazz, classical, rock or country music – or something in between – chances are you can hear it live in Portland. If you prefer the stage, you can see classical ballet or modern dance; Shakespeare or a Broadway musical. While the club scene is varied and a few small theaters are still around, many performances are booked into the Portland Center for the Performing Arts. City boosters will proudly tell you about the performing arts in Portland, and the Center's financial situation is indicative of some of our arts funding problems. So let's take a look at one of the city's loveliest attractions.

Portland Center for the Performing Arts

The 1987 opening celebration program traces the Center's origins back to 1976, when a task force was asked to consider the need for additional performing arts space in Portland. Their recommendation called for at least three new theaters. When Mayor Connie McCready appointed the Performing Arts Center Committee in 1980, her charge to them was simple: "I'm not asking you to do another study. I'm asking you to build a performing arts center."

The story has many twists and turns: renovation plans that fell through, land acquisition problems, strikes, and the like. But Portland voters approved a $19 million bond measure in 1981, private donors contributed, and the city added some funding, enabling the Performing Arts Center Committee, under the direction the Chairman Ronald K. Ragen, to see it through to opening night.

The Portland Center for the Performing Arts, or PCPA, is under the jurisdiction of the Metropolitan Exposition-Recreation Commission, or MERC. MERC is a METRO commission. The PCPA is actually four theaters in three buildings:

- ▸ the Arlene Schnitzer Concert Hall – fondly called the Schnitz – a renovation of the old Paramount Theatre;
- ▸ the Intermediate Theatre, located in the New Theatre Building that opened in 1987, just across the street from the Schnitz;

▸ the Dolores Winningstad Theatre, sometimes called the Winnie, also in the new theatre complex;

▸ and the Portland Civic Auditorium, built in 1917 and renovated in 1968, and located on 3rd between Market and Clay.

You'll also hear people talking about the Performing Arts Center. That's an alternate name for the New Theatre Building. Indeed, many Portlanders confuse the whole Portland Center for the Performing Arts with the New Theatre Building/Performing Arts Center. PCPA staffers are considering ways to resolve the name confusion.

Voting With Their Feet?

But it's not keeping anyone away. By seat count, the PCPA is fourth largest in the United States. With almost one million tickets sold in 1990, the center is extremely well-attended. In fact, it's the fifth most popular performing arts center in the United States. And those that top the list are located in far bigger cities, like New York and Los Angeles.

But the Portland Center for the Performing Arts is also the only comparable facility that is expected to be self-supporting. In the same year that the Center opened its doors, voters refused to approve a 2% increase in the hotel/motel tax, which would have assured the PCPA stable operating funds. While some Portlanders are apparently voting with their feet when they attend performances at the PCPA, others are less enamored and refuse to support the Center with more tax dollars.

Blazers and Ballet

Revenues from the Memorial Coliseum, as administered by MERC, have been used to keep the PCPA afloat. But that arrangement will change soon, for the Trail Blazers are building a new arena, and will be managing the Coliseum – which means that by 1994 or 1995, the Coliseum revenues will no longer be available to bail out the PCPA.

METRO and MERC are committed to the long-term health and survival of the PCPA. In 1992, the Metro Arts Funding Task Force estimated that about $2.31 million is needed for

Center operating expenses, theater improvements, rent subsidies, and programming needs. METRO is considering a variety of measures, including an increase in the hotel/motel tax, a bond measure, a regional income tax and/or an admissions tax on tickets to entertainment events.

Many arts supporters would like to see a broad, regional tax plan put in place to address a variety of other needs too, including funds for libraries, greenspaces, historical societies, and the like. But the post-Measure 5 climate is difficult and voters may once again nix any new tax plans.

Bringing the House Down

The METRO Task Force included rent subsidies in its funding estimates. Until mid-1992, the companies that book space at the Center – like the Oregon Symphony Orchestra, the Oregon Shakespeare Festival/Portland, and the Portland Opera – were paying what were comparatively high rents. The PCPA couldn't afford to give them the rent discounts that are typically given to non-profit groups in other cities. Other groups that were once PCPA tenants, like the Music Theatre of Oregon, the Storefront Theatre, and the West Coast Chamber Orchestra, went out of business in 1991 because of financial problems that were caused in part by the high rents.

Fortunately, MERC and the Portland City Council came up with a plan to provide rent relief. But it uses some of the Coliseum revenues. Which means that they will dry up about a year earlier than originally anticipated. Most arts observers agree that the new rent arrangement was appropriate: you can't bring down the house if you can't pay the rent, and it is clearly in our long-term interest to keep our arts organizations afloat. But it makes METRO's search for arts funding all the more critical.

Happy Endings

The happy ending depicts the active performing arts groups surviving until a stable funding source is in place. It portrays the birth of new companies that draw even more arts attenders. The sad scenario shows arts organizations that are afraid to try anything new or experimental, for fear of a financial flop. It depicts some performing arts groups homeless and others disbanded, while the Center is mothballed for lack of operating dollars.

Those who juggle the figures want to see a solution in place by 1994. The Portland Center for the Performing Arts reports considerable economic impact, noting that "for every $20 ticket sold, an additional $55.80 is spent on restaurant meals, parking, clothing, babysitting, hotel rooms, etc." The *Arts Plan 2000+* survey found that 80% of those surveyed believe that municipal governments should support cultural activities. Let's hope the voters look at both the economic and the cultural benefits, and choose to support the arts the next time they have the chance.

"All That Jazz"

There are many world-class performers who do not usually play at the PCPA – like our jazz musicians. Back in August, 1986, *Oregon Magazine* quoted pianist Tom Grant, noting that "Portland probably ranks among the top five cities in the country in terms of the seriousness of the local jazz scene." More recently, Lynn Darroch wrote in the June 2, 1991 *Oregonian* that Portland has been called "the best jazz town on the West Coast."

This reputation comes in part courtesy of neighboring Gresham – the home of the Mt. Hood Festival of Jazz. On the festival's tenth birthday in 1991, about 28,000 people heard great jazz during its three day run in early August. The festival did post a loss in 1992, but organizers are committed to making the changes necessary to wipe out the red ink.

While the festival is great, the truth is that Portlanders can hear exceptional live jazz just about every night of the year, in various clubs around town. In her June 2, 1991 article, Darroch mentioned Tom Grant, Glen Moore, David Friesen and Dave Frishberg as "just a few of the virtuoso players who can be heard almost any night in Portland's nearly 20 jazz clubs." Writing again on Portland's "flourishing jazz community" in the July 27, 1992 *Oregonian,* Darroch mentions more "jazz immigrants with national reputations" like Red Mitchell, Leroy Vinnegar, Andrew Hill, Tad Weed, Andrei Kitaev, Bob West, Jessica Williams and Dick Berk. It's a great town if you love jazz.

Multiple Museums

...right here in Puddle City we have a dazzling array of museums. Whether your taste is vacuum cleaners, chronometers, talking trees, carousel menageries, or Renoirs, this town has a museum for you. Along with their variety of subjects and artifacts, the museums have one nice thing in common: They're all within easy reach. Several are in the heart of downtown; others are a quick bus or MAX hop from downtown, and only a few require a short car trip.

> Lois Allan, "Museums Galore!" *This Week Magazine,* March 20, 1991.

Pick up one of the guidebooks mentioned on pages 245-246 for the whole scoop on museums. Portland may not have museums of the stature and breadth of New York or Chicago, but there is an eclectic selection with enough to please both the "culture junkie" in you as well as your fun-loving kids. Here's a quick list to get you started:

- ▸ American Advertising Museum
- ▸ Children's Museum
- ▸ Cowboys Then and Now
- ▸ Jeff Morris Memorial Fire Museum
- ▸ Kidd's Toy Museum
- ▸ Metropolitan Center for Public Art
- ▸ Oregon Historical Society
- ▸ Oregon Jewish Museum
- ▸ Oregon Maritime Center and Museum
- ▸ Oregon Museum of Science and Industry
- ▸ Pittock Mansion
- ▸ Portland Art Museum
- ▸ Portland Carousel Museum
- ▸ Portland Maritime Museum
- ▸ Portland Police Museum
- ▸ State of Oregon Sports Hall of Fame and Museum
- ▸ Stark's Vacuum Cleaner Museum
- ▸ Washington County Museum
- ▸ World Forestry Center

And while they may not qualify as full-fledged museums, don't miss the following exotic downtown attractions:

- ▸ Nike Town, Nike's fancy store that seems more like a museum than a retail establishment;
- ▸ and the 24 Hour Church of Elvis – which may or may not be open and may or may not be in business – but is worth a visit to SW Ankeny to check it out.

As we write, two more projects are in the works. Oregon City hopes to be the site of a proposed End of the Oregon Trail Center. And the Evergreen AirVenture Museum plans to build near McMinnville. Evergreen already has the exhibit that will be the main draw: the Spruce Goose, also known as the Flying Boat. Built by Howard Hughes during World War II, the Spruce Goose is the world's largest airplane.

While we'll let you explore the more exotic collections on your own, here's some information on two of the bigger museums; those known affectionately as OMSI and PAM.

On to OMSI

Amidst totally appropriate hoopla, the Oregon Museum of Science and Industry moved to its new east side home in October, 1992. It's now almost three times bigger than it was in its old Washington Park location, making OMSI the fifth largest science museum in the nation. Attractions abound, including:

- ▸ six exhibit halls – one each for the earth, life, physical, space and information sciences, and one for changing exhibits
- ▸ two theaters – the giant screen OMNIMAX and the Murdock Sky Theater
- ▸ Discovery Space, an early childhood education area with lots of hands-on science for the littlest visitors
- ▸ an environmental hallway
- ▸ as well as lab areas for science demonstrations, classrooms, a restaurant, science store, and an auditorium

OMSI's Washington Park building will be reborn as the OMSI Educational Resource Center, a home for the many outreach programs – like science camps, classes, and traveling programs – that are offered by the museum.

From OMSI to PAM

Most Portlanders know just what you mean when you say OMSI. Fewer are aware that PAM stands for the Portland Art Museum. In 1991, the Oregon Art Institute changed its name to the Portland Art Museum. The museum, which also includes the Pacific Northwest College of Art and the Northwest Film Center, celebrated its 100th birthday in December, 1992.

PAM began its second century with both promise and problems. Just days after the birthday festivities, director Dan Monroe announced his resignation. Museum supporters did not agree in their reactions. While they were familiar with his accomplishments – like raising almost half of the $4.5 million needed to purchase the Masonic Temple, which sits next door and will provide badly needed expansion space – Monroe presided over a museum with budget troubles and a staff with low morale. Barry Johnson explained in the September 12, 1992 *Oregonian*:

> The museum ran up a $389,000 deficit last year. To make matters worse, infighting among its component parts – museum, art school and film center – and its central administration over resources proved to be both paralyzing and demoralizing.

But by the time of the December, 1992 birthday celebration, the museum administration was reorganized and a new budget had been adopted. At press time, the board was in the process of selecting a new director. Many see Monroe's departure as a great opportunity to hire a new director who will not just oversee PAM, but will strive to champion the arts in Portland, along the lines suggested in *Arts Plan 2000+*.

PAM's Paintings

There are paintings to be sure. They include works from the Renaissance, as well as Impressionist works by Renoir, Monet and others, and Albert Bierstadt's *Mt. Hood*. But the paintings are just one part of the museum's holdings. Other permanent collections include Native-American, Asian, Pre-Columbian, and West African art. There is also a collection of English silver, and works of modern sculpture. The print collection, which includes more than 20,000 prints, photographs and drawings, will be part of the museum's new Gilkey Center for Graphic Arts, which is scheduled to open in 1993.

Museum After Hours . . . and During Hours

One of the more popular events at PAM is Museum After Hours, when you can hear great live jazz in the sculpture court. Museum After Hours happens on Wednesdays during the cool and rainy months, in the hours just after work. The museum is also the regular destination of those who take classes at the Pacific Northwest College of Art, or see flicks at the Northwest Film Center. And more than 45,000 Oregon school kids participate in museum programs each year.

Yesterday, Today and Tomorrow

Just across the Park Blocks from the art museum is the Oregon History Center, home to the Oregon Historical Society, museum exhibits, a research library, a bookshop, and the society press. A large variety of events take place at the center, including ethnic festivals, workshops, author parties, seminars, and exhibits. Those in the know consider the Oregon Historical Society to be one of the best in the nation. But they too may face some challenges over the next few years, for the state may be forced to cut some society funding, courtesy of Measure 5.

A number of exciting events and exhibits are in the works. The center will soon open three new, interactive exhibits on Portland, the Willamette Valley, and the Trail Blazers. And while he may have been trained as an historian, Chet Orloff, the society's Executive Director, clearly thinks in terms of the future. In April, 1992, Orloff proposed plans for a bicentennial celebration of the Lewis and Clark Expedition. As 2005 Project Director Bruce Hamilton described it, Orloff envisions "an international fair of the world's great minds here in Portland." So mark your calendar for the year 2005. It should be great!

Galleries Galore

When *Travel & Leisure* profiled Portland in January, 1991, they wrote that we had "far more galleries than a city of less than a half-million people should hope to have." An Association for Portland Progress brochure reports that there are 50 art galleries in the Rose City. Art Media, an art supply store, includes 53 in their free gallery directory and map. And *Portland Best Places* notes that about two dozen galleries participate in First Thursdays, a monthly gallery-hopping night when many of the city's downtown galleries stay open late.

While the number varies, there is general agreement that the Pearl District in Northwest Portland, and the Skidmore and Yamhill neighborhoods downtown, are good places for gallery-hopping. But don't miss the Contemporary Crafts Gallery on SW Corbett, or the Hoffman Gallery on SW Barnes Road at the Oregon School of Arts and Crafts. They're a little out of the way, but they're worth it.

"Expose Yourself to Art"

Yes, Portland is the city whose mayor exposed himself to art. The famous "Expose Yourself to Art" poster shows Bud Clark – a tavern owner who was not yet mayor – flashing *Kvinneakt*, the nude statue on Fifth Avenue. According to Phil Stanford's column in the October 18, 1991 *Oregonian*, the photo was taken by Mike Ryerson in March, 1978 for a small neighborhood newspaper.

The newspaper sponsored a contest to select a title, and Ryerson sold 800 of the first 1,000 print run on the very first day. Ryerson sold 425,000 copies of the poster – not counting the perhaps 500,000 bootleg versions that have been sold too. In 1991 and 1992, the poster was in the news again, when autographed copies were being sold to help Clark retire an old mayoral campaign debt.

Portlandia

She is – shall we say – a titan of estrogenic prowess. And with her nine-foot-long thighs and plunging decollétage, some have even called her X-rated. At once heroic, revealing, and statuesque, Portlandia, the monumental figurative sculpture commissioned to grace the entrance of Michael Graves' Portland Building, has finally arrived....

Gideon Bosker, "Long-Awaited Portlandia In Place on Portland Building," *Architecture*, December, 1985.

Perhaps the most famous piece in Portland's public art collection is *Portlandia*. This 36 foot hammered copper sculpture of a kneeling woman was designed and executed by Raymond Kaskey. Her inspiration was Lady Commerce, from the Portland city seal. As *Portlandia*, she kneels above the entrance to the Portland Building, hair flying, with one arm reaching down, perhaps to us below, and the other holding a three-pronged spear.

Whether you like her or not, she is impressive; the only larger hammered copper sculpture is the Statue of Liberty. She certainly caught Portland's fancy when she arrived in October, 1985. More than 50,000 people cheered her trip from a Portland warehouse to her perch on the Portland Building; first by barge down the Willamette, and then by truck through thick crowds in the street.

And despite occasional protests that she – like Lady Commerce on the city seal – ought to be at the water's edge, there she crouches, to the delight of some and the mild amazement of all. So head back for a visit, or go make her acquaintance. She's quite a lady.

In the Public Eye

At noon in [Pioneer Courthouse Square] I joined a crowd staring up at a silver globe atop a mast. A fanfare of trumpets erupted, and the kinetic sculpture called the Weather Machine went into action. Would the coming day's weather be fair – or unfair? Three symbols in succession rose from the globe: a blue heron (indicating mist and drizzle); a golden sun goddess (clear skies); and a copper dragon (approaching storms, heavy wind, rain). As sprays of water misted the globe, the heron re-emerged to reign over the day.

> Jerry Camarillo Dunn, Jr., "Portland: Thought-ful, Playful – an Eyeful," *National Geographic Traveler*, March/April 1991.

Not all of Portland's public art is as whimsical as the *Weather Machine*. According to *Arts Plan 2000+*, Portland's percent-for-art programs have been models for other communities seeking to develop their public art programs. By law, both the City of Portland and Multnomah County must set aside 1.33% of their new public construction budgets for public art. METRO passed a similar ordinance, and the County recently broadened its program to include new parks, the EXPO center, and purchases of existing buildings. While a portion of the money is used to administer the program and maintain the art, most is for the commission or purchase of works for the public art collection.

On the Streets and Around the Town

The percent-for-art works join a variety of other pieces that dot the city, indoors and out. A Metropolitan Arts Commission pamphlet describes eight walking tours that take you past more than 100 works of art. They include famous pieces, like the *Allow Me* businessman and the *Weather Machine* at Pioneer Courthouse Square; *Kvinneakt*, the nude woman on Fifth who costars with Bud Clark in "Expose Yourself to Art"; and the stately *Elk* on Main. If the copper dragon emerged from the *Weather Machine* and the rain is too heavy for an outdoor tour, try the Oregon Convention Center, where you'll find a Foucault pendulum and Asian temple bells among a diverse collection that decorates the building.

While *Arts Plan 2000+* recognizes Portland's leadership in public art programs, the report also argues that Portland's public art collection is "an aggregation rather than a collection, lacking the kind of coherence and depth which normally characterize a collection." Not all within the arts community agree. Go see for yourself. And there is one part of the collection that has a definite coherence: the coherence of "Portlandness."

"Portlandness"

Portlanders often try, sometimes unsuccessfully, to describe their city to visitors, new residents or the folks back home. Perhaps they should send the curious to see Portland's Visual Chronicle. According to a Metropolitan Arts Commission flyer, Portland

> ...has a small but growing collection of art that is unique in the country: the Visual Chronicle. Now in its seventh year, the Visual Chronicle documents Portland's changing urban environment by inviting local artists each year to submit works...that portray some aspect of the city's life....
>
> Artists are invited to submit either existing works for direct purchase, or proposals for the creation of new works. In either case there are two main criteria for selection: quality of execution, and "Portlandness" – subject matter that is recognizable as pertaining specifically to the people, topography, or civic or cultural events of the city.

There's even a proper catalog, complete with pictures, that you can send to the folks back home. As for the works themselves, you can usually see selected pieces from the Visual Chronicle on display in the Portland Building. So after you visit *Portlandia*, go on in and see what's there. For information about where other pieces might be on display, call the Metropolitan Arts Commission, or just go up to their offices. They are in the Portland Building too.

Let's Get Literary

In the beginning, there was Powell's - open 365 days a year and rumored to have broken up marriages of people who spent too much time in its endless aisles. Twenty years after the nation's largest literary institution opened its doors, Portland boasts more than 100 independent new-book shops and probably just as many, if not more, dealers in used and rare books, all for roughly 650,000 residents. No less staggering is the fact that more than 70 percent of Multnomah County residents hold active library cards.

Portland Best Places, 1992.

We are indeed a literary bunch. According to figures from the American Booksellers Association, Portlanders are confirmed book buyers:

▸ Folks in New York City, which is the largest book market in the U.S., spend $82.93 per household in bookstores each year. Portland households spend $84.50 a year in bookstore purchases.

▸ Portland has 1.7 bookstores per 10,000 households. That's more than many other cities. For example, LA has 1.33, Boston has 1.67, Chicago has 1.13, and New York has 1.0. With 1.8 per 10,000 households, Washington, D.C. beats Portland by a tad.

100 and Counting

There's plenty of local evidence too:

▸ Powell's City of Books – which occupies a complete city block – is indeed the largest independent bookstore in the U.S. Devotees sip espresso at the Annie Hughes Coffee Room, listen to readings in the evening, and lose their companions in the seven rooms that house books on hundreds of topics. Even some of the regulars need the poster-size map that's provided to find one's way. With more than one million books in 43,000 square feet, it's easy to get lost.

▸ Powell's has branches at the airport, on SE Hawthorne and in Cascade Plaza. There's also Powell's Technical Bookstore, Books for Cooks, a gardening bookstore in the Portland Nursery, and Powell's Travel Store at Pioneer Courthouse Square.

▸ We'll give you just two more Powell's statistics: their used book buyers buy about 2,000 titles a day from the 6,000 to 8,000 they are offered. And it was Powell's that sent the first U.S. commercial shipment to Vietnam since the end of the war – a shipment of more than 17,000 books.

▸ At last count, Portland had seven children's book stores, more than most comparable and many larger cities. And Portland is one of the few cities that has an audio bookstore. Talking Books rents and sells tapes for readers to enjoy while they drive, garden, cook, or relax.

▸ LitEruption, in its 5th year in 1992, has become an annual March event. Readers, writers, publishers and booksellers gather to mingle, read, listen, autograph, and browse among the latest Northwest literary offerings. It gets bigger and more successful each year.

Find Your Favorite

As for favorite bookstores, that of course varies by the Portlander. But we can't resist mentioning our personal favorites: Catbird Seat, on SW Broadway and Annie Bloom's, in Multnomah.

Catbird Seat's downtown location is great, as is the complimentary coffee (usually Kobos) and comfortable chairs. Their comprehensive collection is especially strong in psychology, self-help books, women's studies, Judaica and Northwest writers. And the avid readers who staff the store are wonderfully helpful.

Annie Bloom's is small, but it usually has the book we seek or a good substitute. They aim to be a "world-class, neighborhood bookstore" and have a distinctly literary flavor. The children's book section, which is up on a raised platform, is particularly inviting to our small companions.

And of course there's Powell's. But that's only three of the more than 100. We even know a few Portlanders who intend to visit them all, before they settle on their very favorite.

Love Your Library

"Love Your Library" was an American Libraries Association slogan back in the 1970s. Clearly, many Portlanders took it to heart, for more evidence on well-read Portland comes from the library world.

Portland has enjoyed library service since 1864, when a core of citizens formed the Library Association of Portland (LAP) as a reading room and subscription library. The People's Free Reading Room and Library Association officially opened in March of 1891. A few years later, that free library merged with the LAP. Library service was soon expanded to include Multnomah County residents too.

The LAP continued to manage the county's library services until July, 1990, when – amidst a bit of a scandal – ownership of all books, buildings and other property was transferred to Multnomah County. The Library is now a county department under the jurisdiction of the county commissioners.

In addition to the Central Library, which occupies an entire city block in downtown Portland, the library system operates fourteen branches throughout the city. The collection is a heavily used, substantial one:

▸ At the end of the 1990/91 fiscal year, there were approximately 725,000 books in the Central Library. Central subscribed to 50 newspapers and more than 6,000 magazines and journals.

▸ Systemwide, the Library had about 1.2 million books, video tapes, CDs, audio tapes, records, maps, documents, and other library materials.

▸ Library users borrowed more than 6 million items in 1991/92. That was about 200,000 more than the 1990/91 total of about 5.9 million.

▸ More than 18,000 people came to the Central Branch each week in the 1990/91 fiscal year.

▸ Children are regular users. They borrowed more than 36,000 items each week in 1990/91.

▸ According to Library Director Ginny Cooper, who was quoted in the September 21, 1991 *Oregonian*, the circulation figures put the Library "in the top 15 percent of libraries our size...."

Thanks to reciprocal arrangements, the Multnomah County Library will issue library cards to residents of Washington, Clackamas, Clark, Klickitat and Skamania counties. So the above numbers tell only part of the story. Not all of the Library's users are from Portland or Multnomah County, but Portlanders also use libraries that are located in other areas.

As for the scandal that led to the Library's transfer to Multnomah County? It flared in the spring of 1990, when the Association's president was accused of misdoings, and questions arose regarding the endowment funds, closed meetings, ownership of art valued at $2.5 million, and the composition of the private, non-profit association. But it quickly became old news, as the transfer – an idea that had surfaced many times in the past – was smoothly accomplished.

Support Your Library

While many Portlanders clearly love their library, not everyone wants to support it. Measure 5 cutbacks brought numerous reductions that were implemented in the summer and fall of 1991:

▸ The smaller branches were closed one more day each week, so they are now open only four days weekly. Hours on those days are shorter than they were before the cuts were implemented.

▸ Some vacant jobs go unfilled, and some staff have been demoted or relocated.

▸ The book budget was cut 25%. Director Cooper noted in the article quoted above that the Library is "in the bottom 10 percent for the amount of money spent on books."

An unexpectedly high jump in property assessments in November, 1991 brought the county an increase in tax revenues, and county commissioners were able to restore some money to the library budget. But Measure 5 will necessitate more cuts in the future. And the tax levy that provides about two-thirds of the library's funding expires in July, 1993.

There's another serious problem: the walls of the Central Library – which was designed by A.E. Doyle and is on the national historic register – have shifted and are cracking. Scaffolding is in place to protect staff and library users until money can be found to fund renovations.

To provide the library with stable funding and money for repairs and renovations, the county commissioners passed a Libraries Utilities 2+2 Tax in August, 1992. But opponents quickly mounted a successful petition drive to challenge the ordinance. When a few new commissioners took office in January, 1993, it was repealed. Voters will be asked to decide how to fund the library in the spring of 1993.

On the Lecture Circuit

Another indication of literary Portland is the successful and critically acclaimed Portland Arts and Lectures Series. According to *Arts Plan 2000+*, the series had larger audiences than comparable programs in bigger cities. In fact, the series is typically sold out, with subscribers filling the almost 2,800 seats in the Arlene Schnitzer Concert Hall for each lecture.

Among the speakers who came since the series began in 1984 are: John Updike, Garrison Keillor, John McPhee, Fran Lebowitz, Norman Mailer, Tom Wolfe, Susan Sontag, Alice Walker, Garry Trudeau, Wallace Stegner, Robert Coles, William Styron, Philip Roth, Doris Lessing, Joan Didion, and John Gregory Dunne.

Another notable series is the Science, Technology and Society Lecture Series, which is sponsored annually by the Institute for Science, Engineering and Public Policy. Among the speakers who came to town for this series are: Carl Sagan, Stephen Jay Gould, David Suzuki, Jane Goodall, James Burke, Richard E. Leakey, and Jeremy Rifkin.

On the Magazine Scene

According to an article by Randy Gragg in the February 2, 1992 *Oregonian*, "the only thing rivalling Portland's gallery boom is the explosion of local culture magazines." The July 9-15, 1992 *Willamette Week* agreed, noting that "Portland has more than its fair share of independent rags."

Portland is indeed a great town in which to start a magazine, and it seems that we find or hear about a new local title every few months. In 1992 alone, we came upon a variety of new literary, arts, and music magazines, including *Left Bank, Glimmer Train, The Feminist Broadcast Quarterly of Oregon, Metropolis, Plazm, Bread and Roses, Motes, Plant's Review of Books* and *Black Lamb.*

"Westward Hoe"

But locals aren't the only ones to notice our thriving literary scene. Commenting that "budding writers...often appear first in underground magazines and small presses," the July 1992 issue of *Esquire* prepared a gardening graphic entitled "A Down-to-Earth Guide to Where Budding Writers Come From." *Glimmer Train* and Powell's appeared in the "Westward Hoe" patch. Another Oregon literary magazine, *Mississippi Mud*, showed up too, in the "Underground." So while you're finding your favorite bookstore, check out the local magazine scene too.

Paradise on Earth

Finally, if you're in the market for magazines, you may find heaven on earth at Periodicals Paradise. According to proprietor Neil Hutchins, this SE Belmont store carries almost 10,000 titles, and they have the last twelve months of those that are current titles. He believes that his store is the largest back issue retail magazine store in the U.S. As he has noted, it's pretty amazing to think that Portland has both the biggest bookstore and the biggest magazine store in the country. For lots of Portlanders, that might just be the definition of paradise.

Movies 'n Music

Despite the statistics in *Let's Get Literary*, Portlanders do not always have their noses in books. That's probably because it's too dark to read in most movie theaters. We've also been known to toss our books aside so we can kick up our heels.

On the Big Screen

Portlanders really like movies. According to Randy Blaum of Act III Theatres, Portland is one of the best movie-going markets in the country. Portlanders see more movies per capita than New Yorkers and Los Angelenos. While rankings vary by the season and the choice of new movies, attendance at the ten screen Lloyd Cinemas puts the Lloyd among the top ten movie theaters in the U.S. The Lloyd Cinemas cater to 1.3 million movie-goers each year, and if the Lloyd is showing a blockbuster, as many as 16,000-20,000 people can attend on a Saturday.

As for alternative films, *Portland Best Places* finds that "the number of art and novelty film venues is growing, providing a pleasing variety of films that the studio-bound theaters fail to book." You can also see films at the non-profit Northwest Film and Video Center, which sponsors a variety of films all year round, as well as the annual Portland International Film Festival, usually in February and March.

It's Act III Country

While we may see a lot of flicks, we're not always happy to plunk down our movie money. Act III owns more than 90 theaters in the Portland/Vancouver market, which means that to a great extent they control the movie offerings. Act III was also criticized because few black films played at the Act III theaters that were closest to the neighborhoods with the largest proportion of African-Americans.

Although the chain had promised to remedy the situation, the controversy flared again in November, 1992 when Act III decided to open *Malcolm X* in the suburbs. In the end, *Malcolm X* did play at Act III's Lloyd Theatre, which is just across from the Lloyd Cinemas. But the process was troubling to many. And according to the October 19, 1992 *Oregonian*, Portland was apparently the only U.S. city where the screening caused any controversy.

You Oughta Be In Pictures

Like other cities, Portland has been the backdrop for many movies. And it's becoming a more popular one. A few recent movies that shot here include *Drugstore Cowboy, Cops and Robbers, Body of Evidence, Frozen Assets, The Temp, Free Willy, Dr. Giggles* and *Breaking In*. The highly acclaimed *My Own Private Idaho* by Portlander Gus Van Zant was also filmed here. Portlanders turned out for the in-town opening, and got a laugh at the scenes that showed local notables. Knowing the geography, they were also amused when views of Mt. Hood popped up in unlikely places. Old Town, with its historic buildings, is a favorite shoot location.

"The Animation Capital of the World"

When the Festival of Animation came to Portland in November, 1991, Kristi Turnquist wrote "that Portland often feels like the animation capital of the world." Her November 15, 1991 *Oregonian* article mentions a few reasons why. One is that Portlanders really like animated films. Another is that many successful and creative animators hail from or work in Portland. Jim Blashfield, Matt Groening, Bill Plympton, Joanna Priestley, Chel White, Joan Gratz and Will Vinton are among those who keep Portland on the animation map.

As for the animation fans, Turnquist quotes Eric Jacobsen, spokesperson for a company that distributes animated films, who estimated that Portland was "in the top 10 or 15 markets in the country." In addition to the Festival of Animation, 1991 events included the Animation Celebration, the British Animation Invasion, and the International Tournee of Animation, among others. With about 10,000 people attending the Festival of Animation, Portland crowds matched those in Seattle.

"The Disney of the Pacific Northwest"

There are various kinds of animation. One, using clay, is a particularly Portland variety. Which is why – when the world famous California Raisins™ danced into the Smithsonian in November, 1991 – people back in Portland cheered. Portland is home to Will Vinton Studios, the animation studio that created the Claymation® Raisins for the California Raisin Advisory Board.

The Raisins are only a few among a host of Claymation® characters that have brought Will Vinton and his staff hundreds of awards – including an Academy Award, Emmy Awards, Clios, and international film awards. With such renown, it is easy to understand why those in film and advertising refer to Vinton and his studio as "the Disney of the Pacific Northwest."

Creatives Confer

Will Vinton is also the founder of the Portland Creative Conference. Since 1990, this event has brought filmmakers and television people together with just plain folks who like movies. Each September, nine hundred directors, writers, producers, animators, composers, cinematographers, sound technicians, and movie buffs descend upon Portland in general, and the Portland Center for the Performing Arts in particular, for meetings, screenings, lectures and conversation. Typically, both the famous and the not-so famous rave about the three day event.

A Great Slacker City

When the movie *Slacker* opened, director Richard Linklater told reporters that Portland is a great slacker city. Bill Donahue explained why in the October 30, 1991 *Oregonian*:

> ...Coffeehouses and used bookstores abound, and there's a plethora of movie theaters and funky nightclubs. Best of all, from a slacker's point of view, rent in Portland is still relatively cheap.
>
> If you're an enterprising young social deviant, you can evade real work almost forever here, and sway every night to the raucous sounds of Crackerbash, Smegma and other Portland bands of hip alienation.

Even if you are not "an enterprising social deviant," Portland offers many diversions for those who like "bands of hip alienation." In its July, 1991 issue, *Details* magazine mentioned three Portland clubs in "an essential guide to the radio, club, and music scene" for rock and roll in selected U.S. cities. They were the Lotus Card Room and Cafe, Satyricon, and the X-Ray Cafe.

There are many more clubs, for music lovers of all stripes. In an article on Portland's main music clubs, the October 22-28, 1992 *Willamette Week* reported that a total of 75 clubs are "providing live music at least one night each week." As for the local performing artists and groups that you might catch at the clubs, Curtis Salgado, Back Porch Blues, Crackerbash, Sprinkler, Sweaty Nipples, the Dharma Bums, and the Crazy 8's are among the more well-known ones. Plus, of course, the jazz greats we mentioned on page 256.

For nine years, the annual Mayor's Ball was a popular Portland event. It began in 1984 when about 40 local bands held a fundraiser to help Bud Clark retire his campaign debts. In 1993, Vera decided to turn the ball over to the Portland Music Association, the group that had been organizing the event, which had continued as a fundraiser for a variety of local charities. Although it won't be called the Mayor's Ball, look for a big PMA music event each spring.

There's even a store on SW 2nd called Locals Only that sells the music of local recording artists. They carry about 1,300 titles in records, tapes and CDs. About 80% are Portland artists, and the remainder are by other Northwest musicians. And in the fine tradition of Powell's and Periodicals Paradise, it also has a claim to fame, for it's reputed to be the first music store anyplace to specialize in exclusively local talent.

Culture Comments Too Good To Miss. . .

It was a standing ovation with a difference.

This is Portland, remember, where a slide show on wildflowers can bring an audience to its feet, where almost any amateur thespian's curtain call will start people cheering. Still, the reception Alvin Ailey's dancers got last Thursday at the Schnitz was off the meter....

Terry Ross, "America's Troupe," *Willamette Week*, April 25 - May 1, 1991.

An Architectural Antipasto

In *Winning on the Willamette*, we wrote about Portland's award-winning architecture. Over the years, many honors have been awarded for the design of individual structures; structures as small as transit stops and as large as skyscrapers. Perhaps more significant, Portland has been praised for showcasing, all within a reasonably small area, stellar examples of critical architectural styles of the last 100 years. In their book *Frozen Music*, Gideon Bosker and Lena Lencek say it far better:

> We discovered, in short, a city that could best be described as an intelligently curated architectural museum. In little over a century, Portland had jelled into a magisterial modern metropolis, in which ancient spaces and futuristic skyscraper-sculptures were brought together on miniature, two hundred foot blocks. What we had first seen as a quietly exotic outpost of American civilization revealed itself as an exquisitely architectural microcosm, an extraordinary tapestry in which relics of the past were fantastically interwoven with buildings that pointed the way toward the world of tomorrow.

Just about all the guidebooks include descriptions of the most notable buildings. We'll leave it to them to provide guidance, directions, and full information. We'll simply mention a few of the Portland buildings that have commanded the attention of both architectural critics and wandering Portlanders, to give you a flavor of Portland's architectural antipasto:

▸ New Market Theatre, on SW 2nd, dates to 1872. It was built, as O'Donnell and Vaughan explain in *Portland: an Informal History & Guide*, "to be both a produce market and a theater, cabbages on the first floor, tenors on the second."

▸ The Old Church, on SW 11th. This High Victorian Gothic church dates to 1882 and has been lovingly restored.

▸ Portland City Hall, on SW 4th. This 1895 Eastern Classical Revival building is where you'll find the Mayor.

▸ The Multnomah County Library, on SW 10th. This Georgian style building was designed by A. E. Doyle and built in 1913.

▸ Pittock Mansion, on NW Pittock, was built by *Oregonian* publisher Henry Pittock in 1912-14 in the style of a French chateau. It sits on a rise with wonderful views in all directions.

▸ U.S. National Bank, on SW 6th; another building by A.E. Doyle. Built in 1917, it has six 54 foot terra cotta Corinthian columns and enormous bronze bas-relief doors.

▸ Temple Beth Israel, on NW Flanders, is a Reform Synagogue that was built in 1927 in a Byzantine style.

▸ The Equitable Building, on SW 6th, was designed by Pietro Belluschi and completed in 1948. As *The First Portland Catalogue* explains, it was "the first building in the country to be completely sealed, the first to use double-glazed windows, the first to be air-conditioned, the first to be sheathed in aluminum, and the first to employ traveling cranes for window washing!"

▸ The World Trade Center, on SW Salmon, was designed by the award-winning Zimmer Gunsul Frasca Partnership. A PSU Summer Session Walking Tour brochure calls this 1980 building an example of "Northwest Modern."

▸ The Portland Building, on SW 5th, was designed by Michael Graves and built in 1983 in a post-modernist style. People seem to love it or hate it. During 1992, renovations were made to brighten up the lobby. *Portlandia* graces the entrance.

Just to name a few more, there's also the Oregon Convention Center and the Performing Arts Center, as well as U.S. Bancorp, the city's tallest building; Pioneer Courthouse, one of Portland's oldest buildings; the Justice Center, another post-modern building on Chapman Square, just opposite the Portland Building; and the Charles Berg Building, the only glazed, terra cotta, Art Deco building in Portland.

Speaking of terra cotta, Portland has a large number of buildings that were constructed with glazed terra cotta. The Portland Development Commission has a brochure called "Glazed Terra Cotta Historic District: A Walking Tour of Historic Buildings" that is a wonderful guide to 22 such buildings in the downtown area.

So if you're inclined, grab one of the maps or guidebooks described on pages 245-246 and see our architectural antipasto – which offers a taste of just about everything – for yourself.

"Meet the Press"

It's almost enough to give you stage fright. Every day over 800,000 people gather in dining rooms, breakfast nooks, corner cafes, buses, trains and couches to stare at your ad.

And, on Sundays, a couple hundred thousand more join them.

That's one ad. One day. Four-fifths of a million people. No other media alternative comes close.

> Advertisement in the April 30, 1992 *Oregonian* based on information in the 1991 Portland Scarborough Report.

Amazingly enough, people soon discovered that a small, underfunded newsweekly [*Willamette Week*] with fewer reporters than the daily [*Oregonian*] has photographers *can* make a difference in the lives of Portlanders and Oregonians. How? By choosing our stories carefully and then outthinking, outreporting and outwriting the competition. By challenging preconceived ideas, both our readers' and our own. By rattling the cages of the institutions that run a community. And by understanding that the true honor of journalism is in kicking aside the sacred cow of objectivity to include context, analysis and even a point of view.

> Mark L. Zusman, in the 15th Anniversary Issue of *Willamette Week*, November 2-8, 1989.

According to *Arts Plan 2000+*, most people turn to *The Oregonian* or *Willamette Week* to learn about cultural offerings in the Rose City. So it seems appropriate to end *Expose Yourself to Portland* with a quick look at the media.

Portland Papers

If you go by circulation figures, *The Oregonian* and *Willamette Week* are the newspapers in town. But they are by no means the only ones. According to the *Oregon Bluebook*, more than 25 newspapers are published in the three metropolitan counties. The *Business Journal* is well read and well respected, and the *Portland Observer* has been serving the African-American community for more than 20 years. And thousands of subscribers regularly read the local papers that emphasize community news in Portland's suburbs.

There is also a number of smaller papers, many of which are free, that appeal to a particular slice of the population. For example, both *Portland Parent* and the *Portland Family Calendar* focus on news, events and resources for parents and families; *PDXS* and *The Portland Alliance* lean to the left; and *Just Out* focuses on news of interest to the gay and lesbian community. For a full list of the major papers, complete with addresses and circulation figures, check the latest *Oregon Bluebook*. You can usually find the alternative papers free for the taking, at bookstores, cafes, public libraries and selected stores.

The Big O

Yes, we are referring to *The Oregonian*. *Willamette Week* appears to be the most frequent user of the nickname, but it occasionally shows up in columns of *The Oregonian* too. *The Oregonian* has won its share of awards. For example, the Association of Opinion Page Editors named the Sunday Forum Section the best in the U.S. in 1991.

The Oregonian surprised some people in 1992, when editors at this traditionally Republican paper broke with tradition to endorse Bill Clinton for President. Their endorsement of Bob Packwood was not a surprise, but shortly after *The Washington Post* broke the story on Packwood's alleged sexual harassment, *The Oregonian* called for his resignation. The Big O's favorite slogan is "If it matters to Oregonians, it's in *The Oregonian*." But it wasn't long before an enterprising entrepreneur began marketing a bumpersticker that read "If it matters to Oregonians, it's in *The Washington Post*."

The Oregonian came out strongly and repeatedly against Measure 9, the anti-gay initiative that was on the 1992 ballot. And they have run a number of lead editorials criticizing the state legislature for their inability to pass tax reform legislation, and their reluctance to face the crises wrought by Measure 5, 1990's property tax limitation initiative.

WW

Willamette Week is a weekly newspaper that is distributed free throughout Portland. WW is an award-winner too. As the May 16-22, 1991 issue reported, WW won 29 citations at the Society of Professional Journalists competition, which was more than any other paper in the region. According to editor Mark Zusman, the paper has won a number of distinguished national awards as well.

As we saw, about four-fifths of a million people read the daily *Oregonian*. So who reads *Willamette Week*? In the November 26-December 2, 1992 issue, publisher Richard H. Meeker included a profile of WW readers, who number about 219,000:

> Thanks to modern market research, we know that more than three-quarters of you are between the ages of 18 and 49. You're nearly equally women (50.1 percent) and men (49.9 percent), and you're 24 percent less likely to be married than the average adult resident of this metropolitan area. Your household incomes are 15.2 percent above average. You're 48.6 percent more likely to be a professional, a manager, or an owner of a business. And you're 58.4 percent more likely to be a college graduate.

At the end of his letter to WW readers, Meeker wrote about the paper's function. His final comment was revealing of the context in which the paper hopes to operate:

> Finally, we aspire to make a difference. *Willamette Week* is the only major medium of communication in the metropolitan area whose owners live here. Thus, as much as it sometimes may appear that we're in the business of tearing things down, this newspaper's overall goal is to be a force for powerful and productive change in its community.

Missing: Portland Magazine

As we saw in *Let's Get Literary*, we are fertile ground for alternative, arts and literary magazines. But Portland has not been able to sustain a general magazine of its own since *Portland Magazine* published in the late '80s. More recently, *Portland Life & Business* published a few issues in 1990, but it did not get enough of a following to continue. Some Portlanders read *Oregon Business*, and others like *Pacific Northwest*. But they rely on newspapers for their quota of printed news.

On the Air Waves

The Oregonian ad we quoted at the beginning of this section happily reported that more Portlanders read the paper than watch TV or listen to the radio. The ad went on to explain that "the average TV commercial on a prime time half-hour show reaches only 106,000 viewers." As for radio, "the best time slot on Portland's favorite station gets you an audience of 27,800."

If you look at the Arbitron ratings for radio, you'll see that the top ranked station in Portland usually pulls in an average of 13,000 to 22,000 listeners, depending on the season, and whether you are counting all listeners 12 and over, or adults in the 25 to 54 age group.

About 40 stations ply the airwaves in the metro area. We have the usual mix of news, talk, sports, religion, and music of all types. Most are commercial stations, but a few, like KOAC (550 AM), KOPB (91.5 FM), KBOO (90.7 FM), and KBPS (89.9 FM) are listener-sponsored.

On the Tube

The Rose City has a typical selection of TV stations, including the network "big three," three independents, Fox, and PBS. Here's a few TV facts that are a little more unusual:

▸ According to Kim Skerritt Duncan of Oregon Public Broadcasting, "OPB is consistently the most watched public broadcasting station in the nation based on Nielson metered markets."

▸ Portlanders also set records when they tune in to watch the Blazers. According to the July 15, 1992 *This Week Magazine*, "for the 15th-straight season, the Trail Blazers had the highest local television rating among the 27 teams in the NBA....The Blazers' numbers are nearly double that of any other NBA franchise."

▸   As for local viewing preferences, the article stated that "the Portland Trail Blazers were the highest-rated prime-time television show in the Portland area during the 1991-92 rating period, beating out the likes of the Winter Olympics, which nationally was the top-rated prime-time program."

On the Cable

According to the *Oregon Bluebook*, about 140 cable companies serve the more than 650,000 cable subscribers in the state. Five cable companies serve most of the Portland area:

- ▸ Paragon Cable serves Portland's east side and East Multnomah County.
- ▸ TCI Cablevision of Oregon serves West Portland; West Linn; Oregon City; Gladstone; areas east of Beaverton, north of Tigard, north of Lake Oswego, and around Milwaukie; and some sections in Clackamas County.
- ▸ Columbia Cable serves Lake Oswego, Beaverton, Aloha, Hillsboro, Banks, Forest Grove, King City, Sherwood, Tualatin, Wilsonville, and some areas of Tigard.
- ▸ Jones Intercable handles cable service within the city limits of Milwaukie.
- ▸ North Willamette Telecom in Canby serves cable subscribers in parts of Oregon City and other areas south of the metro area.

The cable companies in the metro area each offer between about 25 and 40 channels. While most users get cable for the extra channels, some subscribe because the reception in their neighborhood – perhaps due to the hills – is utterly hopeless without cable. Although it's not well publicized, some of the companies offer ultra basic service, which simply provides good reception to the regular stations.

Though we end with cable TV, our focus here has been on Portland's cultural offerings. But there are other offerings that deserve our attention too – like the parks, carousels, fountains and markets; and a variety of other local institutions that are part of daily life for many Portlanders. We look next at some of them.

Rose

City

Recreation

Green, Greener, Greenest

Fabulous Fountains

To Market, To Market

Attention Sports Fans!

Pint-Sized Portland

Green, Greener, Greenest

...Lieutenant William R. Broughton of the British Royal Navy, who in 1792 set down the first written description of Oregon, called it the "most beautiful landscape that can be imagined." David Douglas, the Scottish botanist who inventoried Oregon plant life on an 1825 trip to the Northwest (the Douglas fir is named for him), walked among firs that were five hundred years old and three hundred feet high....Members of the Lewis and Clark expedition, who camped out in 1805 along the Columbia Slough, the slow-flowing wetlands-bordered backwaters of the Columbia River in what's now North Portland, complained that they couldn't sleep at night because of the "horrid noise" made by thousands upon thousands of cranes, swans, geese and other waterfowl.

> Tony Hiss, "The Wild Side of Portland," *House & Garden*, May 1991.

A city like Portland, to which nature has been more prodigal in climate, diversity and grandeur of surroundings than any other in the country, should provide itself the name of having been worthy of its heritage. A park system embracing riverside, mountains and plains, and connected by wide boulevards, would go far to make this the most beautiful city in the world.

> Portland Parks Commission, 1901, as quoted in *Portland Parks: A Vision and Blueprint for Preserving and Enhancing our Park System*, November 1991.

Whether you prefer a manicured rose garden or a wildlife refuge; a community baseball diamond or a swampy marsh; a simple picnic table in the shade or a hike through old growth forest; Portland has places to go and people who share your interest. The choices are truly vast. We can't possibly do justice to the more than 700 public parks and natural areas you'll find in the metro area. As we've said before, we don't pretend to be a guidebook. Rather, we aim to give you a sense of the green places – parks, gardens, and natural areas – that Portlanders know and love. We begin with Portland's parks.

Parks For All Seasons

The city of Portland has more than 200 parks, gardens, natural areas and recreation sites. Plans for parks date back to 1848, when Daniel Lownsdale set aside a strip of his land, with the intention that it would be used for public parks. He didn't actually deed it to the city, but his land would eventually become part of the Park Blocks. The city bought the land for Washington Park about 20 years later, in 1871.

Landscape architect John Olmsted was brought to town in 1903, with two purposes: to develop a citywide park plan, and to design a site plan for the Lewis & Clark Exposition. Some of the Olmsted recommendations were eventually implemented a few years later, including the construction of the Terwilliger Parkway, and the acquisition of land for Mt. Tabor Park, Laurelhurst Park, Peninsula Park and Sellwood Park.

Portland's biggest park is Forest Park, in northwest Portland. With more than 4,600 acres, Forest Park is the largest park within a city in the United States. Portland wins in the smallest park category too. Measuring just 24 inches in diameter, Mills End Park – in the crosswalk at the intersection of SW Taylor and SW Front – is the tiniest park just about anywhere. And then there's all those in between.

There are probably as many ways to enjoy the parks as there are parks themselves, and parks are frequent destinations for both visitors and those who live here. For example, you can:

▸ Enjoy the view from the city's highest elevation in Council Crest Park

▸ Jog through Duniway Park, off Terwilliger, and stop to see the famous lilacs there

▸ Spend a summer's evening at a concert or festival in Waterfront Park

▸ Play tennis at one of the more than 100 park courts

▸ Plant vegies or flowers in a community garden plot

▸ Launch your boat at Willamette Park in southwest, or Cathedral Park near the St. John's Bridge

▸ Picnic on an extinct volcano in Mt. Tabor Park

- Run the Rose City Relay, an annual 70 mile race through the city parks system

- Play baseball or basketball at Gabriel Park, while your small companions swing in the playground

- Take a swim lesson in one of the 11 city pools

- See old growth forest up close at Macleay Park

- Breathe air perfumed by more than 10,000 roses at the sunken rose gardens in Peninsula Park

- Cheer one of the 40,000 little leaguers at the many neighborhood parks throughout the city

- Watch butterflies and hummingbirds at the pocket park at Butterfly Bay

- Tee-off at one of the four public golf courses

- Feed the ducks at Laurelhurst Park

- Stroll along the Park Blocks during your lunch hour

- Remember Lewis and Clark at Kelley Point Park, which sits at the confluence of the Columbia and the Willamette

- And, although it's not a city park, many Portlanders find their way to the hiking trails and Nature Center at Tryon Creek State Park, which sits between Southwest Portland and Lake Oswego.

Into the Forest and Through the Trees

Forest Park well deserves a section of its own. It was not established until 1948, when the City Council finally implemented a recommendation by the Olmsted brothers, whose 1903 city plan described "a succession of ravines and spurs covered with remarkably beautiful woods."

The Olmsteds acknowledged that some might see the woods as "a troublesome encumbrance standing in the way of more profitable use of the land." But they urged the city to preserve them, since "future generations will not feel so and will bless the men who were wise enough to get such woods preserved."

The land remained privately owned, and some of the land was logged. During the Depression years, some land owners in the area defaulted on their taxes, and the city decided to finally create the park the Olmsteds had envisioned.

A wonderful guide to the park's hiking trails as well as park "geology, history, vegetation, and wildlife" is Marcy Cottrell Houle's *One City's Wilderness*, which was published in 1988 by the Oregon Historical Society. According to the introduction, Forest Park has about 50 miles of trails. As Houle explains, the park is "an example of a western Oregon coniferous forest ecosystem. Hundreds of species of native Oregon plants and animals live and range within its borders. From this forest sanctuary, panoramic views of the city of Portland, the Willamette and Columbia rivers, and five major peaks of the Cascade Range – Mts. Rainier, St. Helens, Adams, Hood, and Jefferson – can be seen through the tall fir trees."

Adopt a Tree

But all was not tranquil in the park. Because of private development and clearcutting in adjacent areas, many Portlanders began to fear for the park's wildlife. A Friends of Forest Park brochure explains the connection between the adjacent land and the park's wildlife:

> Within 20 minutes of downtown Portland lies the last remnant of ancient forest that once covered all of Portland's hills....The old growth grove lies in the heart of a fragile habitat connecting Forest Park to the Coast Range. This biological link enables many of the more than 100 bird species and 60 mammal species to live inside or range through the park, including black bear, elk, bobcat and rare birds.

About 50% of these "crucial close-in corridor lands" were clearcut by private owners between 1989 and 1991. In an effort to save the old growth, both for itself and to preserve it as a wildlife corridor, the Friends of Forest Park are in the process of purchasing 38 acres of the land in question. They've been able to do so in part because of the success of their Adopt a Tree program. By the end of 1992, more than 40,000 Portlanders had contributed. As we expect you'll agree after a hike through the park, all of us are beneficiaries.

Washington Park

By comparison to the natural forest in Forest Park, Washington Park — the oldest of the city's parks – is far more organized. Many of Portland's favorite places are within the park boundaries. Among the choices:

▸ The Washington Park Zoo

Home to more than 600 animals, the Zoo has a world famous breeding program for Asian elephants, an award winning colony of endangered penguins, and the largest chimpanzee exhibit in the U.S.

▸ The International Rose Test Garden

With more than 400 rose varieties, the Garden has been testing roses since 1917.

▸ The Vietnam Living Memorial

Constructed from black indian granite, the Memorial spirals up a hill in the southwest corner of the Hoyt Arboretum.

▸ The Japanese Garden

With five traditional gardens and a pavilion, the Garden is one of the most authentic outside Japan.

▸ The Hoyt Arboretum

The Arboretum, which is known for its large variety of conifer trees, has wonderful trails, including some that connect to trails in Forest Park.

▸ The World Forestry Center

This museum has exhibits on logging, wood products, fighting forest fires, the tropical rain forest, and wood carving, as well as a huge talking tree to charm the kids.

The Rec in Parks 'n Rec

As wonderful as they are, the parks are just one part of the Portland Parks and Recreation Bureau. Some of the gardens and wildlife areas we'll consider are also within the Bureau's responsibility. The best way to learn about all the offerings is to ask for their free brochure and facilities map. Then you'll be able to locate all the parks, natural areas, public gardens, golf courses, tennis centers, swimming pools, community centers, and art centers. As you'll discover, you can make jewelry, develop outdoor skills, go to camp, or play sports, among a host of other activities, all under the auspices of Portland Parks and Recreation.

Preserving Portland's Parks

As we saw with Forest Park, effort must be expended to preserve what we have. The Bureau faces many challenges, including inefficient irrigation systems, play equipment in poor condition, vandalism, limited wheelchair access, a shortage of athletic fields, an insufficient number of swimming pools, aging buildings that are in need of maintenance, needed signage and the like.

While money may be tight, planning staff at the Parks and Recreation Bureau are attempting to address these and many other pressing needs. For more information on both problems and strategies, ask the Bureau for a copy of their November 1991 *Portland Parks: A Vision and Blueprint for Preserving and Enhancing our Park System*.

Happy Trails

Portland has many trails within its park system, including the Wildwood Trail and the 40-mile Loop. The Wildwood Trail, made up of more than 24 miles of trail, winds through Washington Park, Hoyt Arboretum and Forest Park. The 40-mile Loop is actually a 140-mile connected system of hiking and bicycle trails encircling Portland and linking its major natural, scenic and recreation resources. Parts of the loop are already in use, and completion is scheduled for 1995.

"Discover Portland Parks and Recreation," Portland Parks and Recreation Bureau, 1990.

Gardens Galore

> Our passion for parks may be outdone only by our infatuation with gardens! And although roses get a great deal of press, there's no shortage of evidence suggesting that they share equal time with a multitude of other wonderful varieties. What better place to garden than Portland?
>
> "Parks and Gardens," *The First Portland Catalogue*, 1987.

Apparently, there are not many. Portland was among the "great garden cities" in the September-October 1990 *Flower & Garden*. The May 1990 issue of *Town & Country Monthly* agreed: "Blessed with loamy soil, abundant rainfall, an early spring and mild winters, Portland is a gardener's paradise, especially for aficionados of bonsai, boxwood and Japanese maple."

Portlanders have always taken gardening quite seriously. Garden societies were formed early on; the Portland Rose Society, which began in 1887, is the oldest such group in the United States. With the help of the rain and temperate climate, gardens were soon flourishing, and they continued to, as Portlanders became converts to the City Beautiful movement that was prevalent in the early years of the 20th century.

Today, the Chamber of Commerce lists 15 gardening and horticulture associations. There are countless garden shows and garden sales, and many impressive public and private gardens. In addition to the Japanese Garden and the International Rose Test Garden, you can also explore the following:

▸ the Crystal Spring Rhododendron Garden, which is lovely all year, but spectacular in the spring when the 600 varieties of rhododendrons and azaleas bloom;

▸ the Leach Botanical Gardens, with more than 1,500 species of plants in rock gardens, bogs, woodlands and meadows around Johnson Creek;

▸ Bishop's Close, which overlooks the Willamette from a high bluff above Elk Rock; an Olmsted garden with awesome views, quiet corners, and surprises for strollers who meander around the trail's next bend;

▸ the neighborhood gardens in Ladd's Addition, that remain

an integral part of that community since they were designed in the 1890s;

▸ the Berry Botanic Garden, with a plant collection that
includes rare and endangered Northwest natives, alpines,
primroses, rhododendrons, and lilies;

▸ or the Grotto, where botanical gardens, towering redwoods,
and a stunning view of the Columbia enhance a Catholic
shrine carved into the face of a 110 foot cliff.

Wild Things

While "the overwhelming profusion of wildlife" Tony Hiss
described in the introductory quote is long gone, Portlanders
are realizing that they must take steps to preserve what does
remain. Mike Houck, Urban Naturalist for the Portland
Audubon Society, is at the forefront. As Cliff Collins wrote in
the August 26, 1990 *Northwest Magazine*, Houck "is no less than
a modern-day Moses to local folks intent on preserving urban
natural areas." Together, they have accomplished a great deal.
Thanks to their efforts, you can visit these preserved natural
areas:

▸ Oaks Bottom, on the east bank of the Willamette, is Portland's only officially designated wildlife refuge. Great blue
herons feed in the marshy wetlands there.

▸ Beggars Tick Marsh, about 20 miles east of Oaks Bottom, is
the new county wildlife refuge. Dozens of ducks and mink
make their homes there. The marsh is located near Johnson
Creek, one of the few free-flowing streams that still runs
through the Portland area. Efforts are currently being made
to solve the erosion, flooding and water pollution problems
that have plagued the creek in recent years.

▸ Powell Butte Park is another new park, that is about ten
miles due east of Beggar's Tick Marsh. Powell Butte is
actually an extinct volcano. Views of the Cascades will
demand your attention, but so will the wildflowers, red-
tailed hawks, black-tailed deer and old fruit orchards.

▸ The Columbia Slough area in North Portland has lakes,
rivers, wetlands, forests, and parks. As Mike Houck writes

in "North Portland Naturally," a brochure with maps and descriptions, "North Portland has a strong claim to the distinction of having some of the most beautiful scenery, wildlife habitat and open space in Portland."

▸ Farther north is Sauvie Island, with 12,000 acres for wildlife. Lucky visitors might spot one of the 35 bald eagles that roost there.

For the Birders Among Us

Birders – or bird watchers – might be interested to know that Portland participates in the annual National Audubon Society bird count. In 1991, Portland volunteers counted 96 species in the Portland area. The 1990 count was better; its bird count was 108 species. And, according to the August/September 1989 issue of *National Wildlife*, "Portland's wetlands are home to the northernmost colony of tri-colored blackbirds...."

As for the great blue heron – the official bird of Portland – if you have no luck at Oaks Bottom, you might see birds feeding at the West Delta Golf Course. There are two great blue heron rookeries nearby, one at West Delta Park and another on Ross Island.

There are other good places for bird-watching. The Portland Audubon Society, in northwest Portland, has an indoor viewing area for its large feeders. And the public Heron Lakes Golf Course, along the Columbia Slough, is within viewing distance of a heron rookery.

Metropolitan Greenspaces

While a few natural areas have been preserved, there is concern that, as the metro area builds to accommodate its growing population, we will lose our "greenspaces." Metropolitan Greenspaces began in 1989, as a way to "preserve and manage a system of open spaces, trails, and greenways." Their hope is to "link a mosaic of natural areas into greenspaces, preserving wildlife habitat and creating greenway corridors for animals, plants and people." Hikers could follow these continuous corridors, which would form an "emerald necklace" around the metro area. Wildlife would make their way around too, as they moved, unimpeded, from one natural area to another.

The program has already inventoried the metro area, using special infrared aerial photography to map natural open spaces. They found about 119,000 acres of natural areas. When wildlife biologists visited some of the sites, they were delighted to find some habitats they had not known before. But they were troubled because 10% of the areas they had planned to explore were purchased – for development – between the time the photos were taken and the field visit was scheduled. In fact, most of the inventoried greenspaces could disappear almost overnight, since less than 10% of the inventoried areas are public lands that are protected from development.

Green, As In Dollars. . .

So the folks at Metropolitan Greenspaces – with Mike Houck at the helm – are working to educate everyone else. They joined forces with METRO, and have been urging more than 50 public and private agencies in the region to work together to acquire, manage and protect natural areas. In July, 1992, the METRO Council voted unanimously to place a $200 million bond measure on the 1992 ballot, to raise funds to acquire some of the critical properties. But it did not pass.

Some analysts felt that the Greenspaces measure was lost amidst the controversy over Ballot Measure 9, the anti-gay initiative. Others attributed the defeat to the "no new taxes" mood that seems so pervasive. Still others believed that voters were uneasy to vote for the acquisition of lands now, knowing that their maintenance will mean more taxes in the future.

Try, Try Again

Supporters hope that Metropolitan Greenspaces will try again. As *The Oregonian* noted in the lead editorial on November 9, 1992, "building a regional consensus is a process, and a one-time election defeat is no reason to give up." And as it concluded, "Setting something aside for the future is each generation's responsibility to the next. But we can't save what is already gone. The region must act soon to save its natural treasures before they disappear forever." The measure may have failed this time, but we, as a region that values its parks, gardens and natural areas, have clearly made a good start.

Fabulous Fountains

This value given to parks and open space continued and in a sense expanded to include that other prime element from nature, water. Today, relative to its size, Portland must have more fountains than Rome.

Terence O'Donnell, "Reflections of a Streetwalker: An Ode to Life as Seen From Street Level," *Northwest Magazine,* August 12, 1990.

Outpourings of water are to be found in every nook and cranny of the city, cascading in dramatic waterfalls, swirling through twisted tubes, spouting into serene pools. What's amazing about Portland's fountains is that people are encouraged to play in them, whether by a discrete dipping of a toe while eating a brown-bag lunch or a full-scale jumping in after bicycling.

In Waterfront Park, which edges downtown in a two-mile stretch of sophisticated esplanade and meadow, an extroverted fountain of 100 water jets [the Salmon Street Springs Fountain] spurts with a frenzied activity during peak commuting hours and returns to a more restful pace at less hectic times of the day. Not as spectacular, but most beloved, are the two dozen cast-bronze, perpetually running, four-bubbler Benson drinking fountains scattered throughout the city. Simon Benson, an early-day lumber baron...was convinced that loggers tarried at saloons because fresh, cool water was not readily available to quench their thirsts. His bubblers were installed, and Benson was pleased to believe that the saloons suffered a drop in business.

Yvonne Michie Horn, "People-Pleasing Portland," *T.W.A. Ambassador,* April 1991.

Indeed it seems that just about every time you round a corner you come upon another fountain, where you can rest, quench your thirst, or let the kids frolic. Fountains in parks and fountains in buildings. Fountains along the Transit Mall and pools where sculptured bronze animals romp. Fountains where tossed coins hold secret wishes. Here's a peek at some of the more famous of these Portland waterworks. But do see them all!

For "Horses, Men and Dogs"

Skidmore Fountain, in Ankeny Square, is famous for its design and its "good citizens are the riches of a city" inscription. It was a gift to the city, paid for in part from a bequest by Stephen G. Skidmore, who wanted to erect a fountain where "horses, men and dogs" could drink. Olin Warner, a well known sculptor, designed it in his New York studio, and it was erected in 1888. The fountain was praised from coast to coast as one of the most beautiful in the U.S.

For Portlanders, the praise was also a put-down. Critics like W.C. Brownell commented that such a fountain belonged in NY's Central Park instead of in Oregon, with the "buggies and buck-boards, and shirt-sleeves and slouch-hats." Did they know that beer merchant Henry Weinhard had actually offered to pump beer to the fountain, for its dedication? Maybe. For the record, his kind offer was not accepted by the city fathers.

Ira's Fountain

Another highly praised downtown fountain is the Ira C. Keller Fountain, just across from the Civic Auditorium. It's also called the Forecourt Fountain. Ida Louise Huxtable's praise in *The New York Times* is hard to match. She called it "perhaps the greatest open space since the Renaissance." Ira's Fountain – a wonderful combination of waterfalls, terraces, quiet pools and islands – takes up a whole city block.

The Benson Bubblers

As for the famous bubblers, the city actually has 40 Benson fountains. The lumber baron gave the first 20 to the city in 1912 and 1913, and the others were cast from original patterns in the 1960s and '70s. During the 1992 drought, to the chagrin of many, the Benson bubblers were refitted with push button devices. It was mostly a symbolic gesture – for they use only a tiny percentage of the city's water – but it was seen as appropriate by the city managers who were exhorting us all to save water. When the water crisis passed for the season, the fountains were reconverted again, to flow freely. But it appears that the push button devices will be back each summer.

To Market, To Market

Sheri Teasdale and Andrea Scharf missed the Eugene Saturday Market after they moved to Portland in the early '70s. After five months of talking to people from the city, the county, the planning commission and crafts organizations, they were put in touch with businessman Bill Naito. He agreed to let them use a parking lot if they would pay the cost of additional liability insurance. With Naito's help, a bank loan and a $1,000 grant from the Metropolitan Arts Commission, they opened the Portland Saturday Market on a clear day in June 1974. Thirty vendors were there, and some of them still come today.

Located in the Skidmore District of southwest Portland, the market has grown to become the biggest open air crafts market in continuous operation in the U.S. Saturday Market has lots of surprises – including, for those new to Portland, the fact that it is open on both Saturdays and Sundays, from March through Christmas Eve, rain or shine. Saturday Market staff provided the following facts and figures, which attest to the success and continued vibrancy of the market today.

- 300 different vendors sell handcrafted and homegrown goods on each day that the market operates.
- While many vendors are regulars who have reserved spaces, new vendors also exhibit, with more than 1,000 different craftspeople participating each year.
- 5,000 to 6,000 people come to the market on an average day, which totals approximately 750,000 visitors annually.

Visitors are treated to a huge array of crafts, snacks and entertainers:

- Wandering through the booths, a visitor can browse for baskets, clothing, candles, cosmetics, glass, flower arrangements, edibles, jewelry, musical instruments, woodwork, pottery, toys, drawings, photographs, and the like.
- Clowns, mimes, jugglers, magicians, singers and musicians entertain in and around the market, hoping for smiles, applause and generous tips from passersby.
- 26 spaces are allotted to food vendors, who prepare tempting dishes from all over the world.

Items are juried by the market's Product Review Committee. Quality is consistently high, and browsers, who clearly like what they see, soon become buyers. The craftspeople are also the salespeople; in fact, it is required that craftspeople staff their own booths. As for finances,

▸ The market reports gross annual revenues at approximately $5,000,000 per year.
▸ 67% of the vendors obtain the majority of their income from market sales.
▸ The market is completely self-sufficient, with the operating budget raised entirely from space rental fees. As of December, 1992, vendors were charged the lesser of $35 or 10% of the day's sales, with a minimum fee of $14 on Saturdays and $10 on Sundays.

Sheri Teasdale and Andrea Scharf should be proud, not only for the market's continuing success, but also for its impact on downtown Portland:

▸ Portland Saturday Market promotional materials credit the market with fostering the renovation of two adjacent buildings, which now operate as shopping centers.
▸ The market is similarly credited with inspiring other open air events, like Artquake, Neighborfair and Oktoberfest.
▸ The market is both a popular tourist attraction and a contributing factor to Portland's livability.

As For the Farmers

Those with an appetite for a real farmers market have many options. The Portland Farmers Market opened in 1992 in the Albers Mill parking lot on NW Front Street. The cities of Beaverton, Gresham, Oregon City, Hillsboro and McMinnville have farmers markets too. And more than 70 farms where you can either buy or pick produce are listed in the *Tri-County Farm Fresh Food Guide*. The guide is available for free at libraries, bookstores, and OSU Extension Service offices.

Attention Sports Fans!

Sports enthusiasts – who prefer to participate rather than cheer – will find options in Portland for just about every sport they enjoy. But with only one nationally prominent professional team – the Portland Trail Blazers – even Portland boosters agree that it's not the best town for tried-and-true sports fans. If you're not a season ticketholder, it's extremely hard to get Blazer tickets. That may still be the case even when the new Blazer 20,000 seat arena opens, hopefully in time for the 1994/95 NBA season. There are other games in town, like the Western Hockey League's Portland Winter Hawks and minor league Portland Beaver Baseball, but they won't impress real sports fans. So while we'll look at the various spectator sports, our emphasis will be on the participatory ones.

Blazermania

Most Portlanders love the Blazers. Every game is sold out. When the team is ripping towards the finals, Blazermania erupts, and for a few rosy weeks in May and June, Portland truly becomes the Rip City we described on page 11. There are countless anecdotes that recount what it's like when the Rose City becomes Rip City. This one, from a May 17, 1992 *Oregonian* column by Jonathan Nicholas, is our favorite:

> Just how big a Blazer town is this burg? Look at it this way. In Portland you can go to a symphony concert and still not miss the game. Last Monday night, during the Pops concert at the Schnitz, conductor Norman Leyden stationed a musician just offstage – one ear glued to the radio.
>
> At key moments during the key game against Phoenix, Leyden had the score relayed to the podium, and he relayed it to the audience.
>
> Things go so hot during the second overtime Leyden actually brought the radio onstage and let it bask in the spotlight.
>
> Wonder what Beethoven might have made of that?

We'll never know, but the Blazer fans in the audience thought it was terrific.

A Banner Year

While the Blazers did lose the NBA finals to the Chicago Bulls in 1992, it was still quite a year for basketball fans. Portland played host to both the NBA draft and the Dream Team, who came to play in the Tournament of the Americas. As Mike Francis noted in his December 1, 1992 *Oregonian* column, Portland had "a five-week run at the top of sports pages everywhere. Meanwhile, civic boosters were aglow, warmed by the heady publicity and the multimillion-dollar infusion."

According to Francis, they liked it so much that they decided to form the Portland Metropolitan Sports Authority, "to help manage efforts to attract more events." If this group is successful, "more such sports events – and eventually, maybe even a franchise or two" could come to the Rose City.

The Missing Pros

Over the years, teams like the Portland Timbers and the Portland Breakers played – briefly – in Portland. And various groups have tried to bring other pro teams to the city. In 1991 and 1992, for example, the sports pages reported the possibility of Portland franchises in the Canadian Football League, the Professional Spring Football League, and Roller Hockey International. With hopes of luring an NFL franchise to Portland, the Oregon Dome Team tried, but finally abandoned, an effort to build a sports dome.

So while Portland is gaining national recognition as a good sports town, and the Portland Metropolitan Sports Authority is a step in the right direction, those who can't get Blazer tickets will have to settle – at least for now – for the Beavers or the Winter Hawks. Or for a college game at Portland State, the University of Portland, or Lewis & Clark. And both the University of Oregon Ducks and the Oregon State University Beavers are not too far away, in Eugene and Corvallis respectively.

To The Races

There is also horse racing at Portland Meadows, which opened its 47th season in October 1992. Some think that the greyhound racing at the Multnomah Greyhound Track is the best in the U.S. And there's car racing at the Portland International Raceway. Portland is one of just 16 cities that can host CART Indy car racing, and the Indy Car 200 is one of the Rose Festival's featured events each year.

Attention Sports Enthusiasts

No apologies needed here. We remarked that book lovers love Portland. So do sports enthusiasts. *Portland Best Places* provides the particulars on more than 20 outdoor sports, including bicycling, bird watching, canoeing, kayaking, running, walking, climbing, fishing, golfing, hiking, horseback riding, ice and roller skating, river rafting, rowing, sailing, skiing, swimming and tennis. Writing on Oregon's "love affair" with outdoor sports, Jeff Baker's May 13, 1990 *Oregonian* article mentions some of the above, as well as volkssporting, boating and water skiing. We suggest you refer to one of the guidebooks listed on pages 245-246 for all of the particulars, but here's a few facts for the fun of it.

At the Clubs and On the Slopes

▸ The Multnomah Athletic Club, with 19,500 members and a huge building in southwest Portland, is one of the largest private athletic clubs in the United States. Members can participate in 24 different sports. MAC athletes have won hundreds of awards, including about 30 Olympic medals. Unfortunately, the "Big MAC" is not open to new members, and no longer maintains a waiting list. While there were times in the past when the MAC actively recruited members, just about the only way to get your name on the MAC rolls today is to marry or be adopted by a MAC member. Those families that were lucky enough in recent years to make it from the waiting list to full membership paid a hefty $5,000 initiation fee. Monthly fees range from $29-$95, depending on age and membership classification.

▸ There are four ski resorts within 70 miles of Portland, in the vicinity of Mt. Hood. Skibowl and Summit, which are about 55 miles east of Portland at Government Camp, are the closest. Timberline, six miles north of Government Camp, has the highest elevation. Mt. Hood Meadows, 68 miles from Portland, is both the furthest away and the busiest. You can even ski Mt. Hood in the summer, and hundreds of skiers do just that.

▶   *Portland Best Places* counts "at least twenty 18-hole golf courses within 20 miles of the city center, though half are private." Two of them – Eastmoreland and Heron Lakes – are considered to be among the 50 best public courses in the U.S. But just about everyone – including the folks at *Portland Best Places* – agrees that there are either too many golfers or too few golf courses.

▶   As for private links, an article in the September 4, 1991 *Oregonian* reported that only 4 of 15 private area golf clubs had any openings. Joining fees ranged from $2,500 at Arrowhead Golf Club to $40,000 at the Waverly Country Club.

▶   The Pumpkin Ridge Golf Club seems to be the one of choice; its Ghost Creek course tops *The Business Journal* list of the 25 toughest golf courses. The Ghost Creek course was also chosen in 1992 by *Golf Digest*, as the best new public golf course in the U.S. And the Pumpkin Ridge Golf Club was the most popular leisure destination for the Dream Team players.

▶   The Portland Parks and Recreation Bureau maintains more than 175 tennis courts – some where reservations are possible, others on a "first come, first serve" basis. There are also private tennis clubs. The Irvington Club, in northeast Portland, is one of the oldest in the U.S., and is known nationally. The Racquet Club, in Portland's West Hills, is one of Portland's more exclusive private clubs.

On Your Feet

Running, walking and bicycling may very well be the most popular sports among Portlanders. At least it seems that way. Since we all walked and ran before we cycled, let's start there. Portland has been recognized as a great city for both walking and running. Back in December 1984, *The Runner* rated Portland as a gold medal running city. More recently, the August 1991 issue of *Walking Magazine* named the Rose City as one of the ten best walking cities in America. Every day, hundreds of people pull on their Nikes or Avias – both of which are made by Portland companies – and get a move on. Many of Portland's organized runs offer a longish course as well as a shorter run and a walkers event. Some offer wheelchair competitions too. Here are some specifics:

▸ The Oregon Road Runners Club, which is based in Beaverton, is one of the largest running clubs in the country.

▸ One of the more popular Portland races is the 15 kilometer Cascade Run Off. Almost 6,000 participated in the July 1991 race, which followed a route through southwest Portland.

▸ The annual Spring Classic has something for everyone: a one mile Kids for Kids Dash; a four mile walk that, with about 4,000 participants, is Portland's largest walking event; and an 8K Run.

▸ One of our newer races is the Rose City Relay. About 250 runners ran the race in October 1991, in what organizers hoped will be an annual event. They ran in relay teams, on a 70 mile course that took them through ten parks.

▸ The Portland Marathon celebrated its 20th anniversary in September 1991. 4,222 runners competed in that Marathon, while other participants did the Marathon Walk, the Five-Miler, or the Mayor's Walk. About 69% of the Marathon runners were out-of-towners, representing 46 states and 14 countries. Perhaps the most interesting statistic is that the Portland Marathon draws more women entrants than any other marathon in the world: almost 29% of the marathoners were women. Another interesting detail is that the runners get entertained along the way, by clowns, bands, dancers, and cheering spectators.

▸ In the Starlight Run, a Rose Festival event, it's the clowns that run. Cavorting in costume is typical in this short race, which is a lead-in for the Rose Festival's Starlight Parade.

▸ Finally, there's the famous Hood To Coast. In its tenth year in 1991, this relay race drew 10,000 runners, walkers, and wheelchair drivers who went the 192.7 miles from Timberline Lodge on Mt. Hood to Seaside on the coast. The Hood To Coast is the largest road running relay race in the U.S.

Cycling Through

1991 was also the 20th anniversary of the Oregon Bike Bill, which ensures that 1% of the State Highway Fund is spent on bikeways and footpaths. Today, cycling is popular in Portland in many forms: recreational rides, races, bike commuting, and as the vehicle of choice for selected Portland police and around-the-town messenger services. Here's a few cycling facts:

▶ Perhaps the most famous bike commuter in Portland was Mayor Bud Clark. When he served as mayor, he was often seen bicycling to City Hall from his home in northwest. And when left his office for the last time on December 31, 1992 – during a big snowstorm – he left on his bike. Statistics from the city's Bicycle Program indicate that the mayor was one of roughly 10,000 bike commuters. More than 1,000 of them biked to jobs downtown.

▶ There are, of course, many other reasons to go downtown. Other Bicycle Program data suggest that riders make between 1,200 and 1,500 daily bicycle trips to the central business district each day.

▶ The April 1991 issue of *Oregon Cycling* lists 15 cycling clubs for the Portland metro area. An article notes that "Oregon's largest touring club, the Portland Wheelmen Touring Club, has rides just about every day of the year...."

▶ Statewide, there are literally hundreds of fun rides, centuries, club rides, road races, off-road races, and multi-sport races to choose from. *Oregon Cycling*, which is free at bike shops and other locations, prints a calendar in each issue.

▶ Racers can practice and race at Alpenrose Velodrome and Portland International Raceway.

▸ The bridge of choice for cyclists is the Hawthorne. Bike and pedestrian counts done by the Bicycle Program indicate that the Hawthorne carries about half the bicycle traffic. The 1991 count – done on a fair day during peak biking season – found just under 1,000 bike trips across the Hawthorne. Pedestrians made just over 1,000 crossings that day. Other "bike friendly" bridges are the Broadway and the Burnside.

▸ And then there's Cycle Oregon, which held its fifth annual race in 1992. 2,000 riders pedaled the incredibly scenic 450 mile long route in this seven day event. According to the September 9, 1991 *Oregonian*, Cycle Oregon "is ranked among the top 10 major bicycle tours in the United States." For *Oregonian* columnist Jonathan Nicholas – who was an original organizer and pedals each year – it's "the finest week-long bicycle ride in the nation."

Those who prefer a shorter ride can check *Portland Best Places* for some recommended routes. Another fine guide for bike trips is *Best Bike Rides Around Portland*, by Anndy Wiselogle and Virginia Church. The authors include 40 rides, with maps, mileage, elevation charts and directions. And a *Portland Metro Area Bicycle Map* is available from the city's Bicycle and Pedestrian Program, in the Portland Building.

A Few For the Road

▸ Oregon is a big hunting state. Although the number of hunting licenses sold in Oregon is declining, about 347,000 licenses were sold in the state in 1990. Oregon is also a great state for fishing. Local choices for metro area anglers include spring Chinook salmon in the Willamette River, and, depending on the season, salmon or steelhead in the Clackamas River.

▸ The nearby Columbia Gorge is becoming one of the most popular places in the world for windsurfing.

▸ According to an article by Norm Maves Jr. in the August 18, 1991 *Oregonian*, "Irving Park, at Northeast Seventh Avenue and Fremont Street, for years has been the capital of summer hoops in Portland. A. C. Green of the Los Angeles Lakers learned his basketball there." Other good places that Maves mentions are "Wallace Park, Oregon Park, Peninsula and Laurelhurst parks."

▸ Strollers in Waterfront Park may be lucky enough to come upon someone practicing footbag, an unusual sport, which involves keeping a leather pouch in the air, by tossing it around with your feet. The world champion is actually a Portlander named Kenny Shults. And the sport offers lots of variety: there's footbag net, and consecutive footbag, and fancy freestyle moves, and speed footbag.

Nike Town

Some will say that we saved the best for last. Just about everyone – whether a spectator or a participant, a Portlander or a tourist – is drawn to Nike Town. Six months after the official opening, lines still formed outside on weekends. In the May 1991 *Architectural Record Lighting Supplement*, the lighting designer, Robert Dupuy, called it "a cross between a world's fair, a movie studio, and Disneyland." And here's what the December 1991 *Money* magazine said, when they picked Nike Town as the 1992 Store of the Year:

> As you adjust to the dim light, life-size plaster casts of Andre Agassi swinging a tennis racket and Bo Jackson pumping iron appear alongside you. High above, a statue of Michael Jordan, going up for a slam dunk, is eerily suspended from the ceiling. There are manhole covers at your feet and catwalks overhead....Recessed lights overhead simulate dawn turning to daylight, gradually brightening, then dimming again. As the lights come up, you hear the sounds of birds chirping.

Music blares, videos play, fish swim, basketballs dribble. You can buy Nikes, look over the new product lines, or just walk around and gape in amazement. It's quite a place. Enough words. Just go there.

Pint-Sized Portland

As we saw in *Winning on the Willamette*, Portland was among the "ten best family cities" listed in the March 1990 *Parenting* magazine. The magazine's Portland profile included comments on the city's good schools, affordable housing, available daycare, and "environmentally conscious" populous – considerations clearly of concern to many parents. But it also mentioned a few of the attractions that appeal to kids, like OMSI and our parks.

When we've considered Portland's livability, our emphasis has been on what the grown-ups think is important. What do kids like about Portland? As with adults, it varies by the person. Some prefer diversions like the Washington Park Zoo; others, like their literary parents, pick the children's room at Powell's as their favorite destination.

Pint-Sized Rose City Specials

Here are a few of the Portland attractions that we haven't mentioned elsewhere, that, while enjoyable to kids of all ages, are of particular interest to the youngest of Portlanders.

- The Carousels

Portland has been called the Carousel Capital of the World, because there are more restored, operating wooden carousels in Portland than in any other city. During some summers there have been as many as seven! There are four permanent locations:

  - Oaks Park, an amusement park in southeast;
  - Jantzen Beach, a shopping center in North Portland;
  - the Burlingame Burger King in southwest Portland;
  - and the Carousel Courtyard, near the Lloyd Center.

- Peacock Lane

Visiting Peacock Lane, in southeast Portland, is a holiday tradition for many Portland children. Homeowners on Peacock Lane take Christmas lights very seriously. Since the 1930s, they have been lighting up their homes so beautifully each year that

Portlanders literally come in droves to see them. Unless you like bumper-to-bumper traffic, the best way to see the lights is to just stroll down the lane. You can even buy some hot chocolate from one of the neighbors to keep you warm while you walk the two blocks. The lights shine each evening from December 15 to December 31, from 6 to 11 PM.

▸ The Rose Festival Junior Parade

This annual parade, which takes place during the annual Rose Festival in June, is the largest children's parade in the world. More than 10,000 children participate each year. We'll have much more to say about Rose Festival in *June Daze*. As you'll see, many other Rose Festival events are fun for kids.

▸ The Washington Park Zoo

More than 1 million people come to the zoo each year. There they can see more than 600 animals which together represent over 200 species. While watching the animals may be the big draw, the zoo offers many innovative programs too. They include:

- ▸ one of the best zoo day camps in the U.S.
- ▸ Camparoo at the Zoo, a parent-child overnight
- ▸ ZooBoo, a spooky train ride at Halloween
- ▸ the ZooLights festival at Christmas
- ▸ annual poetry contests
- ▸ summertime concerts

Packy's birthday party is a big annual event each April. That's when Portlanders gather to celebrate the birthday of the first elephant to be born at the zoo. In fact, the zoo is known throughout the world for its breeding program for Asian elephants. No spring chicken, Packy turned 30 in 1992.

The zoo is also known for its colony of endangered Peruvian Humboldt penguins, and it has the largest chimpanzee exhibit in the U.S. It is less well known for its Zoo Doo. Odd as it may seem, Portlanders turn out each year, usually around February, to buy this elephant manure by the bag or by the truckload. Those who want a bagful are advised to bring a bag, a dollar and a shovel!

Watching the City Go By

We've mentioned Portland's "fare-less square" – the downtown area in which both TRI-MET buses and MAX light rail is free. Riding a bus or train has great appeal to just about all kids, and it can be a fine way to shuttle your small companions around, whether sightseeing or just running errands.

Another helping hand from TRI-MET is their "Summer Fun For Kids" map. It lists and locates museums, community centers, swimming pools, playgrounds, fishing spots, skating rinks, and the like, providing both suggestions for activities and the bus routes to get there.

For the Kids

For most parents, the facts of life include daycare, pre-schools, pediatricians and toy stores. But they are beyond the focus for our *Facts of Life*. They are beyond our focus in part because there are many useful sources already available. Like the following:

▸ *A Comprehensive Guide to Family Resources & Services in Portland*, by The Family Resource Group, Inc., provides an incredible amount of information on family services of all types in the tri-county area. It includes listings on everything from adoption and foster care to daycare and schools; hospitals and social service programs to parks and community activities.

▸ *Portland Family Calendar* and *Portland Parent* are monthly newspapers that are available free at area libraries, bookstores, pre-schools, and community centers. Complimentary copies of *That's My Baby: The Magazine for Moms & Dads*, "Portland's parenting resource directory," are also available around town.

▸ Two Portland guidebooks focus on children. They are *Around Portland with Kids*, by Judi Siewert and Kathryn Weit, and *Portland Kids*, by Jan and Steve White. Finally, both *The Oregonian* and *Willamette Week* regularly cover children's events.

Between Rose Festival and the Blazer semi-finals, the month of June is usually a busy month in Portland. We've already looked at Blazermania. We look next, in *June Daze*, at Rose Festival and the tourists who come to the Rose City.

June

Daze

Roses and Royalty

Toasting the Tourists

Brews, Brewers and Brewpubs

Coffee, Coffee Everywhere

Regarding Restaurants

Familiar Folks

You Can Get There From Here

Royalty and Roses

For more than 100 years, the month of June has seen a lot of hoopla – for June is Rose Festival time in Portland. In the last few years, the Portland Trail Blazers have put real hoop in the hoopla, as they fought for a national championship. Blazermania in the Mythical Realm of Rosaria – we good-naturedly call it *June Daze*.

You know that Rose Festival is approaching when tiny rose pins begin to appear on collars and lapels all around town. You know it's getting closer when *The Oregonian* announces the names of the festival princesses as they are selected, one by one, at high schools throughout Portland. The roses begin to bloom and speculations on the weather are heard more frequently than usual. (Portlanders rarely complain about the rain, but even they don't like rain on parades.) Carrying on a tradition that began in 1907, these are the trustworthy indicators that the annual Portland Rose Festival is about to begin.

Rose Recognition

Although the first "official" festival took place in 1907, it developed from earlier celebrations. The Portland Rose Society held its first rose show in 1889, beginning an event that would take place annually. In 1904, the Society organized a fiesta in conjunction with the show, which included entertainment as well as a floral parade. The fiesta also became an annual event. According to literature from the Portland Rose Festival Association, the current name can be traced to two civic leaders: "E.W. Rowe is credited with the original idea of a 'rose festival.' Portland Mayor Harry Lane is also remembered for expressing a need for a 'festival of roses,' on the heels of the successful Lewis & Clark Exhibition in 1905."

Reigning over the 1907 festival was Queen Flora, who was actually Carrie Lee Chamberlain, the governor's daughter. The festival's two day festivities featured an electrical parade. Twenty floats, illuminated with bright lights, were set on flatcars that travelled on the trolley line rails. Portlanders were rightfully proud, for the parade utilized one of the world's first electrically propelled trolley systems. The Association notes that it was "the most lavish spectacle of its kind on the continent."

Ninety Years Later

Harry Lane and E. W. Rowe would be astonished to see how the festival has grown. According to the Portland Rose Festival Association, the festival runs for 25 days. Two million people attend the 70 events that are scheduled in conjunction with the festival. These events, which take place in the air, on the ground and on the river, include:

▸ an air show and hot air balloon event;
▸ the arrival of more than 20 naval and coast guard ships, which are from several countries and are open for tours;
▸ fireworks;
▸ auto races;
▸ the rose show;
▸ dragon boat races;
▸ the festival queen's coronation;
▸ concerts;
▸ a food fair and carnival on the waterfront;
▸ and of course, parades.

In fact, there are now three parades:

▸ 400,000 spectators watch the Grand Floral Parade, which is the second largest all floral parade in the U.S.
▸ 23.3 million households tune into the Grand Floral Parade on TV.
▸ Involving over 10,000 children, the Junior Parade is the biggest children's parade in the world.
▸ Reminiscent of the electrical parade in 1907, the evening Starlight Parade draws 150,000 spectators.

Hail to the Queen

Royalty – in various combinations – have always reigned. After Carrie Lee Chamberlain inaugurated the custom in 1907, a king, called Rex Oregonus, occupied the throne from 1908 to 1913. Played by different prominent citizens, the king's identity was kept a secret until his disguising beard was removed at the festival's ball. He normally arrived by boat, and he was greeted with much pomp and pageantry.

The Royal Rosarians began participating in the Rose Festival in 1912, after a select group of business and professional men decided that Portland needed them to serve as the city's official hosts. The Rosarians continue to serve that role today. But they are most visible during Rose Festival, when – dressed in jaunty white suits and straw hats – they escort the Rose Court, knight distinguished visitors, preside at the Queen's coronation, and march in the Grand Floral Parade.

From 1914 to 1930, festival queens were selected from area socialites. The practice used today – selecting a queen from the princesses chosen at each high school – began in 1931.

The Show Must Go On

There have only been a few years when festival organizers have had to cancel or change plans:

▸ The Grand Floral Parade was cancelled in 1918 and 1942, due to the world wars.

▸ The entire festival was cancelled in 1926, because Multnomah Stadium was being rebuilt.

▸ Because of the Vanport flood, the parade was held on the east side in 1948.

▸ The 1980 parade was held as scheduled, but not until the streets were cleaned of ash from the eruption of Mt. St. Helens. In fact, it was not uncommon to see spectators in dust masks during the 1980 festivities.

Making it all happen is a year round job, and the results bring fun, national recognition and tourist dollars to the city:

▸ Over 5,000 volunteers assist a small full-time staff at the Portland Rose Festival Association, which is a non-profit organization.

▸ National, regional and local businesses help by sponsoring events and by contributing goods and services.

▸ Each year the festival generates more than $44 million for the local economy.

So grab your umbrella and pin a rose on your lapel. If the roses are beginning to bloom, the festival is not far away!

The Other Festivals

If the Rose Festival hoopla is not your cup of tea, there are many other possibilities. In the November 2-8, 1989 *Willamette Week*, Doug Marx wrote about his preferences:

> I also like the way Portlanders party. Citywide. I can do without the Rose Festival and the inflated beer cans that always tower wobbly above Waterfront Park, but to boogie down with all those people at the Cascade Blues Festival or simply to drift, shoulders scrunched, carried along with the human swarm during Neighborfair, mitigates my latent misanthropy. The thing of it is, the folks in these crowds seem comfortable with each other, approachable, conversational, and at times my antennae pick up the feeling that they don't take for granted what they hold in common.

Rose Festival is just one of literally hundreds of annual events that happen in and around the Portland metro area. Many draw thousands of people, like the Oregon Brewers Festival, Artquake, LitEruption, the Mt. Hood Festival of Jazz, and The Bite. Most have a more limited following, like the Sullivan's Gulch Blackberry Festival, the Wooden Arts Festival, Rock 'n' Rose, the Portland Poetry Festival, the International Film Festival, the Salmon Festival, Great Blue Heron Week, the Greek Festival and what's billed as America's Largest Christmas Bazaar, each December at the Expo Center.

The Portland/Oregon Visitors Association distributes a detailed "Annual Calendar of Major Upcoming Events." It's a good place to start for info on annual celebrations as well as one-time events. There's a good chance you'll find something appealing; the one we have on our desk right now has 38 pages of fine print listings!

While June may seem like the busiest month, tourists and conventioneers come to Portland year round, as we'll see next in *Toasting the Tourists*.

Toasting the Tourists

> Tourism and travel, in terms of visitor expenditures, now represents a more than $2 billion industry in Oregon. Tourism ranks as the second largest employer in Oregon with an estimated employment of 44,000.
>
> Julie Curtis, "Tourism Gives Economy a Boost," *Daily Journal of Commerce 1991 Industry Edition*, February 21, 1991.

Some may debate the numbers quoted above. They'll point out that most service workers in the tourism industry take home paltry paychecks, since so many make only minimum wage. But the main point – that tourists and other visitors contribute mightily to the state's economy – is not debatable.

What's the impact on Portland? Who comes, and what do they do here? The Portland Oregon Visitors Association (POVA) provided some "Quick Facts," compiled from *Oregon Travel and Tourism,* a study done for the Oregon Tourist Division by Dean Runyan Associates in January, 1989 and May, 1990:

- ▸ 61% of the more than 6,000,000 annual out-of-state visitors who come to Oregon spend at least some time in the Portland area.

- ▸ Only 2% of Portland's visitors are from foreign countries. 38% come from the Far West or Hawaii. 12% are from southern states, 14% are from the Great Lakes, and 16% hail from what POVA calls the "Frontier West."

- ▸ All but 2% of Portland's visitors spend at least one night in Oregon. 35% stay from three to five nights, 24% stay between six and nine nights, and 21% stay for ten or more. The average stay in Oregon is seven nights long.

- ▸ More than half of Portland's visitors – or 54% – say the purpose of their visit is to take a vacation or pleasure trip. Another 13% come to visit with friends or family. 11% combine business and pleasure, and 10% come for a conference or convention. 5% come on business, and another 5% are just "traveling through."

- ▸ 80% of Portland area visitors relax and go sightseeing.

More than half (51%) shop, and not quite half (49%) visit a museum or other historical attraction. 47% spend time visiting family and friends, and 32% dine at restaurants or go to clubs.

Top Attractions

Just where do the tourists go when they do go sightseeing? According to the September 23-29, 1991 *Business Journal*, the zoo can boast the most visitors among the sights in town. Here's the paper's rundown on top attractions in Portland:

Destination:	Visitors in 1990:
Metro Washington Park Zoo	965,000
Oregon Museum of Science and Industry	400,000
Portland Art Museum	171,000
World Forestry Center	60,000

Counts since 1990 are even higher. For example, the zoo had more than a million visitors annually in the last few years. And according to the October 18, 1992 *Oregonian*, about 600,000 people a year had been visiting the old OMSI building at the time of move. OMSI staff expect that the new facility will attract more than 1,000,000 visitors annually. Visitors also go in droves to sights nearby Portland. In 1990, 1.9 million people went to Multnomah Falls and 1.2 million visited Timberline Lodge.

We're In The Money

And all the tourists spend money. An August, 1990 POVA brochure notes that visitors spend $937 million in the Portland area every year, generating 11,700 jobs. Much of the money comes during June, thanks to the Rose Festival and Blazer basketball. With the added festivities for the NBA draft and the Tournament of the Americas, 1992 was a particularly good year.

The June 26, 1992 *Oregonian* reported that the 1992 Tournament of the Americas would be "a potential $40 million boost to the region's economy." According to state economist Paul

Warner, whose comments were summarized in the May 30, 1992 *Oregonian*, the 600 or so reporters that would cover the 1992 NBA championships would spend about $1.5 million. And that doesn't even consider all those Bulls fans who came to town.

Conventions and Conventioneers

Before the opening of the Oregon Convention Center in September, 1990, POVA found that 10% of the area's visitors arrived to attend a conference or convention. With convention bookings running far better than initial projections, it's a safe bet that the number of conventioneers in town is on the rise. According to the Association for Portland Progress, the Convention Center "projects more than 450,000 delegates attending 100 conventions over the next five years."

Using industry standards, POVA estimates that "convention delegates spend approximately $520 per stay" when attending a convention. The "trickle effect" suggests that we can multiply that figure by three to get a sense of the overall economic impact of a conventioneer's dollars.

Twin Peaks

Conventioneers – and the all important people who book conventions – seem to really like the new Convention Center. The *Daily Journal of Commerce 1991 Industry Edition* summed it up nicely:

> The Oregon Convention Center already is pulling down national honors. *Business Week* featured the center among the top three architectural projects in its recent Best of 1990 tribute. Visitors in the know like Bill Taylor, president of the American Society of Association Executives – whose members sponsor virtually all of the nation's conventions – called the center "one of the prettiest I've seen" and said it is capable of handling his members' conventions "marvelously."

Located in northeast Portland, just across the river from downtown, the center is hard to miss. Its two matching, graceful, glass towers – or, as locals say, the Twin Peaks – are truly a shining addition to the skyline. Here are the Convention Center specs, from center literature:

Total capacity:	10,000 people
Banquet seating:	6,000 people
Exhibit space:	150,000 square feet
Ballroom space:	25,000 square feet
Meeting space:	30,000 square feet
Parking for:	900 vehicles

Promoters also note that the Convention Center is conveniently located right on the MAX transit line, only two blocks from the Memorial Coliseum. The center has added roughly 3,400 jobs to the area, generating an additional $4 million annually in tax revenues and $140 million in business revenues.

Reservations Required

One less than perfect piece of this otherwise successful scenario is that hotel space is sometimes scarce. In 1991, Portland had a little more than 12,000 hotel rooms, with about 5,100 in the city center – not near enough for the bigger conventions. When the Rotary International Convention came in June, 1990, its 21,400 attendees were housed all over the metro area. Some Rotarians stayed in hotels or private homes that were more than an hour's drive from Portland. The situation may be similar for the Elks, who anticipate 18,000 attendees for their July, 1993 convention. The National Square Dance Convention will bring a whopping 25,000 attendees in June of 1994.

Fortunately, plans for the Convention Center area do include a large, first-class hotel. According to the terms of their agreement with the Portland Development Commission, the developers who own the land must break ground by mid 1994. The first phase of the project calls for a 400 room "headquarters hotel." If it is successful, the developers will expand to 700-800 rooms.

No Room At the Inn

In the meantime, the hotel occupancy rate is encouraging to area hoteliers and city boosters. For much of 1992, it was in the

75% range. During June, the larger hotels were reporting occupancy rates of 90% or more, with many days of full occupancy.

So where do the tourists stay? Most stay wherever they can get a room. But some movers and shakers have definite preferences. Here's how the May 25, 1992 *Business Journal* saw it:

> The Heathman, by many accounts, is considered the hotel of artists, musicians, writers and other well-funded notables in the creative industries, such as movie producers. The Benson, Hilton and Marriott, which have large banquet facilities, seem to attract many of the political shindigs. The Benson, Hilton, Hotel Vintage Plaza, Heathman and even the new Governor Hotel garner film stars, while film and production crews and opera singers tend to stay at the Mark Spencer. The Cypress Inn and Red Lion Inns also have hosted many film production companies. Sports teams tend to stay at the Red Lion Hotels, the Marriott, the Benson, and occasionally the Vintage Plaza.

Indeed, it was the Vintage Plaza that played host to the Chicago Bulls, when they came to town for the championship games during the 1992 version of *June Daze*.

Don't Forget the Expo Center

In all the excitement about the Oregon Convention Center, the Portland Exposition Center seems to get lost in the shuffle. With more than 220,000 square feet of indoor exhibit space and 3,500 parking spots, you'd think it would be hard to lose. The Expo Center, in North Portland, is one of the largest trade show facilities on the west coast. It regularly hosts some of the area's biggest shows, like the Portland Boat Show, America's Largest Antique and Collectibles Sale, the Pacific Northwest Sportsmen's Show and America's Largest Christmas Bazaar.

Portland's Living Room

Finally, we can't close our section on tourists without a visit to Portland's Living Room. We described Pioneer Courthouse

Square on page 61, in *A Bird's Eye View*. Here's two more descriptions. They say as much about the square as they do about the Portlanders who helped build it, and now enjoy it. The first is from the May 1992 *Travel Holiday* magazine:

> Portland's most important architectural statement is the block that doesn't have a building on it at all. The center of the city, the most valuable piece of real estate in town, is reserved for open space. Pioneer Courthouse Square, a grand, European-style plaza, is the perfect spot for people-watching and for brown-bagging, often accompanied by concerts – impromptu and choreographed.

Another popular square activity was described by Julie C. Sterling, in the September 1989 issue of *T.W.A. Ambassador*:

> In the case of Pioneer Courthouse Square, citizens' outpourings of time and money...transformed it from a parking garage into a spacious playground that pokes fun at the solemnity of a public meeting place. Roses...and ladybugs adorn the capitals of the square's columns. One column, in fact, lies on its side, broken into sections suitable for sitting or playing chess.
>
> Despite its eccentric features, even the most down-to-earth Portlanders have taken a proprietary interest in the square. Less than a decade ago, 64,000 locals helped pay for its construction by buying the bricks that now pave it. On almost any day a random few of these people can be seen wandering around the square as if they were looking for a lost quarter. What they are really doing is searching for the bricks that bear their names.

Among other square "eccentricities" are the *Weather Machine*, a kinetic sculpture that announces the weather daily at noon; *Allow Me*, a J. Seward Johnson statue of a man hurrying across the square, umbrella protecting him from the rain; and the wrought iron gate and fence from the Portland Hotel, which once occupied this city block. Appropriately, the square was dedicated on April 6, 1984. April 6th is Portland's birthday.

Brews, Brewers and Brewpubs

Nowhere in North America do people drink more microbrewed draft beer.

Jim McConnaughey, "Take Me To the River," *American Brewer*, Fall 1990.

Many of the tourists who come to Portland already know the city's reputation for microbrewed beer. The rest learn quick, when they are offered a variety of locally brewed beers at restaurants. Henry Weinhard built the city's first brewery in 1863, and we continue to drink his brew today. But we have, as the above quote suggests, a wealth of other choices.

The Portland Brews

In the mid 1980s, microbrews began appearing on the Portland scene. Bridgeport Brewing Company began in 1984, and Widmer Brewing Company the following year. 1985 was also the year that the McMenamin brothers opened the Hillsdale Brewery & Public House, the first brewpub in Oregon since prohibition.

According to Stuart Ramsay, writer, brewer and organizer of the Oregon Brewers Festival, Portland has indeed become the center of the new Northwest industry of microbrewing. The April 22, 1991 *Business Journal* lists the nine most active Oregon microbrewers. Four of the top five – Widmer, Bridgeport, McMenamins Pubs & Breweries, and Portland Brewing – are located in the Rose City. And new microbrewers seem to be entering the fast-growing market about as frequently as the established ones are announcing expansions.

Good Numbers Getting Better

So it should be no surprise that Portland has more small breweries and brewpubs than any other U.S. city. Depending on the season, Portland brewers offer 30 to 40 or more different beers to increasingly sophisticated Portland palates. They must be on the right track: more than half of the draft beer sold in downtown Portland in 1991 was from local microbreweries.

Another indication of success is the steadily rising sales figures. According to Ramsay, two of the Portland microbreweries enjoyed annual sales increases of 100% and 150% in 1990. And sales totals are respectable: it was announced at the 1990 Oregon Brewers Festival that draft sales for Oregon microbrews make up 7% of the total market share. By 1991, microbrewers had claimed 10% of the draft beer sales in Oregon. And local microbrews are becoming increasingly popular in California.

They Even Have A Festival

The Oregon Brewers Festival is another indicator of the industry's success. Since its inception in 1988, the three day festival has become a popular, annual summer event at Waterfront Park. Small brewers from throughout North America travel to Portland to participate. The numbers are impressive:

- The 500 volunteers who would serve 7,650 gallons of beer at the 1992 festival expected about 35,000 people. Attendees would enjoy the opportunity to taste brews from 51 different breweries.
- The 1991 festival featured 46 different brews. In 1990 there were 39.

Blame It On the Rain

What's the secret of Portland's brewing success? Those in the business offer the following explanations:

- The climate (read rain) encourages a tavern culture.
- Oregonians traditionally support local products.
- Portlanders found the first microbrews to be a welcome change from industrial beers, so they kept on tasting.
- The right raw ingredients are available in the region.
- Restaurant and tavern owners were supportive from the beginning, so much so that local brews are available in most Portland establishments.

The most recent development appears to be public stock offerings. In December 1992, two companies announced plans to go public. Henry would be proud.

Coffee, Coffee, Everywhere

In addition to our penchant for microbrews, tourists are quick to notice our affection for another beverage. They are tipped off by the large number of Portlanders who carry cups. Sometimes they are tall paper ones; often they are large plastic mugs that have the logos of local coffee bars. But they are all filled with the same basic ingredient: aromatic, steaming coffee.

With "the highest per capita consumption of 'gourmet' coffee beans" in the U.S., an August 25, 1991 article in *The New York Times* called Seattle "the coffee capital of the country." A year later, the August 25, 1992 *New York Times* revisited the issue, noting that "the Pacific Northwest is fast becoming known as a sort of 'latte-land,' as Jean Godden, a columnist for The Seattle Times, calls it."

Much of what is popular in Seattle soon hits Portland, and coffee is no different. Although the coffee roasters who participated in the first Portland Cup – a coffee tasting sponsored by McCormick & Schmick's Seafood Restaurant in November 1991 – knew of no definitive studies, they agreed that Portland is quickly catching up with Seattle.

For the Coffee Lovers

According to David Kobos, of The Kobos Company, 90% of the coffee sold in the U.S. is the typical supermarket variety. Specialty coffees account for the remaining 10%. But in Portland and Seattle, about 15% of the coffee sold is gourmet, freshly-roasted coffee. Kobos opened Portland's first pure specialty coffee roaster in 1973. The Kobos Company now operates six stores. Thousands of Portlanders carry the distinctive red and blue Kobos mug to keep their favorite brew hot and close by.

As we'd expect in a growing market, other coffee roasters and retailers have also become well established in Portland. Starbucks, Seattle's first coffee roaster, entered the Portland market in 1989, and had fourteen stores at press time. Coffee People operates seven, including the famous Motor-Moka, a drive-through that serves about 2,500 drivers each day. In fact, Portlanders can order regular coffee, espresso, cafe latte or a whole range of other gourmet coffee drinks at more than 40 coffee bars in the Portland area. And that does not include the many coffee carts that dot the city, the espresso bars in area supermarkets, or the restaurants and cafes that will gladly serve a cappuccino-to-go. We've even seen espresso signs in the windows of gas stations and hardware stores.

The Portland Cup

Six Northwest coffee roasters – Boyd's Coffee, The Kobos Company, Longbottom Coffee & Tea, Millstone Coffee, Starbucks, and Coffee Bean International – were invited to participate in The Portland Cup. They competed in five categories. Looking for the best "unadulterated brew," a panel of six tasters, known "tastemakers" in Portland, scored the black coffee entries in a blind taste test for flavor, aroma, body and acidity. The winner? According to the press release, "Coffee Bean International...was rated the No. 1 best overall cup of coffee." Here are the category winners:

Best Morning Wake-Up:
The Kobos Company, for Kenyan Estate

Best Daytime Interlude:
The Kobos Company, for Guatemalan San Sebastian Estate

Best After Dinner Partner:
Coffee Bean International, for Velvet Sumatra

Best Chaperon for Brandy:
The Kobos Company, for Sumatra Manheling

Best Decaf for All Day Zealots and Late Night Revelers:
Boyd's Coffee, for French Roast Decaf

The organizers were delighted that Portland brews took "top honors," winning handily over Washington-based Starbucks and Millstone. They immediately announced plans for the next Portland Cup, when they'll taste espresso, latte and cappuccino. Which is a good idea. According to Barry Bernard, who opened the first espresso cart in Portland in 1982, latte is ordered "most frequently" but cappuccino is "most representative." You can read his story in the October 25, 1992 *Oregonian*, Or go have coffee. His cart is the one on the Park Blocks near Madison, by the Portland Art Museum.

Regarding Restaurants

All kinds of tastes sweep through the city these days, and even locals dubious about the new subdivisions wouldn't stop the new sauté pans at the border. These days you can get decent New York pizza, reasonable barbecue, flown-in lox, and fettuccine al limone around here. Portland is having its own Northwest cuisine explosion, including nationally known chefs who have moved in. The Vietnamese refugees who provided some of Portland's most exciting cuisine in the '80s are being reinforced by phad Thai purveyors and sushi chefs prepared for customers who last tasted toro in Tokyo. Portland is even making some dents in its Italian food deficiencies, a lasagne lacuna that many thought could be rectified only by forced busing of Italians from Newark. Over one year, deft cucina hands moved in from San Francisco, Atlanta, and Sacramento, and the dominant Portland pasta presence is no longer Chef Boy-Ar-Dee.

David Sarasohn, "Introduction," *Portland Best Places*, 1992.

Much as we may like our beverages, they don't completely substitute for lunch and dinner. At least not all the time. There are many choices for both natives and visitors, and as David Sarasohn suggests, it's getting better all the time. Various city boosters and some of the guidebooks claim that Portland has more restaurants per capita than any other city. None quote a source for that statistic, but it is certainly true that there are many good restaurants in all price ranges. You can find restaurant recommendations in a variety of ways:

▸ The 1992 edition of *Portland Best Places* includes restaurant reviews for the "Top 150 Restaurants" in the Portland area.

▸ Each fall, *Willamette Week* compiles an annual restaurant supplement, which comes free with the paper. The 1992 version included 107 picks.

▸ *The Oregonian* does an annual restaurant guide called "Diner" that also appears in the fall.

▸ Bargain-hunters should get a restaurant coupon book. Many groups sell them as fundraisers. For example, *The Enter-*

tainment Book offers hundreds of two-for-one dinner coupons. For upscale places, it includes typical menus too.

▸ Another way to check out restaurant menus is to get a copy of *The Menu Restaurant Guide to Portland,* a book that came out in 1991. It is "a collection of menus from many of the most popular restaurants in Multnomah, Washington, Clackamas, Clark and Yamhill Counties."

▸ Or just check current issues of *Willamette Week* or *The Oregonian.* Both review restaurants regularly.

Find Your Favorites

As with the bookstores, everyone has their own favorite. We'll defer to the experts and just mention three.

▸ The 1992 *Willamette Week* Restaurant Guide picked Zefiro, on NW 21st, as Restaurant of the Year. According to the review by Jim Dixon, "entrees represent the cuisines of Spain, southern France, North Africa and, of course, Italy, but with the best provender of the Northwest."

▸ *The Oregonian's* pick for 1992 Restaurant of the Year was Esparza's Tex-Mex Cafe, on SE Ankeny. According to the review by Karen Brooks, "the secret of Esparza's cooking is its newness: stuff you won't find elsewhere. An inventory of nightly specialties featuring smoked buffalo, duck, wild boar and other rarities pushes Esparza's to the pinnacle of greatness."

▸ Finally, there's Jake's. When Jonathan Nicholas wrote about Jake's 100th birthday in his column in the February 23, 1992 *Oregonian,* he wrote about "the holy trinity of Jake's bounty: charm, crab and chocolate truffle cake." We'll end with one more of his comments, as a toast to both Jake's and Portland:

> Because it so much personifies the maverick spirit of our city – one part Godiva, one part Gore-tex – Jake's remains the first place on almost everyone's list to take the hungry visitor from out of town.

Whether you opt for Tex-Mex, crab or fettuccine al limone, you'll do fine. Bon appetit.

Familiar Folks

The final explanation we offer to those who come for *June Daze* – or any days – concerns names and nicknames, for Portlanders are very familiar folks. They are quick to be on a first name basis, and they have nicknames for everything from buildings and stores to city landmarks and flowers.

Neil, Earl and Vera

For example, during Neil Goldschmidt's tenure as governor, visitors were often surprised at the number of people who called him Neil. It is true, of course, that Goldschmidt was the popular mayor of Portland from 1972 to 1979. And in a small state like Oregon, it's not unusual to have had an opportunity to meet the governor. But Portlanders were just as comfortable referring to Earl Blumenauer and Vera Katz, the 1992 mayoral candidates, as Earl and Vera. We're a little less likely to refer to Governor Roberts as Barbara, although her critics are fond of calling her Babs.

Perhaps it's just a small state syndrome, because a similar phenomenon is apparently at work in Arkansas. In his July 9, 1992 column in *The Oregonian*, Steve Duin quoted a Little Rock teacher who said that "two-thirds of the people in Arkansas call Bill Clinton by his first name."

Rhodies, MAX and Big Pink

Portlanders also like nicknames. The city itself has many, including the official City of Roses, as well as informal ones, like Puddletown, Rip City and the Carousel Capital of the World. (See *A Rose By Any Other Name* on page 9 for more on Portland's monikers.) But there are many other nicknames you're bound to hear. The nicknames usually convey a fondness for the object so named, or poke fun with no real malice intended.

In our descriptions of Portland, we mentioned some of the more popular ones. Like WW and The Big O, for *Willamette Week* and *The Oregonian*. Like MAX, for the Metropolitan Area Express, the 15 mile light rail line that connects east side Gresham with downtown Portland. Like Twin Peaks, the 310 foot, green, glass and steel towers of the Oregon Convention Center. Although the center's opening celebration was called Party-by-the-Points, and the Portland/Oregon Visitors Association gives Twin Spires awards, the towers were quickly dubbed the Twin Peaks. And of course, the Schnitz, for the Arlene Schnitzer Concert Hall, which is part of the Portland Center for the Performing Arts.

But there's also the Glass Palace, aka the Memorial Coliseum. There's the Winnie, for the Winningstad, another Performing Arts Center theater. And there are two for the lovely *Portlandia*: the Copper Goddess, and Queen Kong. Perhaps this is a good place to mention that she is occasionally the butt of practical jokes, like the morning city workers arrived at the Portland Building to find a giant yo-yo in her outstretched hand. Here are a few more of the nicknames that we haven't mentioned yet, that you might hear around town.

Rhodies

While we're known as the Rose City, it's hard to spend much time in Portland without noticing the rhododendrons. Natives call them rhodies, and you'll see many different kinds, in a variety of colors, all over the city. A particularly good spot to enjoy the rhodies is the Rhododendron Garden, in southeast Portland. This garden is large enough to qualify as a park, and it can be enjoyed all year round – but it's really worth a visit or two in the spring, when the rhodies are in bloom.

Freddy's

Freddy's, or sometimes Fred's, is the familiar way that some Portlanders refer to Fred Meyer stores. A cross between a K-Mart, a supermarket and a lumber yard, you can get almost anything at Fred Meyer's, from a bake-at-home pizza to a rosebush; from jogging pants to a gallon of paint.

In *The Growth of a City: Power and Politics in Portland, Oregon 1915 to 1950*, E. Kimbark MacColl noted that Fred Meyer "created his opportunities by accurately predicting and even influencing where the commercial activity would be centered 10 or 20 years later." That may be why everyone – from the folks who live in style up in the hills to those who live in more working class digs – shops at Freddy's. His "one stop shopping" is a real draw, and with 27 Fred Meyer stores in the area, there always seems to be one close by.

Perhaps another reason Portlanders feel a fondness for Fred Meyer and his stores is the founder's generosity. As MacColl explains, "he left an estate of more than $60 million with nearly the entire amount bequeathed to a charitable trust, the income to be used for 'religious, charitable, scientific, literary or educational purposes.'" While we see the Fred Meyer name most often in advertisements, we also hear frequently of projects funded by the Fred Meyer Charitable Trust.

Nordie's

Nordie's is the nickname for Nordstrom. Offering impeccable service and high quality merchandise, upscale Nordstrom is a favorite department store. A friend confessed that when she left the country to live abroad, she sold her house, her furniture and her car, as she didn't expect to come back. But she kept her Nordstrom credit card tucked away in her wallet. When the overseas move didn't work out as planned, her first stop after the airport was Nordstrom. You really can believe the "I'd Rather Be Shopping at Nordstrom" bumper stickers.

We've also heard mention of Normie's, Mervie's, and Stroh's. Norm Thompson Outfitters is a Portland-based store and mail order company for well made, upscale, often imported clothes and unique gifts. Mervyn's, a department store with good values, is a west coast chain. And Strohecker's is a family owned grocery store on SW Patton that is a favorite among Heightsy-babes.

Heightsy-babe

Actually, this one is not heard "around town" quite in the way the other nicknames are. Heightsy-babes are girls who live in Portland Heights and attend either Ainsworth Elementary School and Lincoln High or private schools. We heard it from a third generation Portlander, who grew up in the Heights, though she now lives in the foothills in a less ritzy area. She called herself "a Heightsy-babe who slid down the hill," and confirmed that the term used when she was a child is still in use today. But its use apparently isn't very common off the Heights. Most of the Portland natives we asked in our unscientific sample had not heard it before.

Schonz

Schonz, or sometimes the Schonz, is Bill Schonely, the Trail Blazer announcer who broadcasts the Blazer games on TV. He made his reputation on the Blazer radio network, where he announced more than 2,000 games before he made the move to TV in 1992. Schonely is responsible for popularizing a "hoopful" of colorful expressions that he uses to call the play-by-play action. Most famous of these is "Rip City" for a shot that touches nothing but net on its way through the hoop. Others include "lickety-brindle," used when a player runs down the court on the way to a fast break; "equator," for the mid-court line; and "climbs the golden ladder," which Schonely uses when a player rises above the rim to get a critical rebound.

Big Pink and the Black Box

Big Pink is our nickname for the U.S. Bancorp Tower, the 43-story building at 111 SW Fifth. With bronzed windows and a facade of pink marble, the building appears rose colored. According to the *Portland Catalogue*, Big Pink, which was designed by Skidmore, Owings, and Merrill, was voted the best-liked building in Portland in 1983.

The Black Box is the building at 200 SW Market. It was built in 1972, and renovated a few years ago when John Russell of Russell Development bought it. The developers wanted a new nickname too. They announced a new moniker – Black Beauty – along with the extensive renovation plans. John Russell's young daughter, who had picked the new name, even arrived to make the announcement atop a black Tennessee walking horse. But Black Beauty never really took hold, and Portlanders continue to refer to 200 Market as the Black Box.

Pill Hill

Like a number of other U.S. cities, Portland has a Pill Hill. Ours refers to the medical campus that sits atop Marquam Hill, in southwest Portland. The Oregon Health Sciences University is there, with University Hospital, and the Schools of Dentistry, Medicine and Nursing. The Doernbecher Children's Hospital is there too, as is the Shriners Hospital for Crippled Children. On the next rise is the Veteran's Hospital. The views are wonderful from Marquam Hill, and the approach via Terwilliger Boulevard is a favorite for walkers and joggers.

Henry's

Henry's is a Henry Weinhard beer, as in "give me a Henry's." Weinhard built the city's first brewery in 1863, only four years after Oregon achieved statehood. By 1907, H. Weinhard Brewers was one of only four locally-owned companies that was worth over $1 million. His beer is still a favorite, although as we've seen, a host of young Oregon microbrewers are giving him some quality competition.

The Ones You'd Rather Forget

Regular readers of The Big O know that Jonathan Nicholas uses lots of nicknames – many of his own invention. Here's a sample, from his April 10, 1991 column:

> Re. my comments earlier this week comparing the 1000 Broadway tower to a doughnut, a Nicholas Notifier with distinct architectural overtones wonders whether I've heard what our burg's blueprint brigade has dubbed the distinctive high-rise: The deodorant roll-on building.

Let's hope that nickname doesn't stick. The same goes for "Three Groins in a Fountain," the nickname for a downtown fountain with three nudes. You can see it near the Standard Insurance Building.

But don't let these last two put you off. The large majority of our nicknames are fun and favorable, and they are used with a real fondness for the object so mentioned.

There's one more thing to tell the folks who come for *June Daze*. And that's how to top off their visit with a look at Portland's environs.

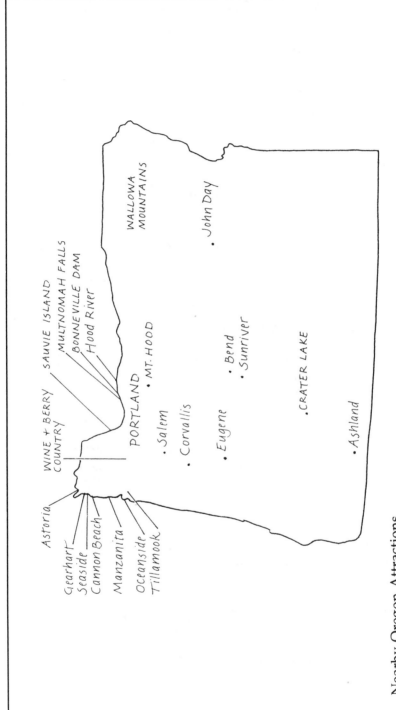

Nearby Oregon Attractions

You Can Get There From Here

Remember the guy from New Jersey who we mentioned on page 107, in *Taking the Trail Today?* Eager to snap up a Portland property – sight unseen – he asked a local realtor to find him a Portland home with a view of the ocean. While those in the know laugh, the story contains a glimmer of truth. There is a sense in Portland that the natural environment is very close at hand. The ease with which we can pursue outdoor sports or simply "get away" helps define Portland's identity. Whether you like fishing, white water rafting, berry picking, skiing, mountain climbing, tidepooling, hiking, fossil hunting or just watching the waves, you can get there from here.

The map on the previous page does not include all the possibilities. But it does help locate some of the diversions we'll mention. Check one of the guidebooks or maps we mention on page 337, and you'll be on your way.

An Hour's Drive

Here's a small sampling of nearby choices. Driving times are always approximate, depending on where you are when you start, but the ones that follow are all less than an hour's drive for just about everyone in the metro area:

▸ Multnomah Falls, or the eleven other spectacular falls along the Historic Columbia River Highway.

▸ A winery; about 25 of the state's more than 75 wineries dot the landscape just west and south of Portland.

▸ Sauvie Island, just northwest of the city, where you can swim, fish, pick berries, or do a little bird watching.

▸ The Bonneville Dam, 40 miles east of Portland; where you can watch Chinook salmon and steelhead climb the ladders. You can also see the fish hatchery, some of the power production facilities, and the navigation locks.

▸ A drive along Washington County's Route 210, through farmland famous for grapes, berries, and nuts, where you can sample the produce at a road-side stand or u-pick farm.

On The Road Again

The next group of destinations are more than an hour's drive, but generally not much more than two:

- ▸ Astoria, Gearhart, Seaside, Cannon Beach, Manzanita, Oceanside, Tillamook, or one of the many other Oregon coast destinations west or northwest of Portland.

- ▸ Mt. Hood, with five ski areas, the famous Timberline Lodge and activities that you can enjoy all year round.

- ▸ Hood River, in the Columbia Gorge, where you can try your hand at windsurfing or watch others do it.

The most popular weekend trips are to the coast or central Oregon, but the state has a host of other appealing destinations. There's the Oregon Shakespeare Festival in Ashland and hiking at Crater Lake in southern Oregon. The Deschutes River, a few hours east of the city, is popular with those who like river rafting. Those who are willing to travel further east can try the more treacherous rapids on the Snake River, along the Oregon-Idaho border. The Rogue River, in southwest Oregon, is also a favorite. The Wallowa Mountains, which have been nicknamed "the Switzerland of America," stand remote and spectacular in northeastern Oregon. Another eastern destination is the Fossil Beds in John Day.

Eugene and Corvallis are frequent destinations for Oregon Duck and Oregon State Beaver fans, as well as those who like wandering around college towns. Oregon school kids take class trips to the State Capitol in Salem. There are a variety of destinations that commemorate the Oregon Trail. And lots of people head north into Washington, for a weekend in Seattle or to do the volcano tour at Mount St. Helens. Here's where to turn for information to help you on your way.

Happy Trails

Just about all the Portland guidebooks include information on other Oregon destinations. Or check these:

- ▸ You can get a hefty envelope full of free information from the Tourism Division of the Oregon Economic Development Department. The same materials are available at tourist information centers around the state. In particular, look for *The Oregon Official Travel Guide, Where to Stay in Oregon, The Official Highway Map of Oregon,* and the *Oregon Bicycling Guide.*

▸ Those interested in exploring wineries should get *Discover Oregon Wineries,* which is available at tourist centers or from the Oregon Winegrowers Association. It has six tour routes, a wineries calendar and information on Oregon's 75+ wineries.

▸ If you stop by the Portland/Oregon Visitors Association, you'll find friendly and knowledgeable people who can give you all the details we don't have room for, along with more brochures than you could possibly want, and a big welcome. It's on SW Salmon at Front Street, in downtown Portland.

It's How Far?

Finally, to give you a sense of just how far we are from other places, here's the mileage from Portland to selected cities:

City:	Mileage:	City:	Mileage:
Albuquerque	1,372	New Orleans	2,653
Anchorage	2,674	New York	3,053
Atlanta	2,664	Philadelphia	2,976
Boise	442	Phoenix	1,268
Boston	3,216	Pittsburgh	2,683
Chicago	2,217	Salt Lake City	818
Cleveland	2,568	San Francisco	658
Dallas	2,146	Seattle	175
Denver	1,302	Spokane	370
Detroit	2,488	St. Louis	2,057
Houston	2,243	Tacoma	142
Los Angeles	1,017	Vancouver, BC	336
Miami	3,257	Victoria, BC	237
Minneapolis	1,799	Washington, DC	2,925

Before we close, let's go back to the City of Roses, to take stock, and to see what we may have missed there.

Last

Licks

"World enough,

and time"

While our Portland picture is long and detailed, it is by no means complete. To borrow a bit from Andrew Marvell's *To His Coy Mistress*, "Had we but world enough, and time," we could have done it all. But we face the joint constraints of page length and timeliness. Those two facts of life forced us to pick and choose among the innumerable facts of life in Portland, Oregon that we could include.

We chose to include the topics that we believe are of the most importance to Portlanders. Like crime and growth, taxes and schools. We also chose to include those things that set Portland apart, like the awards we've won, the arts and cultural scene here, and our concern for the environment around us.

That meant inevitable cuts. We made them – often with regret – but we promise to fill in the blanks in *More Facts of Life in Portland, Oregon*. In fact, it's already in the works. In the meantime, we'll consider, briefly, some topics that you should not overlook. We'll include sources that you can turn to for more information. And we promise a proper examination in *More Facts*.

Economics 101, Portland Style

You'll find economic data throughout *The Facts of Life in Portland, Oregon*. For example, the government section includes information on taxes, the chapters on housing include home prices and apartment rents, and the population profile has figures on income and population growth. But a brief overview of the economy will help fill in some of the blanks. We'll start with a description from a Portland Development Commission brochure that was distributed to the press in June 1992, during the NBA finals, the NBA draft, and the Tournament of the Americas:

> Portland's economy is thriving. Employment is growing at 1 to 2% and population at 3.9% Our economy is one of the most diversified on the West Coast, providing a stable environment for new investment. We are the leading Pacific Northwest warehouse and distribution center, with twice the space of Seattle. Entrepreneurism is very strong; Oregon has the nation's highest percentage of small businesses. And international trade is growing steadily with the Pacific Rim and much of Europe.

Why? William B. Conerly, Vice President and Economist for First Interstate Bank, offered this answer in the April 29, 1991 *Business Journal*:

> The cause of Portland's growth defies the stereotypes about regional economies. The Northwest's largest industry, wood products, is shrinking. Tektronix Inc. has laid off thousands of employees and no longer is Portland's largest private employer. So how do we manage to have one of the strongest economies in the country?
>
> The idea behind the traditional view, a very Keynesian view, is that jobs are created by major industries. The alternative view is that jobs follow people. Both views are right at certain times, in certain places. Right now in Portland, the jobs are following the people who are moving here.

According to Conerly, "Portland's growth will continue so long as the quality of life is perceived to be better here than elsewhere."

It's Job-Related

More than half of the jobs in the state – 51.7% – are in the Portland metro area. Here are some facts and figures about all those jobs:

▸ The Portland area is not dependent on one major employer. The top 50 private sector Portland employers employ an average of 2,000 workers. Firms of less than 100 employees provide jobs for almost half the city's workers.

▸ The largest employers in the area include retail giants, like Fred Meyer and Safeway; high tech companies, like Tektronix and Intel; health care providers, like Legacy Health System, Oregon Health Sciences University, and Kaiser Permanente; financial institutions, like U.S. Bancorp, First Interstate, and PacifiCorp; manufacturing companies, like Nike, Freightliner, and Precision Castparts; and utilities, like the Bonneville Power Administration and Portland General Corp. U.S. West and the U.S. Post Office are also among the area's largest employers.

▸ The work force includes more than 832,000 people. According to the PDC, the work force has expanded 13.9% since 1987.

▸ In 1991, 16.6% of the work force was employed in manufacturing. The average manufacturing wage varies from month to month. In 1992, it fluctuated between a low of $11.74 and a high of $12.70.

There are many sources for more information on local employers and the labor force:

▸ *Largest Employers of the Portland Metropolitan Area* and *Manufacturers of the Portland Metropolitan Area* are available from the Portland Metropolitan Chamber of Commerce.

▸ The "Top 25" lists, which appear weekly in *The Business Journal*, profile area businesses and organizations. For example, recent lists have focused on architectural firms, advertising agencies, art galleries, publicly held companies, hospitals, and universities. Each spring, *The Business Journal* compiles the weekly lists into an annual publication, *The Top 25 Book of Lists.*

▶ *Contacts Influential: Portland Edition* provides business information, including names, addresses, and phone numbers, for local companies.

▶ *Portland Metropolitan Labor Trends,* a monthly newsletter from the Oregon State Employment Division, provides a wealth of statistical information on the labor force, unemployment, and manufacturing.

Pay Dirt

When we looked at the census in *A Portland Profile,* we saw that the median household income in the city of Portland in 1989 was $25,592. It was higher – $31,071 – for the metro area. The 1991 *Editor & Publisher Market Guide* has more recent figures. Their estimate for household income in the Portland metropolitan area is $36,347.

The Bureau of Labor Statistics provides data on average annual pay. According to a report in the January 12, 1993 *Oregonian,* Portlanders were paid an average of $24,577 a year in 1991. That's a 4.8% increase over 1990. We beat the national average of $24,575 by just $2, but we lagged behind the average for metro areas, which was $25,729. On a percentage basis, we did well: our 4.8% increase was better than the 4.1% increase seen nationwide.

There's one more important income fact, that appeared in the Portland Future Focus *Environmental Scan.* Both Portland and Multnomah County have a larger share of the region's disadvantaged than other locations in the metro area. About 60% of the region's registered unemployed reside in Multnomah County. Portland has more people who live on fixed incomes, more people who receive public assistance, more people whose incomes are below the official poverty level, and more homeless people than other areas in the region.

Help Wanted?

What about the unemployed? In February 1993, staff at the Oregon Employment Division anticipated that the final 1992

Portland metro unemployment rate would be verified at 6.2%. That is substantially higher than the 1991 rate of 4.7% and the 1990 rate of 4.2%. The 1990 *Environmental Scan* projected that the unemployment rate in the region would vary from 4.8% to 6.0% through 1995. In 1992, the Employment Division projected that the unemployment rate for 1993 would be about 5.8%.

As we'd expect from the rising unemployment rate, the number of help wanted ads in *The Oregonian* fell between 1990 and 1992. There were 285,852 ads in 1992, down substantially from 422,864 in 1990.

High Hopes for High Tech

Experts see the high technology industry – and the business high tech companies generate for accounting, advertising, law, real estate, and public relations firms – as critical to diversifying the economy of the state. Oregon high tech companies are involved in many aspects of the industry, including the development, design, and manufacture of semiconductors, engineering tools, parallel processing, software, computer peripherals, and systems products. Oregon companies are also involved in telecommunications and biotechnology. Despite the layoffs that periodically plague this industry, high tech should continue to be a growth area in the '90s. And much of it will happen in the Portland metro area.

According to the Portland Development Commission, about 900 high tech companies are located in the metro area. They are responsible for about 75% of the state's high tech jobs. In recent years, both people and companies have left the Silicon Valley in California to head for the "Silicon Forest" in Oregon. New nicknames are even popping up, the latest being the "Parallel Valley," a reference to the high concentration of parallel processing companies and research centers that are located in Washington County.

Although we hear most often about Tektronix, Intel, Mentor Graphics, and Sequent – high tech firms that employ thousands of workers in the Portland area – the Silicon Forest also includes a host of smaller spin-offs, start-ups, suppliers, and service providers. And they do a lot of business. An article in the December 3-9, 1992 *Willamette Week* indicated that in 1991, about 35% of the state's exports were high tech products. That topped the 28% that were agricultural exports and the 27% that were wood products exports. Clearly, the Silicon Forest is a place to watch. These directories may be of interest to both watchers and participants:

- ▶ *Resource Guide: Oregon High Technology*
- ▶ *Advanced Technology in the Pacific Northwest*
- ▶ *Northwest High Tech: A Guide to the Computer Industry of the Pacific Northwest and Canada.*

Pacific Rim Profit

Another place to watch is the Pacific Rim. According to the PDC, Portland ranks first in wholesale trade among Northwest cities and first in export tonnage among west coast ports. Figures from the International Trade Institute at PSU indicate that most of this trade involves other Pacific Rim countries.

The numbers are pretty staggering. In 1991, total exports were valued at about $5.9 billion. Imports were slightly less, totalling about $5.5 billion. In terms of total value, Japan is our leading trading partner for both imports and exports. South Korea is second in both categories. We'll take a peek at the Port of Portland – where all this trading takes place – shortly. But first we'll look briefly at Japan, since that country factors so prominently in both high tech and trade.

The Japanese Connection

During America Japan Week, the May 20, 1992 *Oregonian* reported that "Japanese businesses have a $460.5 million investment in the Portland area. Eventual investment is projected at more than $1 billion." That means "about 6,700 jobs now, more than 15,000 jobs eventually." According to the August 16, 1992 *Oregonian,* Japan is "the biggest foreign investor in the state," with assets valued at more than $1 billion.

While the economy in Japan may slow things down a bit for a while, the August 16, 1992 *Oregonian* reported that "Tokyo money men predict a new wave of yen in about three years, as Japanese firms recover and find the Northwest an attractive alternative to the Sunbelt."

All this activity translates into lots of business travel. Fortunately, Delta Airlines offers daily flights to Tokyo. Those flights both grease and fuel Pacific Rim business. For more information on Japanese trade and investment, check Wallace Bain's *Japanese Investment in Oregon: A Case Study*, which is available from the International Trade Institute at PSU.

Retail Heaven

According to the Portland Development Commission, "Portland ranks number one in the nation among the top 50 markets in per capita general merchandise sales." Here's a few more retail sales facts:

- ▸ There are about 1,100 stores downtown, which is many more than the average for most cities of our size.
- ▸ The Lloyd Center is the largest mall in the Northwest.
- ▸ Nordstrom is expanding its Washington Square store. When the expansion is done it will be the largest Nordstrom in Oregon.
- ▸ Meier & Frank is also expanding at Washington Square. The expanded store will be the largest of all their stores in terms of both selling space and sales volume.
- ▸ Two remarkable stores picked the Portland metro area as the place to open first. Both Nike Town, in downtown Portland, and Tandy's Incredible Universe, in Wilsonville, have attracted national attention for their unique marketing concepts.

As for space, the PDC counts about 28 million square feet of retail space in the metro area. According to the January 14, 1993 *Oregonian*, the vacancy rate in 1992 was 5.4%. Real estate experts expect that retail sales space vacancy rates in 1993 will be in the 4.5% to 4.8% range.

As for more information, if you want to buy or build a store, you might begin by contacting the PDC. If you just want to shop, *The Portland Super Shopper*, by David and Carolyn Gabbe, is a good source for info on Rose City bargains.

Need A Building?

What about the office space market in Portland? The January 14, 1993 *Oregonian* reported a 1992 vacancy rate of

12.3% in the metro area. That's down from the 1991 rate of 15.3%. Experts project a rate of about 10.3% in 1993. They do not foresee any new buildings going up downtown. If you're in the market for an office building or want more info on office space, the *Portland Metropolitan Office Guide,* an annual publication from the Portland Metropolitan Association of Building Owners and Managers (BOMA) is a good place to start.

As for industrial space, PDC brochures report that there are more than 135 industrial parks in the metro area. They also note that Portland has "the lowest land and building costs of any major West Coast city...." Both the Chamber of Commerce and the PDC cite the same suburban areas as the main locations for recent and future industrial development. They are:

▸ The Columbia Corridor, a 16 mile long section just south of the Columbia River, which includes the Port's marine terminals and Portland International Airport;

▸ The I-5 Corridor, from southwest Portland to Wilsonville, which is part of the larger corridor that runs from Seattle to Eugene;

▸ The Sunnyside 205 Corridor, at the intersection of Highway 212/224 and I-205, a fast-growing, mixed use area that is home to the large Clackamas Town Center mall;

▸ And the Sunset Corridor, west of Portland along U.S. 26, which is known nationally as the high tech area of the region.

Experts quoted in the January 14, 1993 *Oregonian* project an industrial space vacancy rate of about 12.2% in 1993.

Is It Spendy?

How does it all add up? Is it expensive to live in Portland? Or, as Portlanders might say, is it spendy? The American Chamber of Commerce Researchers Association (ACCRA) prepares a cost of living index four times a year, which considers necessities like housing, health care, groceries, transportation, and utilities in selected metro areas. A score of 100 is equal to the national average. According to the September 1991 issue of *Portland Metropolitan Labor Trends,* which included the following data, "costs are weighted to reflect expenditure patterns for mid-management households." Here is a sample of west coast city scores, for the first quarter of 1991:

City:	Score:
San Diego	131.4
Los Angeles	120.9
Sacramento	106.3
Seattle	115.1
Portland	109.2

Labor Trends cautions us that the ACCRA index "does <u>not</u> measure price changes over time. Each report is a separate comparison of prices at a single point in time, and the number and mix of participants may not remain the same from quarter to quarter." But we've checked the index from time to time in the course of researching this book, and Portland usually has one of the lowest scores among major west coast cities. For example, Portland's third quarter 1990 score was lowest of the five cities noted above. The second quarter 1992 index did not list Sacramento or San Diego, but the Portland index of 109.7 was substantially less than Seattle's 118.1 and LA's 131.7. For more information, check the *ACCRA Cost of Living Index*, or contact the Portland Metropolitan Chamber of Commerce.

Economics From Day to Day

This is just the tip of the economic iceberg. In addition to the sources we've mentioned already, the weekly *Business Journal* is a great source for up-to-date economic information. *The Monitor*, a quarterly supplement to *The Business Journal*, may be especially helpful. For daily business news, try the business section of *The Oregonian* or the *Daily Journal of Commerce*.

With a passing grade in *Economics 101* under our collective belts, we can move on to *Keep On Trucking*, where we'll consider a variety of transportation, trade and transit topics.

Keep On Trucking

In a literal sense, we need to keep the economy moving. We've mentioned Tri-Met and trade, bike commuting and bridges. Here's a quick survey of a few more topics that are too important to miss, to round out the transportation picture.

The Port in Portland

Portland was not named for the Port, but it may well have been, for the Port is a crucial factor in Portland's identity and economy, and it has been for 100 years. Speaking at festivities in honor of the Port's centennial anniversary in February 1991, Portland historian E. Kimbark MacColl called the Port "the most significant public agency in Portland in the past century." According to a recent study done for the Port, Port activities generate almost 17,000 jobs.

When the legislature created the Port in 1891, its mission was to dig and maintain a 25 foot channel from Portland to the Pacific. Concerned that the city's shallow channel might affect ocean commerce, the legislature acted to protect and strengthen the city's growing function as a regional trading center. Port responsibilities grew steadily. They now include marine, aviation, ship repair, and industrial land development operations.

The Port intends to maintain its competitive edge. It has continually upgraded and expanded facilities. The Port is currently involved in a $111 million expansion at the airport, and Port officials expect to spend about $185 million in the next 20 years to expand, repair, or replace marine terminals. Here's a few more fast facts selected from Port of Portland brochures:

- More than 7.2 million passengers flew into or out of Portland International Airport, or PDX, in 1992.

- Fourteen passenger airlines fly daily between Portland and more than 120 cities.

- The Port is first among west coast ports for total export cargo tonnage.

- Because Portland is served by 18 cargo airlines, more than 100 truck lines, 17 tug and barge lines, and 3 railroads, marine shippers can arrange easy connections for cargo.

▸ The Port's intermodal service is top notch. For example, the on-dock rail facility provides Port customers with "the lowest import rates and the shortest transit time from the Pacific Northwest to most major U.S. cities."

▸ The Portland Ship Repair Yard is one of the largest in the world. The Port owns the yard, maintains its facilities, and moves ships. Private firms perform the repairs.

Go see for yourself. The Port offers tours on Saturdays in the summer. Tours take you through the marine terminals, the shipyards and the airport.

The Best Transit in America

Those who have read prior sections know that Tri-Met was named the Best Large Transit Agency by the American Public Transit Association. They've read about MAX, the light rail line that connects Gresham and downtown Portland, and "fareless square," the area downtown in which the buses and MAX are free. Here's a few more details from Tri-Met literature:

▸ In 1992, Tri-Met had about 200,000 riders each weekday. That's up from about 146,000 in 1991. Tri-Met projects weekday ridership to total 216,000 in 1993, 310,000 in 1997 and a whopping 690,000 by 2005.

▸ As long as it isn't rush hour or Rose Festival, you can take your bike on MAX. Tri-Met is experimenting with bikes on buses, by allowing them on buses on selected routes.

▸ Plans are in the works for low-floor light rail line cars, which will make MAX more accessible to people in wheelchairs and those who find steps difficult.

▸ Regular adult fares are $.95 or $1.25, depending on the distance traveled. Senior and disabled riders pay $.45. The youth fare, for those 18 and under, is $.70. Reduced fares are available by purchasing monthly passes or discount tickets.

▸ The downtown transit mall on SW Fifth and Sixth Avenues has exclusive bus lanes. The brick mall makes transfers easier and helps minimize conflicts between buses, cars and trucks. Covered bus shelters provide computerized transit information.

The mall is being extended to NW Fifth and to NW Sixth. By 1994, it will reach Union Station.

▸ The boundaries of fareless square may be expanding. Plans for Portland call for a truly unified downtown that spans the river, and some have suggested that one way to facilitate that goal would be to expand the free ride zone to some close-in areas on the east side.

▸ Drivers will stop anywhere along late-night routes to discharge passengers who are travelling alone.

▸ Each commuter who uses Tri-Met instead of a car keeps 78 pounds of pollutants from entering the air annually. More than 110,000 cars remain off area roads daily, because their owners opt to ride Tri-Met.

▸ A western extension of MAX is being built. When it is completed in 1997, commuters will be able to travel on light rail to go between Hillsboro and downtown Portland. Long-range plans call for a regional light rail system connecting downtown Portland with Vancouver, the airport, Clackamas, Milwaukie, and Tigard.

▸ There are occasional complaints. One is heard from would-be riders. They note that while Tri-Met is great for getting from outlying areas to the center city and back, travel between two suburbs (or even two bordering neighborhoods) can be inconvenient, especially during the middle of the day. Others would like to see more late-night bus routes and service to more areas and neighborhoods in the region. For complete information on schedules and routes, call the Tri-Met trip planning desk.

Car Commuting

What about the folks who still drive to work? How long does it take? Are there parking spots downtown? Here are some commuting facts of life:

▸ The 1990 census found that the average commute for those who live within the Portland city limits takes 20.3 minutes. Looking at the entire metro area, the average commute takes 21.7 minutes. In 1993, most observers estimated that the average commute was between 20 and 25 minutes.

▸ According to the Association for Portland Progress, the downtown is within a 20 minute commute for about 75% of the area's work force.

▸ But, according to a Tri-Met informational ad in the April 29, 1990 *Oregonian*, "the average speed on the Sunset Highway during peak rush hour is only 15 MPH." For those not in the know, the Sunset Highway is the local name for the often congested part of Highway 26 that runs through Washington County, connecting Portland with places west like Beaverton and Hillsboro.

▸ To keep air quality high, Portland restricts the number of downtown parking spots. In January 1993, the "parking lid" – which includes both on-street and off-street parking – was 44,220 spots. It breaks down as follows:

42,359	existing parking spots
1,201	approved but not yet constructed spots
660	reserve spots (that could be approved and constructed)

▸ With the lid on, parking in the central part of the city is tight. Some people rent spots, for roughly $100/month, in private parking lots. Others park on the east side and walk or hop a bus across the river.

▸ If you don't have a monthly spot, plan to pay $.75 per hour for the first four hours at both metered parking on the street and in city lots. It's $1.50 for each hour after the fourth, up to a max of $7.00. You can park all evening for just $1.50. Many stores and businesses will validate parking tickets, providing up to two free hours of downtown parking for their clients and shoppers. If you opt for a private lot, you'll pay more.

At the Pumps

For a variety of reasons, gas prices tend to be high in Portland. Self-service gas stations are not legal in Oregon, and taxes are high here. We're also located at the very end of the Olympic pipeline, and have a variety of environmental regulations that can up the price. Experts don't always agree on the reasons or on the impact of supplies and profit margins on prices, but the fact remains that prices are high. During the spring and summer of 1992, they were among the highest in the country.

Get A Horse?

If the parking lid and the gas prices get you down, there are a few other options. Like the trolley that connects Lake Oswego and Portland, a water taxi that may soon make stops along the river, or one of the horse-drawn carriages that can be hired downtown. As for cabs, you'll have the most success if you phone for one, since they don't cruise around as they do in some other cities. Or just look for one in front of a hotel.

Traveling to the Future

Just about everyone agrees that growth in population and employment will affect commuting and transportation needs. According to the *Tri-Met Strategic Plan* of December 1992, "current projections show the number of total trips within the [region's] suburbs will increase by 72 percent over the next 20 years." As for the state, "the number of vehicle miles traveled increased **eight** times faster than the population" in the 1980s.

In his article in the November 1992 issue of *The Atlantic*, Philip Langdon notes another sobering statistic: the "total miles driven in the Portland area jumped 55 percent during the 1980s." Langdon also describes a solution:

> Many planners believe that if a number of sizable mixed-use centers, incorporating offices, stores, housing, and parks, are built – dense, walkable, and connected to public transit – people will have more choices of how to get around and the region can remain compact.

Mixed-use strategies are mentioned in the Tri-Met plan too, and they are certainly part of the solution. Planners are considering other options too. For example, should the region implement congestion pricing, which would charge rush hour commuters for their use of certain roads? Should traffic impact or transportation development fees be assessed when land is developed? Would a west side bypass that connects I-5 with Route 26 help or harm? What will be the impact of planned light rail extensions? What road improvements will be necessary during the '90s? For more information on questions like these, and the interrelationship between growth, land use, and transportation, check the following sources:

▸ The *Regional Transportation Plan*, which is available from METRO.

▸ *The Land Use, Transportation, Air Quality Connection*, also known as LUTRAQ, which is a 1000 Friends of Oregon study that looks at the issues that give it its name.

▸ The *Tri-Met Strategic Plan: Pursuing A Shared Vision*, which is available from Tri-Met.

Do As I Do . . .

As we think about transportation in the future, we can't help but remember that Mayor Vera Katz doesn't drive. Staff members do help out by driving her to some of the meetings and events that fill her schedule, but she is no stranger to public transit. As for the city commissioners, Gretchen Kafoury walks to work, and Charlie Hales rides the bus. Earl Blumenauer and Mike Lindberg drive to work, although Earl "bikes on and off," according to his staff. Ex-Mayor Bud Clark was often seen biking to and from City Hall. When he left for the final time on December 31, 1992, he was on his bike, despite a snowstorm that swirled around him.

If we Portlanders can just imitate this mix, we can go a long way towards solving many of our transportation troubles. With one exception: you might want to consider Tri-Met – or cross country skis – in the snow!

Two more sections remain. *Choices and Challenges* looks at a variety of urban problems and state-wide issues – like higher education, drug use, race relations, and conservation – that impact on Portland. *Body and Soul* looks at topics like health care, philanthropy, religion, and clubs. Most of the topics we'll consider are part of the fabric of life in all cities. But a look is necessary, because it will tell us a bit more about the particular fabric that we weave in Portland, Oregon.

Choices and Challenges

A number of serious issues face urban dwellers. Portland is not immune to any of them. And as Portlanders, we confront issues that are facing all Oregonians. In both cases, the problems and their resolutions will inevitably affect the quality of life in Portland. Here's a survey of some key topics to watch.

Critical Critters

It's impossible to spend any time in Portland without hearing about old growth forests and the spotted owl. Conversations about salmon runs and the rivers are becoming as commonplace. For the survival of these critters – and the implementation of federal legislation that protects them – has an enormous impact on people and the economy. A look at the spotted owl will help explain the connection.

For several years, the northern spotted owl has been the focus in a battle between environmentalists on one side, and the timber industry and its workers on the other. Because the spotted owl is an endangered species, federal law can in certain instances restrict logging to preserve owl habitat. To timber workers and mill owners, that means job losses and fewer logs to sell. To environmentalists, it means that the owl and old growth forests may have a chance to survive.

The timber industry stresses that the owl's survival should not be at the expense of loggers and logging. Environmentalists counter that the owl is only one of many species supported by old growth forests. With little old growth left, they say, we must preserve it for future generations. Moreover, they believe that the industry is in trouble more from weakening demand, mechanization, and raw log exports than from the owl. The controversy has innumerable twists, and the battles are being waged in court, in Congress, at federal agencies, in suffering timber towns, and in the media.

Critical Critters, Part 2

It may be hard to imagine a similar controversy with even broader impact, but that is exactly what is on the horizon. As J.D. Hultine wrote in *The Oregonian* on July 8, 1991, "Unlike the northern spotted owl vs. the timber industry, the salmon issue facing the Northwest involves a much larger and more diverse group of businesses and potentially every person who pays an electric bill or ships an agricultural product down the Columbia." An *Oregonian* editorial hammered the point home on September 4, 1991: "Make no mistake, protecting fish, if done right, is likely to raise electric rates, raise transportation costs, reduce irrigation water for farmers and reduce the catch of commercial, sport and Indian fisherman."

The August 22, 1992 *Oregonian* listed 17 plants and animals that "live or once lived in the Pacific Northwest that have been listed as endangered or threatened." The marbled murrelet, a small seabird, has been added since then, and environmentalists are petitioning the U.S. Fish and Wildlife Service to consider other critters that they believe are at risk. With the Endangered Species Act up for reauthorization in 1993, future installments in these sagas are anyone's guess. But the critters and the legislation merit our attention, for the decisions that are made will greatly impact our lives right here in Portland.

The Powers That Be

The Portland metropolitan area has long been known as a place of abundant, pure, and clean water; inexpensive electricity; and competitively priced natural gas. But a variety of factors have combined to change that picture, particularly for water and electricity. They include recent droughts, increasing demand fueled by population growth, restrictions on river use to help save critical critters, and the decision to close the Trojan Nuclear Power Plant. We considered the water situation and Trojan in *An Environmental Report Card*. Let's look now at some of the players in the power game:

▸ The Northwest Power Planning Council is an eight member group with representatives from Oregon, Montana, Washington and Idaho. The Council implements the Pacific Northwest Electric Power Planning and Conservation Act, which governs electricity generation in the Northwest.

▸ The Bonneville Power Administration (BPA) is a power marketing agency that was created by Congress in 1937.

The BPA sells and transmits power produced at 30 federal hydroelectric dams in the Northwest. The BPA serves Oregon, Washington, Idaho and parts of Montana, by selling power wholesale to public and private utilities as well as a few large industrial customers. The BPA is also involved in programs to conserve existing power resources, develop new resources, and maintain fish and wildlife in the rivers that generate our electric power. With headquarters in Portland, more than 2,500 employees in metro Portland, and an annual payroll of $68.8 million, the BPA has considerable impact on the Portland area.

▸ The Portland General Electric Company (PGE), which is part of the Portland General Corporation, is one of the two investor-owned electric utilities that serve the Oregon part of the Portland metro area. PGE is one of the BPA's customers.

▸ Pacific Power, a division of PacifiCorp, is the other electric utility that serves the metro area. Pacific Power works with the BPA too.

▸ Northwest Natural Gas is the local gas distribution company that serves northwest Oregon and southwest Washington. Since they are an exclusive distributor, anyone in the metro area who needs gas service will join their more than 350,000 current customers.

▸ Finally, it is the Oregon Public Utility Commission that regulates rates and services.

All of these power players agree that we need to conserve, make more efficient use of electricity, and develop new sources of power. But given the current situation, it's a good bet that both industrial and residential rates will be on the rise, and that industrial customers may face power cutbacks.

Higher Education Blues

When he was Governor, Neil Goldschmidt formed the Governor's Commission on Higher Education in the Portland

Metropolitan Area. Their charge was to analyze the current situation and to propose a vision and blueprint for the future. What's happening at Portland's colleges and universities? Why was a higher education commission necessary? Their findings go a long way to explain why Goldschmidt saw the need for a commission in the first place. The November 1990 report described "a diverse set of strong institutions" and "new and enlightened leaders at many institutions." But the Commission also identified serious problems and called for many changes.

For the Portland metro area falls below national averages in the granting of bachelors, masters and doctoral degrees. And some companies chose not to locate here because they could not find the educational support and graduate programs they sought. Community colleges are overcrowded, and tuitions are on the rise. Most metro area students who seek a four-year college education enroll in a school elsewhere.

In terms of educational expenditures, the Portland metro area compares poorly to other medium sized cities. We receive comparatively low amounts of federal research funds, and, by national standards, our college and university faculty are underpaid. In the face of Measure 5 budget cuts, there is evidence that the situation is worsening.

Everyone we spoke to in the academic community was eager to tackle the problems. But some solutions cost money, and money is short. For more details, see the Commission's report, *Working Together: A Community and Academic Partnership for Greater Portland*. For information on individual colleges and universities, check the *Oregon Bluebook* or contact the school in question. And the media should provide news on how the public colleges and universities are coping with Measure 5 cuts.

A Place to Hang Your Hat

Not everyone worries about their electric bill or college tuition. Like other American cities, Portland has a sizeable homeless population, as well as a substantial number of people who are at risk for homelessness:

> ▸ An exact count is hard to come by, but most experts believe that, annually, between 17,000 and 20,000 people in Multnomah County are homeless.

▸ One night counts done for the 1990 census and by the Oregon Shelter Network indicate that between 1,700 and 1,800 people are homeless each night in the Portland metro area.

While census takers did try to include homeless people on the streets, the above numbers basically count homeless people in shelters. Scores of other homeless people take refuge with friends or relatives, or live on the streets, in cars, under bridges, or in other locations not intended for shelter. And while it may be the single adults who we notice on the streets, the problem is not confined to them:

▸ *The County-Wide Housing Affordability Strategy*, known as the CHAS, reported that about 2,300 Multnomah County families are homeless each year.

▸ The Multnomah County Youth Program Office estimates that between 1,500 to 2,000 youths were homeless in 1991.

For information on homelessness and low income housing issues, contact the Housing Authority of Portland (HAP). Their 1989 report, *Resolving Homelessness in Portland and Multnomah County*, is the most comprehensive study of Portland's homeless population. HAP can also provide information on the CHAS. The CHAS numbers that we cited were from the Public Discussion Draft of September 1991.

A Few Helping Hands

While the problems are serious, Portland can report a few successes. A number of public and private programs, like Operation Bootstrap and Central City Concern, have won national recognition for their efforts to fight homelessness. The Sisters of the Road Cafe was the first restaurant in the U.S. to accept food stamps, and their voucher program – that enables people to give meal vouchers rather than spare change to panhandlers – has become a national model. Finally, what began as the sharing of picnic leftovers has become a weekly Potluck in the Park. Every Sunday afternoon, thanks to Sharon

Darcy and her friends, volunteers meet on the South Park Blocks, where they feed more than 250 hungry people. Stop by any Sunday from 3 to 5 PM, with a dish to share, to find out more about these issues firsthand.

A House Is Not A Home. . .

Sadly, it isn't enough to have a roof over your head. Thousands of Portlanders are victims of domestic or sexual violence each year. According to *The County-Wide Housing Affordability Strategy*, between 1,550 and 1,650 people are housed annually in emergency shelters. About 350-400 are served annually in transitional housing. Unfortunately, the number in need far exceeds the beds available. Experts believe that only one of about six victims is ever served by the system.

Before One More Woman Dies, a report from the Tri-County Domestic and Sexual Violence Intervention Network, echoes the same tragic tale. The report estimates that almost 1,200 women and close to 1,000 children sought and found emergency shelter in the tri-county area in 1991. They represent just 10-15% of those in need of shelter. In all, more than 40,000 women called shelters or crisis lines in 1991.

Race Relations

Skinheads make headlines. An Afro-American *Oregonian* reporter writes of her experience when a Portland businessman verbally assaulted her at a downtown restaurant. *Willamette Week* reports that most of the board rooms in the city are overwhelmingly occupied by white men. There are charges of discrimination at the Portland Development Commission, and minority business owners protest that few public works contracts are awarded to minority-owned firms. And a June 6, 1991 report to the Metropolitan Human Relations Commission notes that "the past ten years have not been a decade of significant progress for equal opportunity at the City of Portland, in particular for minority group members."

While there are problems, Portland may have a better record than other places. According to Darrell Millner, who was Head of the Black Studies Department at Portland State University when he was quoted in the July 4-10, 1991 *Willamette*

Week, Portland is a tolerant place. "Despite the presence of white supremacist groups in the region, Millner says, there's less hostility toward minorities here than in other large cities. It's a factor he attributes not to any inherent open-mindedness on the part of Oregonians but to the small black population, which is seen as less threatening."

"Less hostility" is still hostility. While Portland may be seen as a pretty progressive place, there is clearly room for improvement. A good place to look for a full analysis of race relations in Portland is the City Club of Portland's 1991 *Study of Racial and Ethnic Relations in Portland*. This six part study looked at social associations and citizen participation, health and welfare, law enforcement and the administration of justice, housing, education, and employment. It provides a detailed and well-researched analysis of both the current situation and possible solutions in each area.

The Drugs Dilemma

We wrote of the general connection between crime and drug use in *Mean Streets*. That section also told of the connection between gangs and drug dealing in Portland. For a more complete picture of substance abuse in Portland, you can contact the Regional Drug Initiative (RDI), which is a "task force of concerned policymakers from business, government, education, housing, health care, law enforcement, treatment organizations and community groups." Their mission is "to reduce both the supply and the demand for illegal drugs."

The RDI has received national recognition and its programs have served as models for similar initiatives elsewhere. RDI efforts include:

- ▸ programs to help employers fight drugs in the workplace;
- ▸ conferences to encourage cooperation and communitywide strategies that go beyond law enforcement;
- ▸ a comprehensive listing of more than 200 prevention programs in Multnomah County;
- ▸ and the Drug Impact Index, which uses ten indicators to measure illegal drug use.

Another source for more information is the Multnomah County Alcohol and Drug Program. You can also check the following publications:

▸ The *Annual Oregon Crime and Drug Report* is available from the U.S. Attorney for the District of Oregon. It provides both statistics and narrative information on crime and drug use in the state.

▸ The *Oregon Public School Drug Use Survey* has information on drug use among youth. It was done by Doug Egan in 1990, for the Oregon Department of Human Resources, Office of Alcohol and Drug Abuse Programs.

As this section shows, not everyone enjoys our city's famous livability. Fortunately, many good souls − like the volunteers who feed hungry Portlanders each Sunday along the park blocks and those who answer the crisis line phones − are aware of the situation and are working toward solutions. We'll look at volunteerism and philanthropy, among other topics, in the final section, *Body and Soul*.

Body and Soul

Health care options. Exclusive social clubs. Women in government. Volunteer activities. Charitable donations. The unchurched. Evangelicals. What well-traveled celebrities think. Topics like these can teach us a little more about our city, and the people who call Portland home. Let's start with the ladies.

Ladies' Choice

According to the 1990 census, Portland has 225,405 females. That's 51.5% of the city's population. Nationally, females comprise 51.3% of the population, so we do have a slightly higher proportion of females here, but the number is not significantly higher. But in many ways, Portland seems to be a particularly comfortable place for women.

For example, as we saw in *Attention Sports Fans*, women like to run in the Portland marathon, and they do so each year in record numbers. According to an article in the February 16, 1992 *Oregonian*, "the Portland Symphony Orchestra – with 43 women and 44 men – has the largest number of women and the highest proportion of women of 10 comparable operations."

We also have a fairly large number of women in prominent government posts. They include Vera Katz, the Mayor of Portland and Rena Cusma, Executive Officer of Metro. Gladys McCoy, who died on April 11, 1993, was in the middle of her second term as chair of the Multnomah County Board of Commissioners. She had served on the Board since 1979. And several metro area women serve in the state legislature:

▸ Shirley Gold and Joyce Cohen are State Senators from Portland and Lake Oswego respectively;
▸ Gail Shibley, Mary Alice Ford, Lisa Naito and Beverly Stein are State Representatives from Portland;
▸ Sharon Wylie represents Gresham, and Delna Jones is the representative from Aloha.

There's also Judith Ramaley, who is President of Portland State University; Marilyn Eichinger, who heads OMSI; and Sherry Sheng, who is Director of the Washington Park Zoo.

Although we've tried to confine this book to Portland information, the following statistic was just too good to miss. During her first ten months in office in 1991, Governor Barbara Roberts – Oregon's first woman governor – appointed women to 49% of the appointments she filled. Not everyone likes it, but Roberts believes it's right on target.

Portland is also popular among lesbian women. Donna Red Wing, Director of the Lesbian Community Project, estimated that there are about 50,000 lesbian women in the Portland metro area. Those who are part of the lesbian community jokingly call Portland the "Lesbian Capital of the U.S." They speculate that there are more lesbians per capita in Portland than in any other U.S. city.

Friendly, Lenient and Comfortable?

For a number of years, members of the Portland gay community described Portland as a friendly, lenient and comfortable place. But that was before Measure 9 polarized the state. Although that anti-gay initiative was defeated in the November 1992 election – and Multnomah County voted more than 2-to-1 against Measure 9 – it is doubtful that very many gay men or lesbian women would choose those words to describe Portland in 1993.

Despite their 1992 defeat, the Oregon Citizens Alliance continues to push their anti-gay agenda. The OCA has identified 25 cities and 8 counties where Measure 9 support was high. There are a number of metro area cities on the hit list, including Canby, Cornelius, Forest Grove, Gresham, Hillsboro, Oregon City, Troutdale, and Wood Village. The OCA will try to pass "Son of 9" anti-gay amendments or ordinances in each jurisdiction. Their intent is to deny both minority status and civil rights protections to gay men and lesbian women, and to prohibit the use of government funds and public resources for anything that could be seen as promoting or approving of homosexuality.

Although the OCA casts a dark shadow, we can report a few local victories. For example, the Portland City Council approved an ordinance in October 1991 that prohibits "discrimination in housing, employment and public accommodations on the basis of race, religion, color, sex, marital status, familial status, national origin, age, mental or physical disability, sexual orientation or source of income...." And medical coverage is available to partners of unmarried Multnomah County employees who are in permanent domestic relationships, without regard to their marital status or sexual preference.

If you'd like more information on any of these issues, or on the gay and lesbian community in general, there are a number of resources available. They include:

▸ *Just Out*, a free bi-weekly newspaper;
▸ *The Just Out Pocketbook*, a free annual "resource guide for lesbian and gay Oregon";
▸ the more than 100 Portland gay and lesbian organizations and services listed in *The Just Out Pocketbook*;
▸ and *The Alternative Connection*, a free monthly newspaper "serving the community of alternative lifestyles."

"What's Up Doc?"

The Portland metropolitan area gets high marks from proponents of both traditional and alternative health care. Traditionalists boast of advantages like the high doctor-to-patient ratio and the nationally prominent research programs at the Oregon Health Sciences University (OHSU). Those who prefer alternative approaches boast that Portland is a good place to both learn and practice wellness and healing arts like acupuncture, naturopathic medicine, chiropractic, and massage therapy. Health maintenance programs are alive and well here too. The February 24, 1992 *Business Journal* lists six metro area HMOs. Their combined membership totaled almost 573,000.

What about medical costs? According to the August 8-14, 1991 *Willamette Week*, the Seattle actuarial firm of Milliman and Robertson Inc. looked at "dollars spent on hospital care, surgery, radiology, pathology and prescription drugs" in fifty large U.S. cities. Portland spent only 89% of the national average. Forty-five of the fifty cities spent more. But, as the article explains,

...the study doesn't prove that health-care costs are lower in Portland....Oregonians simply use the system less. [Chad] Cheriel [of the Oregon Office of Health Policy]

points out that, when compared to the rest of the country, state residents have fewer hospital admissions per year. And when they do go into the hospital, Oregonians don't stay as long....Although the average *per person* cost of health care may be relatively low in Portland, Cheriel contends that medical treatment here is not necessarily more affordable.

For more information, contact the Oregon Office of Health Policy.

What About AIDS?

Since 1981, the Oregon Health Division has kept a cumulative count of diagnosed AIDS cases. There were 1,024 AIDS cases reported in Multnomah County between 1981 and September 1992. The 1991 total was 173 cases; the 1992 total, through September, was 151. There are undoubtedly more people with AIDS in the county. But statistics are kept by state of diagnosis, so there is not an exact count.

How does Oregon compare to other states? State by state comparisons indicate that Oregon has a lower percentage of AIDS cases than many other states. The October 28, 1991 *Oregonian* reported 10 cases for every 100,000 Oregonians. The article included a few state comparisons: 25 per 100,000 in California; 36 per 100,000 in Florida; and, highest in the nation, 44 per 100,000 in New York. North Dakota, with just under one case per 100,000 people, was lowest.

While the state may have relatively fewer AIDS cases per 100,000 people, Multnomah County proportions are much higher than the state-wide figure. In August 1991, the Health Division calculated a case rate of 134.8 cases per 100,000 people in Multnomah County.

On the Health Horizon

Oregon made headlines in 1991 when the state legislature debated the budget for the new Oregon Health Plan. As health professionals and government staffers across the country looked on, Oregon took another step toward the implementation of universal health insurance for all Oregonians. Although our focus is on Portland, we mention the plan because it is unprecedented in the U.S., and because it will have great impact on poor and uninsured Portlanders, as well as Portland health providers.

The plan was authored by Dr. John Kitzhaber, a physician who served as President of the Oregon Senate. It is controversial in some circles, because it rations medical treatment, using a prioritized list of procedures and conditions. Critics decried the idea of rationing and priorities that choose between competing treatments and conditions. Supporters responded that, in reality, all health plans ration; typical Medicaid cutbacks simply slice out whole categories of people from receiving any care at all.

With bipartisan support, the plan was overwhelmingly passed in the Oregon legislature. But we still needed a federal waiver that would allow the state to modify Medicaid guidelines. The waiver was finally granted by the Clinton administration in March 1993. So the ball is back in the state legislature's court, for the folks in Salem must fund the plan – not a small task in the wake of Measure 5. It is not an exaggeration to say that the whole nation will be watching.

A More Holistic Approach

Portland offers many options for people who seek alternatives to traditional medicine, in part because Portland is home to the following schools:

▸ the Oregon College of Oriental Medicine, where students learn acupuncture, nutrition, oriental massage, use of chinese herbs, and the traditional or "western" sciences;

▸ the National College of Naturopathic Medicine, which trains naturopathic physicians;

▸ the East-West College of the Healing Arts, for massage;

▶ the Oregon School of Massage, another massage program;

▶ and the Western States Chiropractic College, which trains chiropractors.

It's quite a collection, considering that there are only two naturopathic colleges, ten nationally accredited acupuncture schools, and seventeen chiropractic colleges in the U.S. While people come to Portland specifically to study one or more of these healing professions, Portlanders also enroll in the programs. Many of the students who complete them remain in the area after graduation.

In general, Oregon is a good state for those practicing or seeking alternative medical care. Oregon is one of only eight states that licenses naturopaths as primary care providers, and Oregon naturopaths have the most leeway in the medical procedures that they may perform. Oregon acupuncturists can treat patients as independent practitioners.

The *Reflections Quarterly Resource Directory* is another good indicator of the range of alternative health care that is available here. This free directory "serves as a link between people who are interested in a holistic framework of personal and global change, growth, and health; and people who serve this community with professional services and businesses." It lists more than 250 services and products, including chiropractic care, massage therapy, stress management, counseling, naturopathic medicine, intuitive arts, yoga, reiki, meditation, hypnosis, wellness, tai chi, aromatherapy, acupuncture, relaxation, and a host of other holistic and alternative services.

According to publisher John Stuart Ivy, most major American cities have similar publications. But Portland has one of the highest per capita coverage rates. For example, the comparable directory that is published in New York distributes about 70,000 issues. Portland's *Reflections Quarterly Resource Directory* distributes 38,000-40,000 issues. If you prefer alternatives to traditional medical care, there's a good chance that there are providers here who are trained in the alternative you seek.

The In Crowd

If joining a club or working out is critical to your mental or physical health, you'll find many options for that too. There are more than 500 associations listed in the January 1991 edition of the *Portland Metropolitan Chamber of Commerce Associations Directory*. And estimates indicate that there are more than 4,000 philanthropic organizations in the Portland area. That's more than enough for even the most enthusiastic joiner around. We can't possibly tell you about them all, but we will mention a few of Portland's more prominent clubs and organizations. Two observed milestone anniversaries in 1991: the City Club of Portland celebrated its 75th anniversary, and the Multnomah Athletic Club its 100th. These organizations are Portland institutions, and a good number of Portlanders hold memberships in both the MAC and the City Club. But there the similarity fades.

"Forward-Looking Young Men"

As its 1991 Annual Report explains, the City Club sees its mission "in shaping public policy, spotlighting issues, and developing the leadership capacities of members." The Club's "legacy of progressive thought and action" goes back to the "forward-looking young men" who began the City Club in 1916. With about 2,600 members, the City Club "offers a nonpartisan public platform for the debate and discussion of civic issues." They invite all with an interest in such issues to join and participate.

The City Club is often controversial. Over the years, reports have examined problems like venereal disease, corruption in city government, and the status of race relations. The Club has called for legalizing prostitution in specific zones of Portland; merging Washington, Clackamas and Multnomah counties; and improving minority participation in city government, private organizations and community groups. Despite the controversy, the City Club rightfully deserves its "national reputation as the most prestigious platform in Oregon."

"Big MAC"

The Multnomah Athletic Club, on the other hand, brings a different kind of prestige to its members. The MAC, which began as a men's athletic club, is where affluent and well-connected Portlanders exercise, socialize and do business. With

19,500 members using extensive facilities at its SW Salmon Street location, the MAC is one of the largest private athletic clubs in the U.S. For more information on the "Big MAC," turn to page 301 in the section on sports.

Elite and Exclusive

When the MAC opened, the Arlington Club had already been around for 25 years. Established in 1867, the Arlington Club began as an exclusive men's club. Writing about the club in his July 30, 1986 *This Week Magazine* column, Karl Klooster explained that the club's "influence on its city, state and region in the early 20th century cannot be understated. During the two decades when Portland's growth was at its greatest, the decisions made within those walls determined much of the Northwest's economic and political direction."

Like so many other upper class men's clubs, the Arlington Club did not admit Jews, Asians, Afro-Americans or women until recently. The women came last; they were not admitted until 1990. But in 1991, the Arlington Club was one of the two clubs in the city that refused to answer a City Club survey on the racial composition of its membership. It remains a very private, exclusive institution.

There's also the Waverly Country Club, which is a golf club of 475 members, and the Racquet Club, which is in the West Hills. The Town Club is the female version of the Arlington Club. It began in 1928, with 235 members. Today, both men and women may be invited to join the 400 member club, should an opening become available. The Junior League of Portland, which was once made up of a select group of upper class women, opened its membership in the late '70s. Today, any woman between the ages of 20 and 44 with an interest in volunteer work may join. Finally, we must mention two groups that seem to be "particularly Portland" organizations: the Mazamas and the Royal Rosarians.

Meet You On The Mountain

The Mazamas, an association of hikers and climbers, have been around longer than the Rosarians. They'll celebrate their 100th anniversary in 1994. Membership is not open to anyone, and social ties won't get you in. The Mazama *Bulletin* explains that one must have "climbed on foot to the summit of a mountain on which there is a 'living' glacier...." It's only fitting: back in 1894, those who wanted to start a hiking organization were asked to assemble on a morning in March – on top of Mt. Hood.

Rosarian Reprise

We wrote of the Royal Rosarians in the section on the Rose Festival. They currently number about 200, although their bylaws allow a maximum of 220. Those who would like to join express their interest to a member. If they are approved by the Council, they are knighted – men as Sir Knights, women as Dames – and assigned a rose. Most of the members are men, since women became eligible only in recent years. For more on the Rosarians, turn back to page 315.

For the Masses

If you don't think you'll make it into the Arlington Club, the Town Club, or the MAC, don't despair. There are many other places to work out besides the MAC, and the *Portland Metropolitan Chamber of Commerce Associations Directory* is sure to list at least a few clubs or organizations in areas that interest you. If you prefer groups with a more liberal bent, check the *Portland Alliance*, a progressive, leftist monthly newspaper that prints an organizational directory every month, with a "comprehensive list of social change groups in Portland." The Environmental Federation of Oregon can send you a brochure on environmental organizations, and the National Volunteer Health Agencies of Oregon can send you one with information on health-related groups.

Finally, if you'd like some advice on social climbing in the Rose City, get a copy of the *Willamette Week* from April 12-19, 1990. Bonnie Martin Fazio's tongue-in-cheek article has a host of suggestions for you. For example, she suggests that you live in the West Hills; "the closer to Strohecker's, the better." Friday Evening Dancing Class and the Christmas Cotillion at the Multnomah Athletic Club are "correct" for climbing children. And when the time comes, Trinity Episcopal Church, St. Mary's

Cathedral or Temple Beth Israel should be booked for the wedding. If you're new to Portland and you're into climbing – and we don't mean with the Mazamas – consider her article required reading.

The Most Unchurched?

While a church wedding may be "de rigueur" for some, not very many Portlanders are regular church-goers. We made headlines in April 1991, when newspapers across the country reported that Oregon led the nation as the most "unchurched" state in the U.S. In other words, Oregon had the largest proportion of people claiming no religious affiliation. The data came from a 1989-90 national survey that was done for the City University of New York. 7.5% of those polled nationally indicated that they had no religious affiliation. Among Oregonians surveyed, 17% reported that they had no religion – more than double the national rate.

So it should have been no surprise when the July 18, 1992 *Oregonian* reported that fewer than one in three Oregonians go to church regularly. According a study called "Churches and Church Membership in the United States 1990," just 32.2% of Oregonians attended church regularly. Oregon was tied with Alaska for second-to-last place; just barely better than Nevada, where 32.1% of the population attended church regularly.

Sociologists believe that people in Portland are about as unchurched as those in the rest of the state. Religious leaders and academics offer various explanations. They suggest that we have many newcomers, some of whom deliberately chose to leave their affiliations behind. Other new residents have not yet sunk roots and affiliated. Another explanation suggests that we are not necessarily irreligious; we simply do not opt for organized religion and/or church participation.

The Churches of Choice

But what about those who do join a church or attend religious services? How does the population break down in terms of religious affiliation? Once again, the available numbers are state-wide totals. According to the 1990 study, Catholics are the largest denomination by far.

Denomination:	Adherents:
Catholic	279,650
Mormon	89,601
Evangelical Lutheran	48,958
Assemblies of God	47,035
United Methodist	42,209
Presbyterian Church (USA)	38,086
Christian Churches/	
Churches of Christ	36,650
Seventh Day Adventist	34,468
Southern Baptist Convention	31,260

The other 70 denominations listed in the study all have fewer than 30,000 adherents state-wide.

An Evangelical Hotbed?

While we may indeed have low rates of church attendance and affiliation, there are some indications that church participation may be on the rise in Portland. Or perhaps the evidence just suggests that the churched are making great efforts to reach the unchurched:

▸ More than 290,000 people went to see Billy Graham when he brought his crusade to Portland in September 1992. Organizers had anticipated about 200,000.

▸ According to the August 2, 1992 *Oregonian*, "the Pacific Northwest is a hotbed of evangelical activity." As the article explains, "religion-watchers see a tidal wave of religious fervor cresting in three American cities...Austin, Texas; Colorado Springs, Colo. – and Portland, Ore."

Other Traditions

What about non-Christian denominations? Portland is home to people of many faiths:

▸ According to the September 15, 1992 Portland *Jewish Review*, the American Jewish Committee reported "significant Jewish population increases" in southeast Florida; Atlanta, Georgia;

and Portland, Oregon. Although there are only about 12,000 to 15,000 Jews in the Portland metro area, and many are unaffiliated, Portland has a vibrant Jewish community. It includes eight congregations, a thriving day school, a community center, a retirement home and long-term care facility, and active local chapters of most national Jewish organizations.

▸ There are three mosques in Portland. And although most Asians in Portland are Christian, eight Buddhist centers serve several different Buddhist denominations.

The last group we'll mention are the people who were here first. According to Carl Abbott's *Ethnic Minorities in Portland: A 1990 Census Profile*, there are about 46,000 Native Americans in Multnomah, Clackamas and Washington counties. The Native Americans who were here when the first white settlers arrived were virtually decimated by disease. Those here today are descendants of tribes from all over North America. A small number are from Central and South America.

There are more than 100 federally recognized tribes in the Portland area. In December 1992, the Portland City Council designated a five acre parcel of land at Delta Park as the preferred site for an American Indian Cultural Center. When built, it will be used by members of all the tribes, for ceremonial events, art exhibits, classes, conferences, and other activities.

Money and Time

Some people give of their time; others write checks. Portlanders do both, although there is some debate on the extent of volunteerism and philanthropy in Portland. Here are some of the facts and figures being quoted lately:

▸ According to *Portland – City at a Crossroads*, the May 1990 report of the Portland Civic Index Project, "local trends regarding volunteerism and philanthropy reflect national trends."

▸ According to the Index Project report, individuals are the major source of contributions. But "the percentage of income contributed is not proportional to income; the largest incomes are not giving the largest percentages."

▸ Corporate giving in Portland is nothing to write home about. The typical corporate giver gives annually and has increased their giving budget in the last five years, but most "have no specific charitable giving guidelines." The Index Project also reports "a lack of broad corporate participation."

▸ The *Arts Plan 2000+* also discussed the extent of giving in Portland. That report concluded that "levels of private giving are also low by national standards. Participation levels – the percentage of individuals and businesses contributing to the arts – is within national norms.... However, the giving levels in Portland and the surrounding region, as reflected both in lead gifts and the average dollar level of gifts and sponsorships, are low."

The 1990 Annual Report for the United Way of the Columbia-Willamette presented a more positive picture. It reported that United Way "raised a record $19.6 million" in 1990. In December 1991, United Way announced that, for the first time in their history, they reached the $20 million mark, raising about $20,700,000. When the presidential salary scandal rocked the national offices of United Way, our chapter was the first affiliate to withhold dues, in an effort to force the national president's resignation. More than 10,000 local volunteers help in the United Way fundraising drives, and "hundreds of thousands" contribute.

As for volunteering, Matthew Prophet, who served as the Superintendent of the Portland Public Schools for ten years, offered this analysis in the March 25, 1992 *This Week Magazine*:

> There is a sense of volunteerism in Portland that I haven't seen in other places. Portlanders are very vocal about what they want, but they're also willing to work to help you do it.

The Volunteer Bureau of Greater Portland, which is one of about 100 United Way agencies, helps connect volunteer wannabes with programs in need of volunteers. In 1990-91, 330 volunteer programs took advantage of the Bureau's matchmaking, and the Bureau helped more than 4,400 prospective volunteers.

Etched in Stone

Portlanders gave both time and money to create the truly impressive memorials that we consider next. The Oregon Vietnam Veterans Living Memorial opened in 1987, and the Japanese American Historical Plaza was erected in 1990.

The Japanese American Historical Plaza stands along the Willamette River, across from Old Town. In the years before World War II, this section of Portland was called Japan Town, or Nihonmachi, and it was a thriving Japanese community. The Plaza's story wall recounts the experiences of the Japanese immigrants who came to Oregon. But, as Plaza creator Bob Murase explained in the Summer 1991 issue of *Oregon Humanities*, "a story that began as a somewhat typical immigrant history proceeds as a potent lesson on civil liberties, recollecting the wartime evacuation and relocation of nearly 120,000 Japanese Americans during 1942."

Visitors to the Plaza are reminded of the 33,000 Japanese Americans who served in the armed forces during the war, and of the names of the ten relocation camps, which often housed their relatives. Each part of the Plaza is a symbol that tells a story, from the "broken and fractured paving stones" to the break in the wall, symbolizing the breakup of the community. Poems engraved on the stones describe the evacuation experience. The words of the Bill of Rights remind us that Japanese Americans were deprived of due process. Recognizing mistakes of the past, the Plaza is also a commitment to the future.

More War Stories

While other states have erected Vietnam Memorials, few are of comparable scale to the one in Portland. Veterans donated time, equipment, supplies and money to help make it a reality. The black granite monument spirals up a hill in Washington Park. Names of all of the Oregonians who died, and those who are missing, are inscribed, year by year, on the shiny stone. A text by Terence O'Donnell is also chiseled into the granite, with descriptions of contemporaneous events in Oregon. The long list of names becomes all the more poignant as we are reminded of the lives they left – forever – back home.

In 1992, Portland hosted an exhibit that memorialized another wartime tragedy: the holocaust in Nazi Germany. More than 72,500 people visited the "Anne Frank in the World" exhibit when it was on display at the First Methodist Church. Exhibit organizers noted that Portland set an attendance record for the exhibit, which had been touring since 1985. Clearly, the permanent memorials we have chosen to erect and our high interest in this temporary exhibit have much to say about our collective souls.

Citing Celebrities

What about local notables? Whether they are movers and shakers, those we revere, or the folks who work quietly behind the scenes, their identities should shed some light on Portland and Portlanders, body and soul. In his column on August 13, 1991, Jonathan Nicholas listed "the 266 most interesting people in Portland." Alphabetically. Practically all of them are still here. We can't possibly repeat all the names, but if you're curious, you might have a look at the column the next time you're at the public library.

Finally, it is sometimes strangers who makes the most perceptive comments about the nature of a place. Thousands of visitors come to Portland each year. Unless they are relatives, we rarely hear what they think of our city. But we usually hear about the comments of celebrity visitors. And quite number of celebrities have made very complimentary comments about Portland. They include a wide variety of folks: Arts and Lectures Series speakers like Calvin Trillin, Philip Roth, and William Styron; movie stars like Faye Duniway and Madonna; and basketball players like Buck Williams, Larry Bird and Wilt Chamberlain.

But our favorite comment was one by President Clinton, which he made when he was campaigning in the Rose City in September 1992. The enthusiastic crowd that packed Pioneer Courthouse Square threw red and yellow roses at the candidate, who appropriately had a rose pinned to his lapel. "Of all the things I've had thrown at me," quipped Clinton, "roses are the best."

Legacy For The Future

We end, finally, just as we began. With Lewis Mumford's famous words to the members of the City Club of Portland:

> I have seen a lot of scenery in my life, but I have seen nothing so tempting as a home for man in this Oregon country....You have here the basis for civilization on its highest scale, and I am going to ask you a question which you may not like. Are you good enough to have this country in your possession? Have you got enough intelligence, imagination and cooperation among you to make the best use of these opportunities? Rebuilding our cities will be one of the major tasks of the next generation....In providing for new developments you have an opportunity here to do a job of city planning like nowhere else in the world.

Mumford spoke these words in 1938, but they still ring true. If he could see Portland today, we trust he'd compliment our progress to date. And that he'd wish us well, as we face the challenges of the 1990s and beyond.

Selected Bibliography

Books:

Abbott, Carl. *Portland: Gateway to the Northwest.* Northridge, CA: Windsor Publications, 1985.

Abbott, Carl. *Portland: Planning, Politics, and Growth in a Twentieth-Century City.* Lincoln: University of Nebraska, 1983.

Bosker, Gideon and Lena Lencek. *Frozen Music: A History of Portland Architecture.* Portland: Oregon Historical Society, 1985.

Boyer, Richard and David Savageau. *Places Rated Almanac: Your Guide to Finding the Best Places to Live in America.* New York: Prentice Hall, 1989.

The Business Journal. *Top 25 Lists.* Portland: The Business Journal, 1989-1992.

DeMarco, Gordon. *A Short History of Portland.* San Francisco: Lexikos, 1990.

The Family Resource Group. *A Comprehensive Guide to Family Resources in Portland.* Portland: The Family Resource Group, 1992.

The First Portland Catalogue. Portland: Earthlight Press, 1987.

Hughey, Donna and Karen Minkel. *The School Tool.* Portland: Portland Public Schools, 1992.

Irving, Stephanie and Kim Carlson, eds. *Portland Best Places.* Seattle: Sasquatch Books, 1992.

Lampman, Linda and Carolyn Wiecks. *The Portland Guidebook.* Seattle: JASI, 1989.

MacColl, E. Kimbark. *The Growth of a City: Power and Politics in Portland, Oregon 1915 to 1950.* Portland: The Georgian Press, 1979.

MacColl, E. Kimbark. *Merchants, Money and Power: The Portland Establishment 1843-1913.* Portland: The Georgian Press, 1988.

MacColl, E. Kimbark. *The Shaping of a City: Business and Politics in Portland, Oregon 1885-1915.* Portland: The Georgian Press, 1976.

O'Donnell, Terence and Thomas Vaughan. *Portland: an Informal History & Guide.* Portland: Oregon Historical Society, 1984.

Oregon Secretary of State. *Oregon Bluebook.* Salem: Office of the Secretary of State, 1991-92.

Price, Larry W., ed. *Portland's Changing Landscape.* Portland: Department of Geography, Portland State University, 1987. (Articles by Larry W. Price, Daniel M. Johnson, Nancy J. Chapman and Joan Starker were particularly helpful.)

Smith, Katlin. *Portland Rainy Day Guide.* San Francisco: Chronicle Books, 1983.

Wood, Sharon. *The Portland Bridge Book.* Portland: Oregon Historical Society, 1989.

Reports and Documents:

Abbott, Carl. *Ethnic Minorities in Portland: A 1990 Census Profile.* Portland: Portland State University Center for Urban Studies, 1991.

Citizens Crime Commission. *Public Safety 2000 Draft Report.* Portland: The Commission, 1992.

Governor's Commission on Higher Education in the Portland Metropolitan Area. *Working Together: A Community and Academic Partnership for Greater Portland.* Portland: The Commission, 1990.

METRO. *Recycling Level Survey.* Portland: METRO, 1991.

METRO. *Regional Factbook 1990.* Portland: METRO, 1990.

METRO. *Regional Forecast: Population, Housing and Employment Forecast to 1995 and 2010, Portland/Vancouver Metropolitan Area.* Portland: METRO, 1989.

METRO. *Regional Transportation Plan 1989 Update.* Portland: METRO, 1989.

Office of the City Auditor. *City of Portland Service Efforts and Accomplishments: 1990-91.* Portland: Office of the City Auditor, 1992.

Oregon Department of Environmental Quality and the Cartographic Center, Geography Department, Portland State University. *Oregon Environmental Atlas.* Portland: DEQ, 1988.

Oregon Legislative Revenue Office. *Implementation of Measure 5: House Plan - HB 2550A.* Salem: Legislative Revenue Office, 1991.

Portland Bureau of Planning. *Comprehensive Plan Goals and Policies.* Portland: The Bureau, 1980; latest revision (1991).

Portland Civic Index Project. *Portland – City at a Crossroads.* Portland: The Civic Index Project, 1989-90.

Portland Future Focus. *Environmental Scan.* Portland: Portland Future Focus, 1990.

Portland Police Bureau. *Annual Report*. Portland: The Bureau, 1989-1991.

Portland Public Schools. *Elementary School Profiles*. Portland: Portland Public Schools, 1990-91.

Portland Public Schools. *High School Profiles*. Portland: Portland Public Schools, 1990-91.

Portland Public Schools. *Middle School Profiles*. Portland: Portland Public Schools, 1990-91.

Tri-Met. *Tri-Met Strategic Plan: Pursuing a Shared Vision*. Portland: Tri-Met, 1992.

The Wolf Organization, Inc. *Arts Plan 2000+: A Cultural Plan for Portland and the Surrounding Region*. Cambridge, MA: The Wolf Organization, 1991.

Newspapers:

The Business Journal, 1989-1993.
The Daily Journal of Commerce, 1989-1993.
The Downtowner, 1989-1993.
The Oregonian, 1989-1993.
This Week Magazine, 1989-1993.
Willamette Week, 1989-1993.

Miscellaneous Publications:

A number of organizations and public agencies provided folders, brochures, booklets, public relations materials and other miscellaneous information. They include:

Ambassador Public Relations Network
Association for Portland Progress
Metro
Metropolitan Arts Commission
Oregon Economic Development Department, Tourism Division
Port of Portland
Portland Bureau of Environmental Services
Portland Bureau of Planning
Portland Development Commission
Portland Energy Office
Portland Metropolitan Chamber of Commerce
Portland Office of Finance and Administration
Portland Office of Neighborhood Associations
Portland, Oregon Visitors Association
Portland Parks and Recreation Department
Portland Public Schools
Portland Trail Blazers
Tri-Met
Will Vinton Studios

For Information Junkies

As we went to press, we learned of two new sources that Portland information junkies might appreciate. One became available in January 1993, and the other was in the works as of February 1993.

First, the Inside Line is a free telephone information service from *The Oregonian*. Callers can access more than 1,000 information categories. You simply call the Inside Line (225-5555) and enter a four digit number for the topic of your choice. Recorded messages provide information on everything from the weather in Wichita to the recipe for roast. As you can probably tell already, the focus is far broader than Portland. But the Inside Line is a good source for the latest in local news, weather, sports and the like.

Second, the *Neighborhood Information Profiles* will soon be available from the Office of Neighborhood Associations. They will provide census information at the neighborhood level. If you'd like information along the lines of the data that we presented on pages 97-102 – but for a specific neighborhood – contact the Office of Neighborhood Associations and ask if the new *Profiles* are ready yet.

For information on online access to the database that was the basis for the *Profiles*, or more details, contact Steve Johnson, Manager of Community Resources at the PSU Center for Urban Studies. He prepared the *Profiles* and is currently working on a number of related projects that are designed to inform Portlanders about Portland.

Finally, most people know that area libraries have back issues of newspapers. But not everyone is aware that you can purchase back issues from *The Oregonian*, *Willamette Week* and *The Business Journal*. WW has them all; the others keep a year's worth. Just request the issue you need by date.

Index

Author Note

Elaine S. Friedman fell in love with Portland on her first visit in May 1987. It was a good thing she did, since her family was about to move to the Rose City. When friends back east got tired of hearing her sing the praises of Portland, she decided to write *The Facts of Life in Portland, Oregon.* Elaine has always been in the information business, working as a librarian, database administrator, and research specialist for universities, law firms, urban agencies, and her own freelance research firm. *The Facts of Life in Portland, Oregon* is her first book.

Colophon

This book was set in 10.3 point Palatino, using WordPerfect for Windows 5.1 on a 386-33 DX machine. Camera-ready pages were printed on a NEC Silentwriter Model 95. The author sends special thanks to the kind people at the WordPerfect Corporation. Their knowledgeable and courteous customer service representatives, who were easy to reach at 800 numbers, were extremely helpful throughout the process.

Put our experienced researchers

to work for you!

Introducing. . .

The FAX of Life in Portland, Oregon

Do you need more information on Portland or Oregon? We would be happy to help you.

Just fax us your question, and we'll fax you back a price list and time estimate. Once we get your approval, we'll do the research and send you the information you need.

Small questions are as welcome as large research projects. And phone inquiries are fine too! Just call (503) 697 3391 or fax (503) 244 2099.

Let

The FAX of Life in Portland, Oregon

save time and provide expertise!

FAX (503) 244 2099

Phone (503) 697 3391

Portland Possibilities Inc.
Research Department
6949 SW 11th Drive
Portland, Oregon 97219

Ordering Information

The Facts of Life in Portland, Oregon, by Elaine S. Friedman, is available at bookstores in Oregon, Washington and California. You can also order by mail or through our 800 number.

The Facts of Life in Portland, Oregon	$14.95
Shipping and handling, first copy	2.00
Shipping and handling, additional copies	.75

To order by mail: Please photocopy the form below, or specify your request in a letter. Include a check payable to Portland Possibilities Inc. Mail orders to: Portland Possibilities Inc., Order Department, 6949 SW 11th Drive, Portland, OR 97219.

To order by phone: Please call (800) 858 9055. Phone orders must be charged to Visa or Mastercard. Please have card number and expiration date available when you call.

For information on bulk discounts, call (503) 697 3391.

Order Form

Please send _____ copies of *The Facts of Life in Portland, Oregon,* by Elaine S. Friedman. My check payable to Portland Possibilities Inc. is enclosed.

The Facts of Life in Portland, Oregon	$14.95
Shipping and handling, first copy	2.00
Shipping and handling, additional copies	.75

Name_____

Address_____

City_____State_____Zip_____

Mail orders to: Portland Possibilities Inc.
Order Department
6949 SW 11th Drive
Portland, OR 97219